*By the Same Author*

**BETWEEN ARAB AND ISRAELI**

# MEGAMURDER

# MEGAMURDER

BY

Lieutenant-General

# E. L. M. BURNS

D.S.O., O.B.E., M.C.

PANTHEON BOOKS

A Division of Random House • New York

*To the hundreds of millions of human beings*
*who would like to go on living*

# PREFACE

Today the great nations are piling up armaments for nuclear missile warfare, and latter-day strategists are theorizing about how it should be waged. If the enormous aggregate of destructive power now existing should ever be used, it could destroy the greater part of Western civilization.

In this book I examine and criticize the theory and practice of air war as developed by the Royal Air Force and the United States Air Force up to the end of World War II. In addition, there is a discussion of various policies for nuclear war proposed by American strategic analysts whose researches seem to be conducted under military auspices. Present and recent war plans produced by the professional defence staffs are not, of course, in the public domain.

This criticism from a Canadian, a foreigner, may be thought presumptuous. The burden which the United States shoulders for the defence of Western democracy over the whole world is immense; Canada bears a share which is relatively small, though respectable considering our population and economy. However, the strategies and theories of war propounded in the United States and British defence departments and their adjuncts can result in peace or war, in security or destruction, for Canada and the other smaller NATO nations. Therefore it seems legitimate for a Canadian to examine these theories of war and related concepts, and to condemn them if he finds that they do not seem likely to promote Canada's security in the dangerous world of today. Admittedly, we are faced with hard choices as to how safety is to be achieved.

The above may seem to imply that Canada has no foreign policy of its own and that we are a satellite nation with little control over our destiny. This, of course, is not so, but we have adopted, as main elements in our foreign policy, partnership in the North Atlantic alliance and in the defence of North America. This decision seems inevitable and right. But having entered these partnerships we find ourselves in a junior position because the contribution of our greater partners to the defensive power of the alliance so far outweighs our own. Thus it comes about that the decisive view on strategy is not ours, but today is that of the Pentagon, just as in the past it was that of Whitehall.

My criticism of the theories of air warfare and of nuclear warfare should not be taken as impeaching the airmen, British and American, whether their names are mentioned or not, who have been the principal inventors and elaborators of the policies and strategies of the nuclear age. I assume they all felt that they were faithfully serving their country, hoping to provide in the best way possible for its defence and to ensure its victory in war. While their intentions may have been unexceptionable, the successive courses of action which they chose have turned out, in the long run, to be wrong—and conceivably fatally wrong for the security of the Western world. It is noteworthy that Air Marshals Harris and Saundby, in their retirement, have stated that the world must eventually be secured by an international peace-keeping organization against the immense destruction of war as it could be waged today.

Although throughout this book I stress the threatening dangers of nuclear war and point out its historical derivation, I do not believe that the world would be more comfortable if we could somehow agree to abolish the delivery of explosives by aircraft and missiles and return to the pre-1918 mode of warfare. To think of turning the clock back is a fantasy, and not a tolerable fantasy to one who first learned the realities of war by seeing the bodies of the young dead strewn thickly on the mud of the Somme and Passchendaele battlefields.

I must acknowledge my debt to the many authors whose books are listed at the end of this volume. It is very difficult to think of any aspect of war in the nuclear age, or of disarmament or arms control, that has not been dealt with exhaustively (and sometimes exhaustingly) in the books and magazine articles on the subject which have poured out in an increasing flood during the last five years or more. If I do not quote all authorities, or have slighted any important contributions to the art of strategic analysis, I must plead that I have tried to avoid the error of the learned Procopius of Gaza (a city in which I also have spent some years) whose commentary on the Octateuch was criticized as being unduly extended because he took care to recite all the opinions of all the authorities.

Since this book is intended for the military and general reader, who is apt to be somewhat distracted by footnotes and references, I have generally kept the text clear of these. However there is, at the end, a section of notes which gives, chapter by chapter, the principal authorities I have consulted, as well as the source of a quotation where it was not convenient to include it in the text.

I wish to thank Brigadier J. Stephenson, OBE, executive director of the Royal United Service Institution for his generous help in finding references. My thanks are also due to Miss Royalla Bohlender who typed the many revisions of the manuscript, and helped with the indexing and other tasks.

Finally, it must be clearly understood that the responsibility for the opinions expressed in this book is entirely my own and that they are not to be taken as representing the points of view or policies of the Canadian Government.

E. L. M. BURNS

*New York, November,* 1966

# CONTENTS

# LIST OF ABBREVIATIONS

| | |
|---|---|
| AEC | Atomic Energy Commission (USA) |
| B 17, B 52, B 58 | "B" indicates bomber in the type numbers of US aircraft |
| ENDC | Eighteen-Nation Disarmament Committee |
| IADA | International Atomic Development Authority (proposed, but never set up) |
| IAF | Independent Air Force |
| ICBM | Intercontinental Ballistic Missile |
| IRBM | Intermediate Range Ballistic Missile |
| NATO | North Atlantic Treaty Organization |
| NORAD | North American Regional Air Defence Command |
| OAS | Organization of American States |
| ONUC | *Organization des Nations Unies au Congo* |
| P 51 | "Pursuit" 51; otherwise known as "Mustang"— World War II US fighter aircraft |
| RAF | Royal Air Force |
| RAND | Research and Development—a profit-free corporation mainly concerned with US Air Force problems |
| RFC | Royal Flying Corps |
| RNAS | Royal Naval Air Service |

SAC            Strategic Air Command (USA)

SACEUR      Supreme Allied Commander, Europe

SAM           Surface-to-Air Missile

UNAEC       United Nations Atomic Energy Committee

UNDC        United Nations Disarmament Commission

UNGA        United Nations General Assembly

USAF         United States Air Force

# MEGAMURDER

# 1

## WAR HAS BECOME MEGAMURDER

Murder is the killing of a human being with malice afore-thought; but killing an armed enemy in war is legally not murder. Nevertheless, under the Hague Convention of 1907 the great civilized nations agreed that the right of belligerents to adopt means of injuring the enemy was not unlimited. It was at that time conceived that the laws of war did not permit unarmed civilians to be killed deliberately. However, in the fifty years that followed the Hague Convention, all that has been changed. Sputnik demonstrated in 1957 that a button pressed half a world away can bring death to millions in half an hour.

If the mass of nuclear weapons which now exists is used in war, it will mean the killing of millions of women, children and old men who bear no arms and who bear no responsibility for warlike decisions. Megaton bombs will cause megadeaths. Is it wrong to call this not war, but megamurder? Military advisers have to weigh the possibilities of nuclear war. However diligently they may seek a way to conduct it which will avoid mass murder of civilians, is it possible that they can succeed while these monstrous weapons are retained in the national armouries?

3

How did war become megamurder? The transformation is only in ideas; the awful reality is not on us yet, but ideas are the precursor of action. Is the idea of megamurder a manifestation of the downturn of the cycle, a warning that *homo sapiens* is destined to plunge the world back into the primeval chaos from which he evolved? Did the discovery of the power to fly and of the power to unlock atomic energy inevitably lead to this? Or have certain theories of war adopted by the great military nations brought us to the present nightmare?

The nightmare of the Western world and of the Soviet Union is that any day instantaneous death may come to millions upon millions of their populations, with the simultaneous destruction of the cities, the structures, the machines and the stored knowledge upon which civilization depends.

Herman Kahn, the American writer on war, (or, in the new terminology, the strategic analyst) brought these generally-concealed fears into the open in a way which shocked many people. In his book *On Thermonuclear War* he investigated with scientific detachment, and in a rather optimistic spirit, the results of the destruction of 53 of the greatest cities or metropolitan areas of the United States. This could quite possibly happen in a nuclear war with Russia. The casualties which the American people would suffer might amount to 90,000,000 if no more adequate civil defence measures were in force than at the time he wrote, 1959. If, however, 70 per cent of the population of the 53 great metropolitan areas were evacuated and many billions of dollars were spent to build fallout shelters in the less populated parts of the country, and if great stocks of everything needed to enable the survivors to live and rebuild the shattered country were laid by, then perhaps only 5,000,000 would need to die.

Some reviewers of Mr. Kahn's book denounced him as an ogre, impervious to human feeling. But more reasoned judgement shows that he performed a valuable service by informing at least part of the public what nuclear war would mean. If anyone is wicked, it is not Mr. Kahn, who has given warning of what the results of nuclear war would be. The wicked are those who advocate the preparation for this type of war in spite of what they must have known long before his book was published.

The military profession derived whatever respect it enjoyed because it was supposed to protect the lives and property of the non-combatant population. Now, in the conception of nuclear war, the armed forces of each side take the civilians of the other side as their targets, and are unable to safeguard the lives of their own people. In 1907 it was declared to be against the laws of war for armed forces to take hostages whose lives would guarantee submission. Now, whole populations are hostages.

I do not pretend that the moral questions created by the existence of nuclear weapons are easy to resolve. The moral problem is essentially the same as that involved in the use of force to compel compliance with law, or for self-protection in the absence of a law-enforcement agency. In the world today there is no supranational force to compel nations to obey international law or to behave as the provisions of the United Nations Charter would have them do; therefore the nations have to rely on their own power, or the power of allies, to protect their existence and their vital interests. In short, they must rely on force to repel force. But just as the municipal policeman must not crack an obstreperous drunk's skull with his night-stick, and a private citizen must not shoot someone who pulls his nose, there should be limits to the force that nations may employ to compel respect for their international rights.

The moral problem will not be resolved by any one nuclear power abjuring, and dismantling its nuclear weapons as the unilateral disarmers propose. Nor can safety and honourable peace be found by piling up nuclear armaments and the means to deliver them, while pressing forward research on new kinds of weapons in the hope of making our own nation strong enough to overawe any other. The idea that security can be bought by amassing armaments is not new in the nuclear age. It has been tried before and it has never worked. The result, as is well known, is to stimulate other nations or coalitions of nations to arm themselves in turn. For if one nation builds armed strength, thinking thereby to deter attack, other nations will think that the first is preparing an aggression against them. When one nation has the power to attack, other nations cannot but fear that that power will be used, and they will arm to defend themselves against it.

In this age of nuclear plenty, another profession shares responsibility with the military for theorizing about and even planning the strategy of possible wars. Since World War II the development of atomic and nuclear weapons and other "sophisticated" armaments has constantly been changing the conditions of warfare, with a result that the services of scientists have become essential to the government and the nation in the preparation for war. It is they who must imagine and design the weapons, and they have acquired an increasingly great influence in determining how those weapons ought to be used. They first came into the business of directing war through the development of operational research which attempted scientific evaluation of how newly developed or modified weapons could be used under battle conditions. They began with tactics where the essential question the operational research boffins had to answer was: How can the weapon or weapons system best be used in contact with the enemy? Then their investigations led them to the problems of strategy in its narrow sense; for example, How shall the weapon be brought to the point of contact to the best advantage? From this, and the comparison of the value of different weapons systems, taking their respective costs into consideration, it was a natural transition for them to examine strategy and military policy in its widest scope. This might be generalized as the selection of the best military forces and weapons to attain certain political ends. Nowadays the writings of Kahn, Kissinger and many other academic strategists show that the scientists, whether they were originally nuclear physicists, economists, mathematicians or whatnot, tend to become the predominant military theorists and to lay down the strategical (and even political) principles and rules for the use of the new weapons which they and their brother scientists have helped to forge. This is not altogether surprising, as the power of these weapons transcends everything hitherto known. There have been only two occasions, separated by a couple of days, when they were used in actual warfare; hence it is necessary to imagine what will happen when the thousand-fold more powerful and very numerous thermonuclear weapons of today are used. This extrapolation can be based on the results of high-explosive bombing, the two atomic bomb explosions and the numerous experiments that have subjected structures and living creatures to the effects of thermonuclear and atomic explosions. Therefore, as no general or admiral has any real experience of nuclear warfare, the pre-1945 theory of military tactics and strategy, built up from military history and criticism, provides little guidance. Thus the scientist, by his training, is probably as well able to determine how these new weapons systems should be used as is the military man. It can be seen from their writings that these scientists, or academic strategists, seem quite confident that they are able to perform this task much better than can the professional military and in this, I daresay, they are right.

It must be laid to the credit of the scientists that they perceive the results of using the weapons and modes of war that they have created, and that this has touched the conscience of a majority of them. Even so, for all their thinking and good intent, they have not been able to devise a sure way to safeguard humanity from the monsters of their invention. They have furnished a range of possible answers. Since 1960 they have been publishing many books and writing many articles, much study of which is a weariness of the flesh. But they are more convincing in warning us about the catastrophe to be expected than in devising practical policies to avoid it. In the United States a group, hoping to eliminate or greatly reduce the danger which the existence of nuclear arms creates, developed theories of "arms control." The basic idea was that the nations having nuclear armaments should limit, by treaty or convention, their numbers and deployment, and even their use in war, but without finally abolishing them. It is to be noted that the term "arms control" in the context of disarmament negotiations is coming to have a more restricted meaning, referring to measures, which while not involving elimination of weapons or reduction of forces, are intended to reduce international tension, and thus facilitate and lead toward disarmament.

In contrast to the scientists, the military do not appear to have been much troubled in their consciences as a result of their responsibility for developing nuclear warfare. The military man, soldier, sailor or airman, thinks of himself as the defender of his countrymen and their protector against the nation's enemies. He generally assumes that in carrying out this duty there are no limits and should be none in the degree of force which he can employ. There has certainly been no great chorus of military men denouncing nuclear war. Those protests that have been voiced are generally by soldiers or sailors rather than airmen, and such arguments against unlimited nuclear war are sometimes put down to the older services' jealousy of the air service, on which the nuclear age has conferred great status, glamour and importance.

The main theme of this book will be that it is for the military to think again of their prime responsibility: how to *defend* their civilian fellow-countrymen. Civilians must not be thought of as expendable in the interests of an illusory total victory. Is, in fact, the way of warfare that is being prepared by the nuclear powers and acquiesced in by their allies, right? I mean "right," in being the best and surest means of protecting the nations? And what is to be done so that the world can be freed from the enormous anxieties and neuroses which now afflict it?

Cynics sometimes ask: "What, in any country, is the principal requirement of the military?" and give the answer: "An enemy." The reason, of course, is that if the armed forces are to be maintained at a level of numbers and equipment which will satisfy the professional zeal and enthusiasm of the military, there must be a threat to be countered. Otherwise the government will not spend the money required for a great military establishment. Immediately after the nuclear warfare era began, the Soviet Union, leader of communism in the world, succeeded the shattered German Reich and Japanese Empire in the role of chief enemy. The expansion into Europe of communist political control, under the aegis of Soviet Union troops, produced the initial threat. Reaction and counter-reaction followed and mutual fears were intensified—these fears coming to a focus on the danger of nuclear war. Nourished by the fears of the seemingly implacable and generally mysterious enemy, the armaments budgets of the United States and its allies grew, and so did the importance of the military in the United States. The present status of the American military establishment is astounding when one looks back on what it was between the two world wars, and when one thinks of the widespread American aversion to militarism in former times.

What I have just written may seem very offensive to many honest *militaires*, American and other. But they should also remember that yesterday's enemy is today's ally. In 1945 the Soviet Union was the ally of the United States, France and the British Commonwealth, while Germany, Italy and Japan were the enemies. Now the position is reversed. This might lead to the reflection that the Russians do not have to be our enemies for always.

What the military should ponder on is this: What is this armament, this preparation for nuclear war, this arms race all about? What is the best way to defend freedom, as we know it in the Western countries, from being destroyed by communist armed force or subversion? Is the best defence to kill and be ready to kill millions upon millions of Russians, our allies of only 15 years ago? Should we apply the catch-phrase "Better Dead than Red" to all Communists? Should the military pronounce the judgement that it would be better for millions upon millions of their fellow-countrymen and of their present allies in the NATO alliance and elsewhere to die in the thermonuclear war than that they should run the risk of being persuaded to be Red?

The military should realize that the greatest threat to the survival of democracy is no longer the Russians or the Chinese or any other country professing anti-democratic ideologies, but rather war itself. It is nuclear war against which the military must protect their fellow-citizens. The thesis often appears in defence department public relations pronunciamentos that the armed forces must be super-strong in order to keep the peace, that this great strength alone restrains an enemy thirsty for world dominion. But the weakness of this argument must eventually be apparent to all: no lasting security can be founded on a race for military superiority.

This leads to the examination of a dangerous delusion of such Western nations as the USA, Britain, France and Germany, to wit, that they possess a peculiar and innate capacity for science and technology which will ensure that their armaments will always be superior to those of the Soviet Union. This notion should by now be exploded by the technical successes of the Russians. Their first achievement was to produce conventional, good-quality armaments, such as tanks, artillery, mortars and attack aircraft, more cheaply and in greater numbers than the Western powers have done. Second, of course, was their mastering of the secrets first of atomic and then of thermonuclear weapons very much sooner than Western scientists believed possible. And finally, there is their performance in rocketry and space exploration, and the remarkable accuracy which they have attained. So it is a vain thought that if enough money is spent and enough valuable brains are employed, the West can always stay militarily ahead of the Russians through superior technique.

In Great Britain this wishful thinking probably was due to the long period of history during which her defence was assured by naval power. This, of course, involved very much less sacrifice on the part of the general population than was required from continental peoples, who were conscripted to serve in their national armies. The same idea of relying primarily on a navy for security also influenced American thinking on defence. As for Canadians, we gave little thought to military matters prior to the nuclear age. Until the Second World War we relied primarily on Great Britain for our defence, and after 1940 we acknowledged that the United States would also protect us from invasion. To rely mainly on a greater power for our security, even within an alliance, imposes limits on our freedom of action.

The preference for being defended by a navy perhaps stems back to the Anglo-Saxon aversion to large standing armies, which became most unpopular following the experience of the military and puritan dictatorship under Cromwell in the 17th century. The heritage of dislike and distrust of large armies and the determination to avoid having them has persisted. Hence the predilection for what is sometimes called the armament-intensive kind of military force rather than manpower-intensive armies. Of course, we cannot remove the threat of armament-intensive nuclear war by making treaties to practise only manpower-intensive traditional ways of warfare. That, as we shall see, is not possible. Thus, to repeat what has been asserted above, what we—the Western nations—have to fear now is not another nation or another ideology, but the possibility of nuclear war itself. Unless we can find a way to eliminate that possibility, or reduce it to the very minimum, we shall be delivering millions upon millions of our fellow-countrymen to death.

There is another block to clear and effective thought about the problem of thermonuclear war by the military, and perhaps also by the scientists engaged in developing armaments. This block is the self-interest of the members of these professions in maintaining things as they are, in the continuation of the great military and scientific establishments that give them employment, that provide them with a career and that create for them an important status in the community, which otherwise they might not have. I do not suggest that any considerable number of soldiers, airmen, sailors or scientists deliberately reason in this way. The thought probably does not come into their consciousness; nevertheless, it is there. It does not require any expert knowledge of psychology to know that the emotions which are aroused by a threat to personal and family security and status can vitiate clear thought and fairnesss of decision and judgement on almost any problem. These emotions, rather than cold reason, may prompt the conclusion that nuclear war is inescapable, and that the only sound policy is to prepare for it by piling up ever more powerful armaments.

Thus far I have touched on the thinking of scientists and military men about the means of waging war, and on what they ought to be pondering, namely, how to find ways to protect their fellow-countrymen from the outbreak of a nuclear war with its inevitable results. I have said nothing about the responsibility of the politicians, the elected governors in democratic countries. It is they, of course, who are finally accountable to the people for whatever policies are adopted. But always in time of war, and now in the time of the cold war, politicians are very dependent on their military advisers and executives, and are dependent also on scientific advisers. That is why I have laid stress on the responsibility of scientists and military men. Since the politician must now rely more than ever on technical advice, the responsibility to their fellow-countrymen of those who tender that advice has immeasurably increased.

# 2

## BOMBING IN WORLD WAR I

Nuclear warfare did not come into existence simply because scientists had learned how to release energy by splitting the atom. This achievement of pure science had to find its practical application. A wonderful vista opened before the proponents of air warfare when they were told that the new discovery could multiply the explosive force of the greatest existing block-buster by several thousand times. This would indeed, they thought, place the final decision of all wars in the hands of the air service, a goal on which their eyes had been steadfastly set for a quarter of a century.

In brief, the theory of nuclear warfare merely carries on and extends theories of air warfare concocted before nuclear fission. These theories were born very soon after aircraft had been brought to the point where they could be effectively used in war, that is, during World War I, although it was not until somewhat later that the individual theories were blended into a system. It is instructive to trace the evolution of these theories. We may be able to determine whether there is something in-herently wrong in them, something self-defeating. If so, then perhaps we can abandon them, and turn away from this ex-

treme application of military force which has become so peril-
ous to mankind.

We may find that the development of war to its nuclear
phase has been inevitable and irreversible, a potential tragedy
for humanity as hard to comprehend as the notion of infinity.
But if we do come to this conclusion, we should look for ways
of escape. We need not give way to despair and resign ourselves to immolation, with the fears but without the hopes of
those queer sects that periodically assemble on high places, to
shiver and await the Day of Judgement. What we should aim
for is to minimize the amount of military force to be applied in
the situations which arise between nations, and within nations,
when reason fails and violence supervenes.

Turn back to the beginnings of air warfare in 1914. One
should remember the remark attributed to Foch (later, in 1918,
Marshal of France and Commander-in-Chief of the Allied
armies) when he saw an aeroplane performing some time before 1914. "That," he said, "is perhaps very nice as sport, but of
no importance in war." It makes one cautious about accepting
any general's assessment of the probable development of war
and perhaps should make all generals wary of delivering un-
qualified judgements.

In the First World War, the few aircraft operating with the
armies and navies of the principal combatants, Germany,
France and Great Britain, were at first used mainly for gather-
ing information by visual observation about the location and
movement of enemy troops. Soon aerial photography was used
to make a better record of what could be seen from the air.
Then the aeroplane was found to be useful in directing artillery
fire, particularly that of the heavier guns and howitzers. Fighting in the air soon followed. At first the airmen fired revolvers
and rifles at each other; then machine-guns were fitted to the
aircraft. Special types of aeroplane suited to the rapid manœ-
vres required in air fighting were developed. This was the age
of air chivalry, of single combat between the aces. Each nation
had its heroes, Guynemer and Fonck of France, Immelmann,
Boelcke and Richthofen of Germany, Ball and McCudden of
Great Britain, Bishop and Barker of Canada, Rickenbacker of
the USA, to cite only a few of the great names. These brave

young men, in single combat or in "dog-fights," all sent down to flaming death some scores of opponents of lesser skill, and most of them in the end met the same fate.

The knights of the air were not engaged in merely symbolic combats unrelated to the battle in which the armies were locked. The air fighting was for control of the air space over the battlefield, so that other aircraft would not be stopped from the reconnaissance and the observation of artillery fire that was considered necessary according to the tactics and techniques of the time. All these air activities, including the air fighting, were strictly auxiliary and subordinate to the operations of the troops on the ground.

But it was not too long before airmen began to intervene more directly, and not merely to act as eyes for the ground-lings. They began to use weapons carried in their aircraft to attack the troops on the ground. What they did was to drop missiles, first little grenades, then larger high-explosive bombs specially designed for the purpose. Later, "ground strafing" with machine-guns commenced. Curiosities of this early air-offensive period were the steel darts with weighted heads, which when dumped out of an aircraft at height would attain enough velocity in falling to pierce from stem to gudgeon any ground soldier unfortunate enough to be in the line of its trajectory. Apparently this frightening device claimed few victims, as it was soon abandoned.

For the British, the first serious bombing was carried out by the Royal Naval Air Service. As a counter to raids by Zeppelin dirigibles which had dropped bombs on England, they attacked the aircraft sheds which sheltered them in Germany. Soon thereafter, in the spring of 1915, the Royal Flying Corps began bombing in support of the armies in France. Railway stations and junctions were the usual targets, the object being to disrupt the enemy's rail communications system, making it more difficult for him to reinforce the front under attack. The first bombing attacks were spasmodic and unco-ordinated, because the command of the squadrons of the RFC was decentralized to army corps.

By the summer of 1915, this haphazard use of aircraft in bombing had been seen to be ineffective. General Trenchard, commanding the RFC in France, got General Headquarters to put out a directive that armies and corps must not try to support their operations by using aircraft in this way. Bombing operations were to be ordered by GHQ only, for the purpose of interrupting the enemy's railway communications, and would be planned to fit in with the general strategy of the Allied offensive. The first extensive attempt to practise this sound principle of concentrated effort was made before the Battle of Loos, in September 1915. It was hardly a thorough-going application, since the total bomb load of 5½ tons was distributed over some 35 targets. Only two attacks were moderately successful. Each aircraft carried one or two of the then standard 112 lb. bombs, whose explosive charge was small relative to the weight of the casing. Consequently the damage it could inflict was limited.

When the Battle of the Somme began in July 1916, the RFC was better organized, and there was a larger number of specialized bomber squadrons. In co-ordination with the offensive of the French and British armies, the bomber aircraft, with some fighter support, were given the task of disrupting German rail traffic on the front of attack. But again the number of aircraft was insufficient for the task as a whole, and there was too much dispersion of effort. The results were minimal. The Germans were having the better of the air fighting over the Somme battlefield, mainly owing to being able to assemble practically all their fighter strength there, as they had centralized the command of all air forces under their general headquarters, which could concentrate them on the decisive front. The British RFC was still organized in brigades, under command of armies, and these formations managed to keep control of their aircraft, instead of releasing them to reinforce the RFC Brigade of the Fourth Army, which was responsible for the Somme battlefront.

At this time specialized bombing aircraft with a somewhat longer range were coming into use in the RFC. To restore the adverse situation in the air over the Somme battlefields the new bombers were used to attack German airfields. Again little effect was produced, too few aircraft being given too many targets to attack. In the 1917 spring offensive, the same errors were made, with the same unsatisfactory result.

One sees in this brief résumé the hard way in which the British air forces learned the need for concentration of effort. It was the "soldier" generals who were responsible for setting the tasks of the air forces. When they committed the same errors repeatedly, it was quite natural for the flying officers to feel that their new arm was being misused and that those in control neither understood its essential characteristics, nor had any vision of what it could do. They concluded that they could do better with it if they were free from control by generals who had their eyes on the battlefield at ground level.

About this time the British Government began to realize that its resources in aircraft were not being used to the best advantage. The unsatisfactory results on the battlefields of France and Flanders were not the only evidence. The Royal Naval Air Service had been built up to considerable strength, but because of the Royal Navy's almost complete control of the surface of the seas it had few operational tasks. On the other hand, the RFC in France was fighting hard, had very many casualties and never seemed to have enough resources to make an effective attack from the air or to carry out its other tasks. Field-Marshal (then General) Smuts, of South Africa, was given the task of examining the whole organization of Britain's air effort and making recommendations for its improvement. He reported that the RFC and the RNAS should form a unified service, under an Air Ministry of equal status with the Admiralty and the War Department, and that the Air Ministry should have control of all matters relating to the combined air service, including personnel, supply, procurement and other essential business. The British Government accepted these recommendations, and on 1 April 1918 the Royal Air Force, under control of an Air Ministry, came into being.

The most important new step taken after the change of organization was the setting up of an Independent Air Force, made up of what were for that day long-range bombers. The IAF's mission was to be the bombardment of German centres of production and communication. It was located in the zone of the French armies, to emphasize its independence of the British armies in France. Although it was planned to make this force very large, by the end of the war (11 November 1918) it consisted of only eleven squadrons, mainly equipped with de Havilland 4's and 9's, whose radius of action was about 100 miles, and whose bomb load was about 500 lb. So if all aircraft could reach the target, the IAF could deliver, in nuclear-age terms, one tenth of a kiloton! The IAF made some successful attacks on Ruhr and Rhineland targets, but no one claimed that these attacks had an important effect on the outcome of the war.

Plans were made, if the war had continued into 1919, to attack Berlin and other distant targets in Germany, with 4-engined Handley Page bombers which could carry a load of 2000 lb. of bombs. Presumably such attacks were to be made in revenge for the sporadic attacks on London and other English cities which had been made by Zeppelins and Gotha aeroplanes. These raids caused a great outcry, although they had not caused very many casualties or much destruction. But for centuries the British, behind the North Sea and the Channel, had been unmolested by hostile armed forces, and they did not like the idea that, although geographically they were still an island, insularity no longer meant invulnerability, now that attack could come by air as well as by sea.

Neither the French nor the Germans developed the theory or practice of air bombardment as an independent method of waging war. Their bombing operations remained strictly tied to the fighting of the armies. The United States, for well-known reasons, had a late start in developing its air forces, but intended to devote part of them to the independent mission of attacking targets in Germany. However, the war ended before these plans could be put into effect, and the US Air Corps' actual operational experience was in support of the army, although some fairly distant bombing raids were carried out.

Rudimentary as the air operations of World War I were, and limited as were their effects, we see clearly the main principles of air warfare as they were to be developed to their full meaning in World War II and in the cold-war nuclear age that was to follow. These principles may be summarized as an independent role for air forces, attack on the means of production and communications of the enemy territory rather than on its armed forces, and concentration of effort which was to evolve into saturation bombing in World War II.

Air Marshal Sir Robert Saundby, in his historical book, *Air Bombardment,* quotes from Field-Marshal Smuts' report:

> Air power can be used as an independent means of war operations. Nobody that witnessed the attack on London on 11th July (1917) could have any doubt on this point . . . the day may not be far off when aerial operations with their devastation of enemy lands and destruction of industrial and populous centres on a vast scale may become the principal operations of war, to which the older forms of military operations may become secondary and subordinate.

Air Marshal Saundby goes on to write: "These were truly prophetic words, and today they have been completely fulfilled. . . ." This, of course, must be a source of gratification to everybody.

At this point, we may pause in the chronicle of the development of the theory and practice of air warfare, and consider the meaning of Field-Marshal Smuts' prophecy: ". . . devastation of enemy lands and destruction of industrial and populous centres on a vast scale may become the principal operations of war. . . ." What used to be the rational purpose of war, so far as it may ever be said to have had a rational purpose? To expand a little on Clausewitz's dictum that war is the continuation of politics by other means, we can say that the purpose of war is by the use of force to induce the enemy to acquiesce in our policies, to accept our will, or to abandon his policies if they are obnoxious to us. More specific aims have frequently been to settle a dispute over the possession of territory, or to obtain some other material advantage.

Pressure has to be put on the enemy to make him give up his policies and fall in with ours. This has usually taken the form of occupying his territory, and appropriating, during the occupation, some of his wealth. Prior to the age of air warfare, although on occasion lands were devastated and cities looted or destroyed, this was usually a temporary and incidental pressure during the course of the war. Sometimes it was done for a strategic purpose, such as obliging him to give battle in disadvantageous circumstances or cutting off some resources which he might otherwise have used.

It has usually been considered that the military object in war is to destroy, disperse or in some other way to render powerless the enemy's armed forces. When the enemy's armed forces are no longer able to resist the advance of ours, we can occupy his country and proceed to put the final pressure on him to accept our terms. While he is still able to resist, even if he has small chance of eventually emerging victorious in the war, he will not accept terms that surrender his vital interests.

It is here that a defect of the general theories of air warfare is to be perceived. They envisage the destruction of the enemy's lands and industrial and populous centres, without taking account of the fact that while the enemy still has forces capable of resisting *or retaliating* he will continue to fight, with the possibility of equal damage being inflicted on both sides. If we destroy all the enemy's cities and industries while he destroys all of ours, neither of us can gain anything. We will resemble the celebrated Kilkenny cats, which got into a fight with each other and continued to fight desperately, until nothing was left but the two tails.

The air warfare theorists, of course, have not been quite so simple as to ignore what would happen if two equally matched opponents followed an unmodified strategy of attack on the enemy's population and industry. For one thing, they postulate that their side should have some considerable technical advantage which would enable them to inflict far more damage on the enemy population and resources than would be inflicted on their own people. We shall be discussing this question of technical advantages later on.

Other theorists have reverted more to the classical order of events in war and have devised strategies for air warfare which, by concentrating the offensive against certain of the enemy's key industries or against his air forces in being, would disarm him and make it impossible for him to continue to resist or to retaliate effectively enough to maintain any sort of balance. Thus we would create the conditions where the enemy would see that a continuation of the war would inevitably make his situation worse and worse. We shall review the history of the attempts to apply this kind of strategy in the air warfare of World War II. It will be found that for technical and other reasons it proved impossible to wage air war in this selective way, and the attacks on the German and Japanese aircraft industries developed into a general attack on cities.

The "counterforce" strategy, advocated in 1962 and 1963 as a new war policy for the us "Strategic" Air Command with its included missiles, is the latest attempt to make the strategy of air forces conform to the classical theory that the destruction of the enemy's armed forces should be the prime object. In due course, we shall try to analyse this policy, to estimate whether it could succeed, or whether it might have the end result of bringing on the feared nuclear holocaust of our cities.

# 3

## THEORIES OF AIR WARFARE BETWEEN THE WORLD WARS

Giulio Douhet, an Italian, was first in the field with a general theory of air warfare. He published his book *Command of the Air* in 1921. It can be said that the most significant elements in his theory are elaborations on Field-Marshal Smuts' prophecy.

His writings excited a great deal of severe criticism, which the reader will understand if he puts himself in the place of the people of most of Europe, then just recovering from the effects of World War I. Air Marshal Saundby remarks in *Air Bombardment* that some airmen believed Douhet to have gone too far, but that everything that has happened since he wrote has amply confirmed his theories. I suppose the same endorsement could be given to the prophet Jeremiah.

Douhet rejected the idea that an air force should fight the enemy's armed forces. The primary objective of the powerful air force which he desired his country to create would be the civil population of the enemy state. It is illuminating, reading Douhet's exhortations that Italy should concentrate on building an air force to wage this kind of warfare, to reflect on what actually happened to Italy in World War II. She suffered very severe damage from the air action of her enemies, even though they refrained from attacking Rome and other important cities and tried to restrict bombing to true strategic objectives.

Douhet laid it down that bombing objectives should always be large and that small targets were unimportant. This dictum turned out to accord with the operational limitations of independent bombing forces. He thought that industrial and commercial establishments, important private and public buildings, transportation centres and arteries and, of course, certain areas of the civilian population should be the targets. Three kinds of bombs would be needed: explosive, incendiary and poison gas —the explosives to demolish the target, the incendiary to set it on fire and poison gas to prevent fire fighters from putting the fires out.

Douhet was wrong in predicting the use of poison gas, but we shall see when we review the history of air warfare in World War II that his recommendations were adopted, by and large, in such operations as the attacks on Hamburg and Dresden in Germany and on Tokyo and other Japanese cities. Douhet also overestimated the effect that could be produced by bombarding cities, using such aircraft as existed when he wrote. However, his conclusion that bombing offensives had to be directed against very large centres of civilian population was adopted in practice—even if not openly avowed—by the airmen directing the offensives of World War II.

In some of his ideas he exhibited the one-way thinking which seems to characterize much theorizing on the application of air power. He became lyrical about the advantages which would come with the command of the air: to be able to wield unimaginable offensive power (and presumably he never imagined how great that offensive power would be in 1945 and subsequent years), to cut the communications of an enemy's army (which air power never achieved completely), to ensure the protection of one's own country and to protect whatever operations of one's own army and navy were necessary. A nation vanquished in the struggle to win command of the air would lie completely at the mercy of the victor and be obliged to accept his dictated terms of surrender. Much of what he predicted came true at the time of the surrender of Japan, but the command of the air possessed by the USA in 1945 had been won after nearly four years of hard battle, in which all three armed services played essential parts.

The passage of Douhet which I have paraphrased above seems to be almost a wish-fantasy. In Douhet's imaginary air war, "our" side will be able to do what it likes in the air; "our" aircraft will be able to fly anywhere and bomb any enemy city, while the enemy will be unable to interfere with the operations of "our" bombers. How such a command of the air is to be attained does not seem to be explained anywhere. We know that during World War II pretty effective defences against bombers were built up both in England and in Germany. Furthermore, retaliation followed bombing attack; the British replied to the blitz on London by putting a very great proportion of their total war effort into the bombing offensive against Germany, and the Germans retaliated in turn by developing the V 1 flying bomb and the V 2 rocket with which Hitler intended to take a fearful revenge for the bombing of German cities.

But the most significant part of the Douhet theory, what he calls a fundamental concept in aerial warfare, is that "we" must be prepared to accept any damage the enemy may inflict on "us" and must concentrate on inflicting even heavier damage upon "him." "Our" independent air force must not concern itself with what the enemy air force does; its business is to do the enemy the greatest possible damage in the shortest possible time, employing its resources against the most vital targets. However, Douhet realized that this sort of war would be somewhat distasteful to "our" civil population. Submitting to whatever damage the enemy might inflict would involve a considerable element of tragedy. Nevertheless, it would be futile to divert resources to defence against the enemy's aerial attacks, since no really effective means of stopping them existed.

This argument was used even recently by extreme protagonists of air power. They did not use it in such stark terms, but essentially the thesis ran that any diversion of budgetary funds to building up defensive measures against what the presumptive enemy can do, weakened the power of the offensive air force (sac, for example) to destroy the enemy's lands and population. Of course, the terms were varied; it was asserted that the offensive weapon-delivering force must be overwhelmingly strong, in order that the deterrent should be absolute. In short, it was hoped that the threat of immense destruction by nuclear arms would ensure that the enemy would never resist our will, when it came to the "crunch." But this argument for the absolute priority of funds for the offensive component of air forces is contested nowadays on two grounds. The first is the familiar argument against "overkill." When SAC can deliver enough nuclear explosive to destroy every sizable Russian city and kill most of the Russian population, why kill them twice? Why keep pouring money into the apparatus of megamurder? The air-power protagonists find two answers to this: There must be continual progress in the technology of air warfare, lest the Russians, working while the West sleeps, find some new and more effective vehicle for the delivery of the nuclear weapon, or (most horrid thought) should devise an effective defence against intercontinental missiles. The second answer, camouflaged behind some variant of the first, is that the aeroplane and rocket factories must be kept going with government orders; otherwise they will go out of business, many skilled workmen will be unemployed, secondary "regression" effects will be widespread and the whole United States economy will falter.

But there is a decisive argument against concentrating all expenditure on strengthening the offensive component of the air forces. It is that the people of the USA, or of any country, want first of all to be defended against the assaults of their prospective enemy or enemies, and only secondarily do they want to assault the enemy and bend him to their own country's collective will. So the voters in a democratic country, although most of them may be fooled some of the time, will not in the end tolerate a "defence" system which leaves them hostage to the missiles and bombs of the enemy.

Pondering on this fact, Mr. Herman Kahn, in his vaticinations on thermonuclear war, has come forth with the proposition that for the USA deterrent to be really credible against any Russian warlike act except nuclear attack on the USA, it is necessary to take certain strictly defensive measures. These could include the building of fallout-shelters for the population in the areas not likely to be affected by blast, shock and heat in a nuclear exchange, and the evacuation of 70 per cent or so of the population of the metropolitan areas and cities. He argues that this is necessary if the USSR is to believe that the USA would loose its nuclear might to defend Europe. The argument is straightforward, although shocking to many who read it for the first time or hear about it secondhand. It is this: Would the President of the USA order SAC into action for the defence of Europe if he knew that the Russian retaliation would result in 10, 20, 30 or more megadeaths of Americans? Mr. Kahn concludes that a decision to strike might be taken if the megadeaths were in the lower range. Therefore, civil defence measures to ensure that the population will not suffer casualities in excess must be taken; otherwise the Russians will not believe in the intention of the USA to use its nuclear weapons to prevent an invasion of Europe. We shall return to Mr. Kahn's discussion of this matter in a later chapter.

When the bomber was the principal means of delivering the nuclear weapon, it was obviously necessary to spend a good deal of the defence dollar in building up active defences against it. These comprised fighter aircraft of high performance, anti-aircraft missiles such as Bomarc, Nike-Ajax and its successors, and the associated radar warning systems and all the apparatus of command and control over the North American continent and beyond. This was, and is, contrary to the Douhet theory that all resources should be concentrated on the offensive component. But no one, so far as I know, has used this argument to denounce NORAD as a waste of money. NORAD is now seen to be inadequate because of its inability to defend the continent against attack by missiles. Since Sputnik appeared in 1957 it is the missile delivery of nuclear weapons against the United States and adjoining Canada that is mostly feared. But so long as there is a large USSR bomber force it is necessary to maintain defences against it, and few question this function. It is clearly desirable to cut down the number of enemy aircraft which will reach their target area, even if Mr. Baldwin's dictum that "the bomber will aways get through" still seems to be true in spite of modern developments in air defence.

Douhet justified his theory of offensive air warfare against the objection that it reverses the attempt during preceding centuries to make war less destructive and horrible and less liable to leave hatreds in the ensuing period of peace. He offered the following arguments: He thought that the use of poison gas dropped from aircraft would be much more effective than dropping high explosive. Poison gas would be greatly improved over the early and relatively ineffective chemicals of 1915-18 (it is true that it has been). Anyway, restrictions on the use of weapons agreed to in peacetime would be swept away in war. All means are legitimate to the nation in a life and death struggle. War is essentially inhuman, and the means of waging it cannot be classified into more and less inhuman, with the more inhuman means being prohibited. Finally, Douhet says that the purpose of war is to harm the enemy as much as possible, and that any means to this end are permissible and will be used no matter what they are.

As we know, the Fascists later took the opportunity at the expense of the Ethiopians to put Douhet's theories on the use of gas into practice. The Ethiopians having no means of replying, this seemed a pretty good idea at the time. This, and other less objectionable uses of aircraft in colonial wars, or in keeping the peace in colonial territories, may have moulded the viewpoint of some air officers who came to authority in World War II.

It has never been clearly understood why poisonous gas, freely used against armed forces by both sides in World War I, was not somehow or other brought into use in the Second World War. The Geneva Protocols of 1925, prohibiting its use, which most of the belligerents other than the USA had ratified, can hardly have been a sufficient reason for this restraint. The consensus of military opinion is that experience had shown that poison gas, because of its essential characteristics, was not likely to be of decisive advantage to either side. Hence neither side cared to be the first to introduce it and thus incure a propaganda, or psychological, debit with no offsetting operational gain.

In passing, we should note that the purpose of war is *not* to harm the enemy as much as possible. It is to make him submit to our policy; and the principle of economy of force dictates that ideally we should only harm him to the extent necessary to cause him to submit. I say "ideally," because, of course, war is not a science in which means are precisely adjusted to ends, but a "terrible and impassioned drama" in which men, even in the highest political councils, act more through passion than by reason.

Perhaps I should amend the tense in the above paragraph; that is, "The purpose in war *was* . . . ." This amendment is because if nuclear weapons are used in war (as they almost certainly will in any conflict between the two great world powers) the cost in death and destruction will outweigh any gain that could be expected from obliging the enemy to conform to our policy. And, looking at the proposition from the opposite, or Soviet Union side, the same thing is true.

Douhet quotes Fokker, the famous aeroplane constructor of World War I, in support of his own view that war in the air would be unlimited by any legal or humane considerations. Fokker had said that the enemy would not distinguish at all between the armed forces and the civil population, and would use the most terrifying weapons he had, including poison gas, no matter what commitments he had made in peacetime not to do so. Fleets of aeroplanes would be sent to destroy the principal cities. Douhet, reinforced by Fokker's opinions, concluded that as the enemy was sure to use the most devastating and horrible means of warfare against "us," the only sensible thing to do was to do the same to him, only sooner. (Preventive war, or pre-emptive strike.) All means to this end must be used, despite any treaties to the contrary, which were only "scraps of paper." Douhet conceded that his picture of future warfare was grim and bloody, but it was no good for people to bury their heads in the sand like the ostrich; all this horror was undoubtedly going to happen, and moreover, there was no defence against aerial attack.

There are two points in this passage which seem to deserve additional comment. The first is that the prophet of air warfare discards the possibility of limiting the effects of war, of air war especially, by any sort of agreement. This conclusion, if applied in the circumstances of the 1960's, would mean that it is completely vain and self-deceiving to hope to prevent nuclear war by agreement between the great nuclear powers; no arms control, no disarmament, no kind of limited war is really possible.

There is, in fact, still a stream of thought to the effect that if there is a war (and that there always will be wars), then the most powerful weapons will be used by nations battling for their existence. This means that nuclear weapons will be used. Therefore the only rational policy is to be as strong as possible in nuclear armaments, so that whatever disaster the inevitable nuclear war will bring to "our" nation, a greater disaster will be inflicted on the enemy.

The other point is Douhet's statement that defence against aerial attacks is illusory. As we shall see later, the experience of World War II proved him to be wrong under those conditions, but perhaps Douhet's prophecy is being fulfilled in the conditions of today, when the principal means of aerial offence is the ICBM with a nuclear warhead. No effective defence against the ICBM has yet been devised, nor is one likely to be, in the opinion of most scientists who have studied the problem from an independent standpoint.

The American prophet of air warfare in the inter-war period was Brigadier-General William Mitchell. It will be useful to consider briefly some of his ideas on air warfare in general. By and large his thinking is pretty close to that of Douhet, although he avoids some of the Italian's extravagances.

One must also draw a distinction between his views on air war in general and his views on the effect of air power in naval warfare. He proved by actual test that aeroplanes could sink battleships, but this proof did not convince admiralties, and battleships remained in navies until the proof was repeated in unmistakable fashion in World War II. So General Mitchell was a true prophet on that point. But what of his views on air war generally? He stated, correctly enough, in his book *Skyways* that war was the attempt of one nation to impose its will on another nation when other means of adjusting a dispute had failed. The victor's will could be imposed when he could control the vital centres of the other, who would then be powerless to defend himself. The vital centres were the cities where people lived, the food- and material-producing areas and the transportation systems which carried food and materials to where they were needed. Mitchell then went on to describe the historic form of war: an army on the offensive with the vital centres as objectives, and the army of the other side defending them. In his view, an aberration in strategical thinking developed. This put the intermediate object—rendering the enemy powerless by destroying his army—ahead of the true object, which was to put pressure on the enemy nation by controlling his vital centres. Air power, however, could attack the vital centres directly and entirely neutralize or destroy them. Therefore the hostile army was a false objective and it would be unnecessary to destroy it; a numerically greatly superior army would be at the mercy of an inferior air force, and could be disregarded.

The same error noted in the Douhet theories is apparent here. Mitchell disregards the possibility of improvements in air defence, and also the possibility that the enemy might have an air force (or other means of delivering high explosives) as powerful as that of his own nation. Of course, he was thinking of aircraft as the only means of delivering high-explosive bombs. The ballistic missile, with its invulnerability to defensive measures, was yet to come, and World War II would also show that the high-explosive bomb delivered by aircraft had its limits. The limitation was to be created by increased defensive power based on improved fighting aircraft, and especially on the invention and perfection of radar, which would allow the fighters to be effectively concentrated against the bombers. Moreover, anti-aircraft artillery was to be hooked up with radar through predictor apparatus, resulting in enormously improved effectiveness of anti-aircraft gunfire, further reducing the power of the air bombing offensive.

The Germans, who had not built up an independent air force for bombing enemy cities in World War II, were to react to the terror-bombing of their country by building the V-weapons. With these they were to open a bombardment of London in the summer of 1944. From these weapons, or more particularly from the V 2, a rocket with a range of about 200 miles and a high explosive warhead, would be developed the rocket armament which is now the principal vehicle of the nuclear weapon.

Foreshadowing these rockets, World War I saw the first instrument of long-range bombardment. This was the German supergun, nicknamed "Big Bertha" (after the Christian name of the Krupp heiress). This secret weapon, which fired a shell of about 8-inch calibre with a range of 35 miles, opened fire on Paris coincident with one of the German offensives of the spring-summer of 1918, and was intended to terrify the Parisians and depress morale generally. After the initial surprise and some consternation, for it took some little time for the French to discover how and from where the shells were arriving, the effect was not great. I recall being in Paris on leave when the big gun was still dropping shells into the city at a slow and rather spasmodic rate of fire (for the linings of the gun, under the tremendous pressure of the propellant, did not last for many rounds). The life of the city seemed not at all disturbed. But from this forerunner it could have been deduced that air bombardment would develop as it has, the rocket replacing the piloted bomber aircraft for the delivery of the explosive to a target area of considerable dimensions.

General Mitchell expressed another important idea in 1930. He wrote that a country which made its air power sufficiently great might easily establish world domination. Great industrial countries could be decisively defeated by bombing attacks; furthermore, they could be held in subjection by an air force more easily than by an army and navy. If the defeated country should try to break out of its bondage, aircraft of the conquering nation could destroy the crops and render the fields infertile, and could destroy more of the industry and dwellings as well.

Reading this, it is hard to avoid an impression of megalomania. The idea of world dominion through air power was to reappear after World War II in the first intoxication of total victory and with the possession of the A-bomb, although the realities of world power and politics gradually extinguished such flaming dreams. The vision of air forces policing a world empire may have been agreeable to some airmen. Maybe they pictured an unopposed air force, like Jove, visiting destruction on disobedient groundlings. However, air force policing was applied, in a considerably reduced and milder form, by the RAF in the inter-war years, to the control of British colonial possessions, or mandates, such as Somaliland, Iraq, Jordan and the North-West Frontier of India. The experience of such operations may have moulded the thought of a generation of RAF officers, the successes of unopposed aircraft giving a false impression of the power of the air. Among those taking part in these operations were Squadron Leader Harris, the future Air Marshal and chief of the RAF Bomber Command in World War II, and Flight-Lieutenant Saundby, who was to be his principal staff officer and deputy and an Air Marshal also.

Mitchell thought that the influence of air power had become so great that all conceptions of military strategy, including the handling of armies and navies, would be changed. He also proclaimed that the growing power of the air was for the betterment of civilization, because wars would be decided quickly and not last for years and years. Finally, he warned that if a European country attacked the United States, the first targets would be New York, Chicago, Detroit, Pittsburgh and Washington. However, with the experience of World War II behind us and the threat of nuclear war looming over us, it is doubtful whether we would agree with Mitchell that the development of air power and its employment in war has been "for the betterment of civilization."

A more moderate view of the future of air warfare was held by Lord Trenchard. This was set out in 1928 in a carefully composed letter to Admiral Richmond, the first Commandant of the newly formed Imperial Defence College. Both before and after this, Lord Trenchard expressed more extreme views; but these presentations were probably influenced by Trenchard's need to make as strong a case as possible for the continued separate existence of the RAF. The younger service was more often than not, in the inter-war years, under attack by the two older services in the battle for the greatest share of the Treasury spending budget. There were frequent attempts to re-establish separate air services subordinate to the Navy and Army, to the detriment of the unified air force idea. In fact the

Royal Navy did succeed, in the end, in gaining much of what it wanted in the way of a Naval Air Service under its direct control.

In his letter to Admiral Richmond, Lord Trenchard was doubtless trying to be as reasonable and objective as possible, while at the same time propounding a theory of overall strategy which would emphasize the importance of an independent air force. He stated that the object of all three services in war was to defeat the enemy nation, not merely its army, navy or air force. The air force, however, would not need to defeat the opposing armed forces before it could defeat the enemy nation. This did not mean, in his view, that intense air fighting would not take place; on the contrary, it would be inevitable. But the air fighting would not take the form of directly attacking the enemy aircraft, either in the air or at their bases. The stronger side would develop a powerful offensive against the enemy industries on which he depended for the sustenance of his war effort; this would force the enemy to allocate aircraft to the defence of these areas, and he would thus be thrown on the defensive.

Lord Trenchard answered the question of whether such an air offensive would be contrary to international law or the dictates of humanity by saying that no international convention on how air bombardment should be conducted, restricted or defined did, in fact, exist; this was true. But provided that all reasonable care was taken to confine the scope of the bombing to the military objectives—the factories manufacturing all sorts of war material "from battleships to boots"—then the incidental damage and casualties which would be suffered by the civilian population from bombs that missed their intended mark would be regrettable, but not a sufficient reason for abandoning the policy of direct air attack on the enemy's productive capacity. If the enemy could secure immunity from air bombardment for his war manufactures because of the possibility of damage and death to the civil population, then he would always site his arsenals in the biggest cities.

Trenchard stated that he did not claim that an air force by itself could finish a war. But it would be one of the means of exercising pressure on the enemy, in conjunction with sea-power, blockade and the defeat of the enemy armies. Aircraft would have a necessary role in future land and sea battles, although their primary task should be the direct assault by air on the enemy nation.

Trenchard's forecast turned out to be closer to the actual events of the air warfare in World War II than those of Mitchell and Douhet, although the latter pair may turn out to be the truer prophets in the long run. Doubtless this was due to Trenchard's greater experience and his long-time responsibility for the development of the RAF—the first independent air force.

The bombing of cities during World War I, limited as it was, and the dire prophecies of others besides Douhet and Mitchell predicting that direct assaults on the civil population would be enormously increased in future wars, made many people believe that air bombing should be outlawed, or at least limited. Various attempts were made to do this. A group of international jurists met at The Hague in 1922-23 and drew up a set of rules which would have set limits to the right of air bombardment in war, generally assimilating these to the previously recognized rights of bombardment by artillery from the sea and the land. The rules allowed the bombing of armament industries, but stipulated that this should be done in such a way as to inflict minimum damage on non-combatants. In this, the distinguished jurists showed that they did not understand an essential characteristic of the aeroplane as a means of delivering an explosive charge, namely its lack of accuracy while fighting under the stresses of actual warfare. But one can scarcely blame them for this, as they doubtless had expert advice to the effect that bombs could be dropped in a relatively discriminating manner. Although a good deal of interest and discussion was aroused by the jurists' proposals, they were never incorporated in an international convention, and never became in any sense international law.

In 1925 the League of Nations set up a commission to prepare for a conference on the reduction and limitation of armaments. It held sessions from May 1926 until December 1930. The United States participated in the proceedings from 1926, and the Soviet Union attended from 1927, although they were not members of the League. Litvinov, the Soviet representative, proposed complete and immediate disarmament in December of 1927, an antecedent to Mr. Khrushchev's proposal to the United Nations in 1959 for general and complete disarmament.

While the preparatory commission was struggling with technicalities, a bolder, simpler and more idealistic proposal was put forward by Mr. Kellogg, then United States Secretary of State. The idea was brought to final form with the collaboration of M. Aristide Briand, Prime Minister of France, and became known as the Kellogg-Briand Pact. It was a treaty under which the signatories renounced war as an instrument of national policy, or, in other words, as a means of settling international disputes. Signed in August 1928 by fifteen of the most important nations, by 1930 it had been subscribed to by all self-governing states, except three South American republics. In 1931 it was invoked in vain to stop the Japanese invasion of Manchuria; in 1935 an appeal to Italy not to invade Ethiopia similarly failed. And then came Hitler and World War II. The lamentable failure of this noble experiment does not seem to have lessened the enthusiasm of the Soviet Union, and a few other states, for giving paper promises to be forever virtuous and peaceful.

Finally the League's disarmament preparatory commission adopted a draft convention, and this was submitted to the main conference which assembled in 1932 at Geneva. The draft convention, *inter alia,* provided for military aircraft to be limited in their horsepower, and for the prohibition of chemical and bacteriological warfare. Another proposal discussed was to prohibit air bombardment of any nature. The British Government, having in mind the use of the RAF to control the unruly tribes on the North-West Frontier of India and in Iraq, suggested an amendment allowing this form of air action. The air control, of course, had been exercised in a relatively decent way: warning was given to evacuate villages which were to be bombed as a punishment for tribal forays, abductions and so forth. This, in fact, was an economical and relatively bloodless way of controlling these lawless groups, who had immemorially been given to the practice of raiding and pillaging their neighbours. The former method was to send punitive columns of troops, who generally had to fight pretty hard to reach their objectives—the tribal villages—in the face of great difficulties of terrain and transport.

The British Labour Party, then in opposition, accused the Conservative Government of having blocked agreement to prohibit air bombardment, which it seemed would have been greatly in the interest of Britain, for the comparatively minor advantage of using the RAF to control marginal frontier areas. The Conservatives, of course, denied that this was a substantial cause of the disarmament conference's breakdown.

There were other proposals for legitimatizing air bombing of military targets in support of air or sea operations. But it became clear that it would be very hard to define what was a legitimate military objective. In 1933 a new draft based on British suggestions was unanimously accepted by the disarmament conference as a basis for the future convention. It called for a limitation of the numbers of naval and military aircraft, and for their eventual abolition.

The conference droned along, but the world political situation was worsening. In September 1931, the Japanese had begun a military offensive in Manchuria, which led to the invasion of China. As the League of Nations disapproved of these actions, Japan withdrew from it in 1933.

Germany had been demanding that the other powers should disarm down to her level as stipulated in the Treaty of Versailles, or that she should be allowed to rearm. In October 1933, she withdrew from the disarmament conference, and from the League. Italy threatened to do the same. In the face of the undisguised warlike intentions of the partners of the eventual Fascist alliance, disarmament was manifestly impossible, and on 16 June 1934 the conference was suspended. However, subcommittees to study various aspects of the disarmament problem were set up, and the bureau of the conference continued to exist until May of 1937. Italy had invaded Ethiopia in 1935 and carried on its colonial war there in spite of half-hearted economic sanctions voted by the League. Japan invaded China in July 1937. In the course of their war against China, they bombed Canton in 1938 and Chungking in 1939, causing numerous civilian casualties in each case. The Kuomintang Government protested violently. Madame Chiang Kai-shek's account of the bombing of Chungking rivalled the realities of the Hamburg holocaust. It was claimed that 1500 were killed, and about the same number seriously injured. The world was mildly upset. In July 1936 the civil war in Spain broke out, during which Hitler's Luftwaffe and their Italian colleagues shocked the world by bombing civilians in towns, notably Guernica.

It is instructive to note that all of these countries that initiated the bombing of civilian targets in the 1930's suffered incomparably greater damage when this sort of warfare was waged against them in the 1940's. Could the same kind of thing happen to the initiators of atomic bombing of cities?

The failure of the League of Nations Disarmament Conference, which broke up without achieving any result whatever in June 1934, is frequently recalled with satisfaction by those who are against all disarmament in the 1960's. Presumably they must also be happy about what followed.

# 4

## BOMBING IN WORLD WAR II: 1939-1942

When World War II broke out the airmen could put their theorizings into practice, though it was more than a year before a bombing offensive which could be described as independent of land or sea operations was attempted. Perhaps the beginning of air warfare in World War II should be dated, not from Hitler's invasion of Poland in September 1939, but rather from his occupation of Czechoslovakia in March of that year. He accomplished this without actual fighting, solely by the threat of overwhelming attack. The surrender at Munich in the previous September had shown Czechoslovakia that she had no friends or allies who would fight in her support. Aged and ill, President Hacha was finally forced by Goering's menaces to sign the capitulation. Goering threatened that his bombers would destroy Prague, and what befell Rotterdam some fourteen months later proved that he could have made his threats good.

The ideas of the air warfare theorists had been popularized, if that is the word, by journalists during the 1920's and 1930's, and in England, at any rate, the majority of people thought that if war came, great air attacks on London and other large cities would be inevitable. Indeed, one of the main reasons why

Mr. Chamberlain had agreed to Hitler's terms at Munich was apprehension (based largely on airmen's evidence) as to the great damage which air bombing attacks could cause, Britain's defences at that time being very inadequate. Aircraft had been greatly developed in speed, reliability and load-carrying power since World War I and it was known that Hitler's Germany had a much more powerful air force than had Britain. It was uncertain how many bombing aircraft the Luftwaffe numbered, and there was an exaggerated fear of what it could accomplish. Londoners could remember the air raids of World War I, and could foresee the multiplication of their effect by a factor of 10 . . . 100 . . . 1000. Who knew? Air Force officers had estimated that air attacks on London might cause 150,000 casualties in the first few days.

Minutes after Neville Chamberlain's voice, gloomy and apprehensive, had announced that Great Britain was at war with the Third Reich, the air raid sirens sounded. It was a false alarm, and for ten months all the alarm about air attacks on England's great cities seemed false also. But the compulsory carrying of gas-masks, issued hurriedly to the population of the most threatened centres, was a constant reminder of the danger. These little cardboard boxes, measuring about six inches in each dimension, were remembrancers that death might come out of the sky with little warning. Looking back, it is somewhat ironic that the danger against which the British were most visibly prepared never materialized.

Why didn't the air raids come? It was because Hitler and his advisers had a theory on the use of aircraft in war different from that of Douhet and his disciples. This had been demonstrated in the swift overthrow of Poland, where the Stuka dive-bombers combined with powerful tank formations to disrupt and shatter the Polish Army and Air Force. The long-range bombers were used mainly to destroy the Polish aircraft on their aerodromes, and then for deep attacks on communications. The air effort was co-ordinated with the operations on the ground; the objective of all the German forces was to destroy the capacity of the enemy's forces to resist, and to conquer territory. In this they were completely successful. Polish bravery could do nothing against the powerful armament and new blitz techniques of the Germans.

On the first of September, 1939, President Roosevelt had addressed an appeal to the belligerents to refrain from unrestricted air warfare. This had been agreed to by the British Government the same day. The German Government issued a declaration on the 18th of September welcoming Roosevelt's appeal. But the British were in no position to begin effective bombing warfare, even if there had been no Roosevelt appeal for them to accept. While over fifty RAF bombing squadrons had been organized, there was no reserve of aircraft, no training organization and no reserve of trained pilots. Even when provision had been made for these essentials, the front line operating bomber strength would be only three to four hundred aircraft, about half of them light bombers unsuitable for long-distance attacks on industrial targets in Germany.

In the hurried development before the war to overtake the lead of the German Air Force after Britian had awakened to the danger, priority had been given to the needs of defence: fighter aircraft, fighter control and the radar for detecting the enemy's approach. In the event, the fighter organization brilliantly justified the money and effort spent on it by repulsing the German invasion threat. But the bomber force, which would have to carry out the strategic offensive, lacked the kind of aircraft and the technical aids needed to produce effective results in an offensive against the German homeland, although the Air Staff had foreseen the need for such equipment in the pre-war years and had urged its procurement. Specifications for the four-engined bombers which were eventually the mainstay of Bomber Command were issued in 1936, but the planes only began to be produced in adequate numbers late in 1942.

During the late autumn and in December of 1939, the RAF attempted a number of raids on naval vessels in German waters or harbours, using the Wellington, the latest and best of their bombers. No serious harm was done to the German ships. In the first raid, the Wellingtons were able to fight off the defending Messerschmitt fighters without loss. But after that they suffered increasingly severe casualties. In two separate attacks, the British bombers lost nearly half their number. These operations caused the British air staff to reassess the possibility of large-scale daylight air bombing of Germany which their pre-war strategical thinking had favoured. It had been the majority opinion that if the bombers were armed with machine-guns in multiple power-operated turrets, and flew in formation, they would be able to bomb Germany in daylight with relatively few losses even against fighter opposition. But the experience of December 1939 decided the air operations staffs that this would not, in fact, be possible, and so it was decided to concentrate on night bombing. The RAF had always considered night bombing as an alternative way of operating. However, the difficulties of navigating in the dark to the target areas and then locating the targets accurately enough to permit precise bombing had not been fully realized.

The US Air Force, even before the USA was at war, knew of the early RAF experience with bombing by daylight which caused them to turn to night bombing as the more effective system of attacking the German homeland. However, the Americans were confident that in the B 17 "Flying Fortress" they had a long-range bomber with sufficient performance and carrying sufficient defensive armament to enable them to penetrate to targets in enemy country, even in the face of strongly organized fighter defence. The famous Norden gyro-stabilized bomb-sight, which under peacetime training conditions had enabled very accurate bombing to be carried out from high altitudes, also led the American airmen to overrate the effectiveness of day-bombing operations.

I recall discussions at this time, in the Imperial Defence College and other military circles, showing a cleavage of opinion in the RAF on what the overall policy of that service should be. This argument went on between the "bomber boys" and the "fighter boys" and, like most inter-service controversy, boiled down to how the available money was to be allotted. Generally speaking, the bombers saw the RAF developing in accordance with theories of independent air operations such as those described in the last chapter. The "fighter boys" were those who now were responsible for building up the air defence of Great Britain to cope with the threat of heavy air attack by Germany.

They had to create the organization within which the future heroes of the Battle of Britain—the famous "few"—could effectively defend the country.

The "fighter boys" were dedicated to the proposition that they could defeat any bombing offensive; the credo of the "bomber boys" was that they could get through any fighter defences and pulverize the enemy's economy. In this connection it may be relevant to note that if the war between Great Britain and Germany had been conducted exclusively by air forces, geographical factors and prevailing winds would have been in favour of Germany.

Analyzing the history of air warfare from 1939 to 1945, before the discovery of nuclear fission multiplied the explosive force of the bomb a thousandfold, one could say that neither the champions of the fighter defence nor the champions of the bombing offensive were entirely right, or entirely wrong. A rough assessment would be that a well-organized fighter defence of high morale, such as the RAF Fighter Command in 1940 or the German defending fighters in 1942-43, could make it impossible for a daylight bombing offensive to be sustained. The defending fighters and flak could inflict such casualties that continued attacks on the same objectives would have reduced the effective strength of the bombing crews more rapidly than they could have been replaced, to say nothing of the effect on the morale of the survivors. This high price in casualties would have been paid for only very limited destruction of the armaments factories, oil production installations and transportation key points that were the objectives. The German air defence retained its relative effectiveness until late in 1944, after which it was worn down and gradually lost its power to prevent daylight bombing. This resulted from a combination of factors: the American development of a long-range escorting fighter, which could accompany and protect the bombers far into Germany and inflict heavy casualties on the defending German fighters; the reduction of the German-held area in Europe consequent on the successful invasion over the Normandy beaches; and the cumulative effects of the USAF and RAF attacks against aircraft-production factories and oil-producing installations.

But from 1940 on the RAF carried out its offensive against

Germany almost entirely by night bombing. Concealment by darkness turned the scale in favour of the offensive, once the RAF had acquired enough suitable aircraft and had developed adequate radio-navigational controls. The bombers did get through, and to most of Germany. But this ability to penetrate was achieved at the cost of accuracy in bombing. While it was always maintained publicly that the bombers' objectives were the industries and transportation facilities that supported the German military effort, in fact these targets were being attacked, and could only be attacked, by the indirect method of destroying industrial cities wholesale. And at one stage, the view was held in high quarters that the object should be to burn so many of the industrial workers' homes that production would become impossible.

The controversy in pre-war theory and its working out in actual warfare illustrates what I believe to be a prevailing general error of proponents of air warfare, namely, that air attack by bombing aircraft can be directed at specific military targets of relatively small dimensions, and directed with such effect that the targets will be destroyed. But even when there is no enemy interference by either fighter or anti-aircraft artillery, the problem of dropping a bomb to hit a given spot on the ground from an aircraft at high altitude and moving at high speed is by no means easy. The position of the aircraft in space at the time of release relative to the position of the target on the ground is hard to determine, because horizontal and vertical planes of reference are very difficult to establish accurately, owing to the distortions of instrument reading introduced by the manœuvres of the aircraft. Also, the direction of the flight is greatly affected by the force and direction of the wind, which is only ascertainable by continued observation of the ground. Accurate bombing thus depends on an uninterrupted view of the earth's surface and the target for an appreciably long time; that is, it depends on having a relatively unclouded sky. Given these conditions, and no distraction from the attacks of defending aircraft or flak, it was possible to drop bombs with sufficient accuracy to permit calculation that a certain proportion of all bombs dropped would fall in the target area, and to assume that the target would probably be destroyed. Of course, it was soon realized that in actual wartime operations it was practically impossible to reach the precision obtained under peacetime experimental conditions. So even daylight bombing in late 1944 and 1945 tended to be against large objectives.

Experience of the development of day and night bombing during World War II could be summed up as showing that in the presence of defensive measures, such as fighter aircraft, flak, ground deception and camouflage, bombing attacks have to be made against large targets, that is, against cities and consequently against the whole of the population, or that portion of it living in large cities or industrial complexes. It flouts the lessons of history to assert that in war between first-class powers nowadays, manned aircraft will drop their bombs only on military objectives. While the accuracy of missiles of intercontinental range under experimental conditions in peacetime is said to be very high, it is hardly credible that under conditions of actual war, cities which happened to be anywhere near military targets would not be blasted.

On 10 May 1940, the Germans invaded France and the Low Countries, Winston Churchill replaced Neville Chamberlain as Prime Minister of Great Britain, and three aircraft bombed Freiburg-im-Breisgau, killing fifty-seven people, mostly women and children. The German Propaganda Ministry immediately announced this as a deliberate attack on the German population, and threatened five-fold retaliation on British or French towns if it were repeated. In fact, German planes had dropped the bombs, thinking they were bombing an airfield in France. The British Government responded to this German threat by withdrawing its 1 September 1939 pledge to the President of the United States that the RAF would not bomb civilian populations. Up to this time, the promise to the US President had been scrupulously kept. Now, however, in view of the German threats, His Majesty's Government would reserve the right to take any appropriate retaliatory action if the British civilian population were bombed.

The next event in the chain of developments that eliminated the attempt to protect the civil population by restrictions on air bombing was the notorious German attack on Rotterdam. In the heat of war the true facts were obscured by propaganda exaggerations by both sides: the British and Allied propagandists represented the attack as pure savagery and terrorism; the Germans tried to show that it had occurred in the course of military operations, nothing more than a new kind of artillery support to their troops endeavouring to capture Rotterdam and defeat the opposing Dutch forces. The German command was demanding the city's surrender, under the threat of total destruction and the Dutch authorities had finally submitted, just as the first German bombers appeared. It was too late for them to be stopped from dropping their bombs. About 100 aircraft dropped 94 tons of bombs. Fires destroyed slightly over a square mile of the principal part of the city, 980 civilians were killed, some 20,000 buildings were destroyed, and 78,000 people were made homeless. These statistics are not impressive when compared with those of later air raids on German and Japanese cities, but they came as a great shock to civilian opinion, and not only to the citizens of the countries actually at war. The first official Dutch statement on Rotterdam was published in Washington, and it exaggerated the casualties nearly thirty-fold. It was the propaganda exaggerations which aroused the fear and anger of the British people, and changed the general mood from a hope that the air would spare the cities, to a readiness for retaliation and revenge on German cities. The idea that this would be the only answer to Rotterdams became accepted.

The events just cited began the erosion of the inhibitions against bombing of civilians during World War II, and the process was relatively slow. The question for us in the age of nuclear warfare (or of preparation for nuclear warfare) is whether any inhibitions against direct attack on the civil population now remain, and if they do remain, how long would they be effective in the accelerated tempo of warfare today. While there was a pause, from September 1939 until September 1940, before air warfare really got into its stride, would there be any such pause if war should break out in the 1960's? We are reminded daily that an intercontinental ballistic missile can travel from Russia to the USA, and in the reverse direction, in half an hour. Would any restrictions on targets remain after the first exchange of rockets, that is, after the first half-hour of war? If no restriction would operate then, why should any initial limitations be put on the icbm targets in the strategic thinking of the air war-lords of either side? The purpose of this review of history is to show that the innate characteristics of the air war, and the weapons with which it will be waged, are such that it will be unlimited, without moral or legal restrictions, and that the principal targets and sufferers on both sides will be the civilians. Civilians, of course, will include the wives and children of the air warriors of all grades.

During the May-June campaign in which the German armies overran the Low Countries and France and forced the evacuation of the British Army through Dunkirk, the tasks of the Bomber Command of the raf included attacks on railway centres and supply depots in the Ruhr and Rhineland. Attacking such objectives was opposed by the French, who feared that it would provoke German retaliation without substantially affecting the course of the land operations. The French were right about the lack of effect, and about the end of May it was decided that attacks on the first type of target were no longer worthwhile. The long-range bombing effort was switched to attacking German synthetic oil plants instead—a strategic objective which was pursued sporadically throughout the whole course of the air war against Germany.

After the surrender of France there was a pause while Hitler was preparing the invasion of Britain. To invade, he would have to gain control of the English Channel and other waters over which the invasion fleet would pass. German naval forces in themselves were not strong enough to defeat the British naval forces which could be deployed in the narrow seas, but the Germans hoped that a combined offensive by their powerful air forces and their naval forces could gain the superiority necessary to permit the passage of the invasion barges. It was clear that the prelude to gaining control of the narrow seas would be to gain control of the air space over them. This is what the Battle of Britain was about.

The Battle of Britain began on 8 August 1940: the German Air Force heavily attacked British shipping in the Channel. Thereafter the main object of the Luftwaffe was to break down the resistance of the RAF Fighter Command. The strikes of the German bomber force were mainly concentrated on a score or so of key fighter airfields. These attacks caused serious damage to the ground organization upon which the control of the defending British fighters depended. The Luftwaffe also succeeded in destroying or rendering unserviceable so many of the British fighter aircraft (though suffering more loss themselves) that write-offs were exceeding production, and the reserves of serviceable aircraft steadily declined. A continuation of the German bombing attacks on these objectives might have achieved its purpose in neutralizing the British fighter defence and rendering it impotent to dispute command of the air over the narrow waters.

It was at this point, on 24 August, that the Luftwaffe dropped a number of bombs on London, and Prime Minister Churchill ordered a retaliatory raid on Berlin. During the night of 25/26 August, 81 aircraft of Bomber Command carried out the raid, which produced little damage directly, but perhaps angered Hitler, and may have caused him, a few days later, to switch the main attack of the German bombers onto British cities, principally London, and away from the proper strategic objective of the British fighter airfields. Probably by this time other considerations were influencing him towards postponing the invasion of Britain until the next spring. The actual decision was taken on 17 September. Ten days earlier the first large daylight raid on London had been made by some 250 bombers with hundreds of escorting fighters. This marked the beginning of the London Blitz. From September 1940 to mid-May 1941 about 19,000 tons of bombs were dropped on the capital, killing over 13,000 civilians and temporarily rendering about 375,000 people homeless.

It was during the Battle of Britain that the RAF had their finest hours in public honour and gratitude. The "few" young fighting airmen on whose courage, endurance and skill depended the fate of Britain, and perhaps of more than Britain, were rightly acclaimed as heroes. And it should not be forgotten that Bomber Command was fighting bravely and effectively as well, hitting the concentrations of barges and improvised landing vessels in French and Low Country ports and disrupting other preparations for invasion.

Apart from the attacks on London, the raid on Coventry on 14/15 November 1940 was perhaps the most important carried out by the Germans. Some 450 bombers, using techniques of radio guidance and target marking by incendiaries (later adopted and improved by the RAF in its night raids on Germany), dropped about 500 tons of high explosives and 880 incendiary canisters, resulting in great destruction and in the temporary shut-down of a number of industrial plants which were very important to aircraft production.

In September 1940, Prime Minister Churchill addressed a memorandum to the Cabinet, containing the following passage:

> Our supreme effort must be to gain overwhelming mastery in the air. . . . We must develop the power to carry on ever-increasing volume of explosives to Germany, so as to pulverize the entire industry and scientific structure on which the war effort and economic life of the enemy depend, while holding him at arm's length from our Island. In no other way at present visible can we hope to overcome the immense military power of Germany.

These bold words were written one year after the outbreak of war, at the height of the Blitz, when Britain stood alone, facing not only Germany but also Italy. The concept demonstrates Churchill's superb courage. While at the time it seemed that there was no other way for Great Britain to take the offensive against Germany, the possibility that a single-handed war against Germany could have been won by exchanges of bombs seems, in the light of present knowledge, very small indeed. When the bomber offensive began in October, after the War Cabinet had agreed to the Churchillian strategy, Bomber Command had a daily average of only about 250 light and medium bombers serviceable and available for operations.

At this time, also, the effectiveness of the bombing which had actually been carried out was greatly exaggerated. The British were nourishing delusions. The thought that extensive damage had been caused to the targets attacked in Germany kept up the spirits of British war leaders and the public. This belief was based on what the bomber crews reported on return from their missions. These reports were usually very much on the optimistic side. This is not to accuse the airmen of deliberate misrepresentation, but experience eventually showed that in this type of combat, as in most others, the perceptions and memories of men during the stress and excitement of fighting are not at all to be relied on. American and other neutral press correspondents in Germany had sent back reports contradicting the Air Ministry communiqués which claimed extensive damage. Some of the higher Bomber Command staff officers, too, were sceptical about the crew reporting, especially when they reported hitting targets obscured by cloud. Eventually investigation, and adoption of the practice of photographing targets after the raids, showed that the bombing was indeed very inaccurate; in general, only about one-third of the attacking aircraft had bombed within five miles of the targets. The percentage of effective bombs dropped fell even lower in well-defended areas, such as the Ruhr. This sobering discovery and analysis by Bomber Command, which showed that the bombing up to that time had been relatively ineffective, made it necessary to revise the strategy of the bombing offensive. The conclusion of Bomber Command, that a change was necessary if the air offensive against Germany was to yield substantial results, was put to the Air Ministry and thence to the Government. The Government was reluctant to abandon its stated policy of bombing only definitely military targets, but Bomber Command pointed out that it was impossible for the bombers to drop all their bombs close to the target, and what in effect was happening, and would necessarily continue to happen if bombing of Germany was to continue at all, would be a fairly large scattering of bombs round the target area. They were bombing areas in fact, if not in intention.

The Government eventually accepted the views of the Air Ministry, which then issued directives on the new strategy and conduct of operations to Bomber Command. These stated that a review of the enemy's situation had showed that his weakest points were the morale of the civil population and the inland transportation system. (This was in July 1941, after Hitler had opened his offensive against the Soviet Union, and Britain no longer faced Germany alone.) So the main effort of the bomber force was to be directed against these supposed weak points, especially against such congested industrial towns as Cologne, Duisberg, Düsseldorf and Duisburg-Rurhort, where the effect on the morale of the civil population would be greatest.

It is noteworthy that even when this decision had been taken, and the object of the bombing offensive had been laid down in unequivocal terms to Bomber Command, so far as the public knew bombing was still directed against militarily justifiable targets, such as submarine and aircraft production plants, transportation key points and synthetic oil works. There would have been politically awkward protests if the intention deliberately to destroy German civilians and their dwellings had been bluntly proclaimed. This is not to assert that the majority of the British people, after their experience of being blitzed themselves and convinced that the Germans had really started unrestricted air war by the attack on Rotterdam, were not quite gratified to know that the Germans were now getting a very large dose of their own medicine.

Some of the directors of the bombing offensive were impatient because of what seemed a lack of candour in continuing to represent the bombing as confined to military targets, when in fact areas were being bombed. They knew it was not possible, given the difficulty of finding specific targets of relatively small dimensions, and penetrating the increasingly effective German defences, to do anything else but bomb areas. But when a nation is struggling for survival, dissimulation is often required, and self-justification is not only easy, but is a necessary concomitant of the determination to fight.

A little later than this, a small war between British scientists broke out. The disputed point was the probable effectiveness of direct attacks on the civil population. In March 1942, Professor Lindemann, the Prime Minister's personal scientific adviser, calculated that if the bombing offensive were concentrated on the working-class areas of the 58 largest German towns and cities with a population of more than 100,000 inhabitants each, it should be possible to make homeless one-third of the whole German population by the middle of 1943. For this sort of operation, the resources of the whole British armament industry would need to be employed in providing for the requirements of Bomber Command. Professors Blackett, Zuckerman and Tizard contested Lindemann's calculations, but their objections were overruled. However, the hoped-for results were not obtained during the period mentioned. Bomber Command (and doubtless Professor Lindemann) had the excuse that all the British armament manufacturing capacity had *not,* in fact, been concentrated on providing the required tools.

What is particularly significant, in connection with the general theme of this book, is that is was decided to attack the biggest targets, those that the bombers could be sure of destroying; that meant hitting the biggest agglomerations of dwelling places. This was a direct attack on the whole population, or that portion of it living in cities and towns big enough to present the bombers with easily identifiable targets that could be set on fire by incendiary bombs. It had been learned by this time that incendiaries were the most effective form of missile for mass destruction.

Sir Arthur Harris took over Bomber Command in February 1942. He has been widely represented as the chief designer and executant of the unrestricted bombing policy of Germany. While he was certainly the commander who executed the policy with vigour and ruthlessness, he did not design it; the policy had already been established when he took over. But he immediately began, with great energy, to develop the capacity of Bomber Command to carry out the task which had been prescribed for it. About this time the heavy, long-range bombers, of which the Lancaster was the most famous type, had begun to come off production; radio aids to navigation precise enough to permit area bombing when clouds made the ground invisible had also begun to be available. During the spring of 1942, under Harris' strong leadership, several relatively successful raids were carried out, on Cologne, Lubeck and Rostock. But the policy of concentrating the offensive effort on the bombing of Germany was being contested with violence by the Army and Navy, with leading politicians entering into the dispute.

Therefore Harris and his advisers concluded that something spectacular must be done to convince the Government and the people that great results could be achieved, and perhaps the war could be won outright, if only the strategic concept of bombing the German people into submission were fully accepted, and if the necessary resources were devoted to it.

This led to the preparation and execution of the first great raid by one thousand bombing aircraft on Cologne. It is interesting to note that the operation was given the code-name "Millennium." The Oxford gives a secondary definition of this word as a "period of good government, great happiness, & prosperity." Whether the period which followed this first demonstration of saturation bombing and its fire-raising capacity should be so qualified is left to the reader to decide.

The raid was carried out, and from the Bomber Command's standpoint it was a great success. Out of 1046 aircraft taking part in the operation, only 44 were lost—a rate far less than normal. Air Marshal Saundby, in his book *Air Bombardment* states that the "reports of the crews were wildly enthusiastic." "The news, when released, resounded throughout the world." "The imagination of the British and American publics was captured." (The United States was at this time developing the bases in England from which its bombing forces would carry out their campaign against Germany.) Part of the reason for Bomber Command's Cologne raid was to convince the American authorities and the American public that air attack on the German homeland should be a prime strategic object of the Allies, and to avoid the possibility that the American bomber force intended to take part in it should be diverted elsewhere.

Prime Minister Churchill sent Bomber Command a congratulatory message, concluding: "This proof of the growing power of the British Bomber Force is also the herald of what Germany will receive, city by city, from now on." The Prime Minister and the War Cabinet were persuaded now of the possibility of defeating Germany by bombing attack, and confirmed their tentative policy. Moreover, it was now directed that priority should be given to Bomber Command requirements, not only in aircraft but in the development of radio devices to facilitate accurate position-finding at night, even in unfavourable weather, in order to make bombing relatively more accurate and effective.

The Casablanca Conference in January 1943 set the seal on the bombing policy which should be followed by the RAF and USAF in the European theatre, in the following words:

> Your primary object will be the progressive destruction of the German military, industrial and economic system, and the undermining of the morale of the German people to a point where their armed resistance is fatally weakened.

"Undermining morale" sounds a nice, gentle, persuasive way of waging war, until one realized that it means killing civilian men, women and children indiscriminately, destroying their dwellings and burning and suffocating them by tens of thousands.

# 5

## BOMBING OFFENSIVES AGAINST GERMANY AND JAPAN; INTRODUCTION OF THE ATOM BOMB

By the spring of 1943 the RAF Bomber Command was sufficiently strong and well-organized to begin the continuous offensive which it was hoped would bring Germany to the point of surrender. The USAF had by this time assembled a larger bomber force on airfields in England, and was also ready to conduct large-scale operations. The general lines on which the bombing campaign was to be conducted had been laid down at Casablanca. This directive allowed a very wide choice of targets—anything in the German military, industrial and economic system, plus (most discretionary of all) anything which would undermine the morale of the German people.

The British and American bomber chieftains, Harris and Eaker, adopted different strategies. This came about because, as already indicated, the British and American theories as to the most effective use of bombing forces differed, and as a consequence, types of equipment and training in the two air forces had also diverged. General Eaker decided to concentrate the efforts of his bombers initially against German aircraft and engine factories. When the bombing reduced the output of the factories, fewer and fewer aircraft could be delivered to the

Luftwaffe, and its strength would be progressively reduced. The Luftwaffe would also be wasted by air fighting, both on the home front against the British and American bomber forces, and on the eastern front against the Russians. This idea of attack on the German Air Force was an adaptation to bombing air war of the classical strategical doctrine of attacking the enemy's military forces and reducing their strength until they were no longer able to sustain the struggle. It was intended that the Luftwaffe should be brought to battle by attacking an objective which it would have to defend.

Air Marshal Harris, on the other hand, elected to attack large industrial areas and ports, convinced that this was the best and most direct way to destroy German industry on which the German military strength depended. The experiences which had led the RAF early in the war to decide to do their bombing by night rather than by day have been described (p. 41). But the night-bombing methods developed by the RAF were not sufficiently accurate to ensure destruction of targets of limited area, such as those that the US Air Force proposed to engage.

Some British officials who had a say in the planning of the air offensive, notably in the Ministry of Economic Warfare, thought that the air effort could be more effective if concentrated on more specific targets such as key industries or bottlenecks in production. If these could be put out of action, it was argued, a more immediate effect on the prospects of the war would be produced. Bomber Command, however, was sceptical about all such special objectives or "panaceas," the more so because some of them had actually been destroyed; nevertheless the war and the Germans' capacity to wage it went on much as before. Harris and his men stuck to their guns—or bomb-bays—and maintained that area bombing was the only dependable way of getting results.

In March 1943 Bomber Command began a series of operations against the Ruhr industrial complex; they now had the strength and organization to continue with the attacks until very great damage had been done. Other important industrial cities and towns, including Kassel, Mannheim, Hanover and the ports of Bremen, Wilhelmshaven, Kiel and Hamburg, were also subjected to massive attack. The operations against Hamburg, on four nights between 24 July and 3 August, were of great historic importance. Their most significant feature was the fire-storm which was created. This phenomenon results when a sufficient number of large fires are burning and the ascending column of hot air causes a partial vacuum in the centre of the area of conflagration. Air from outside is sucked in, resulting in winds of considerable force which fan and spread the flames. Tremendous temperatures are reached and the oxygen in the area becomes exhausted, resulting in the suffocation of people in cellars and air raid shelters. Fire storms were also caused in the intensive bombing of other cities, and are promised as one of the effects of attacks by thermonuclear bombs.

Hamburg was in advance of any other German city in its precautions against air raids; it was extraordinarily well prepared. But this was unavailing against attack on the scale which Bomber Command mounted. In this operation the British attacking forces used for the first time the technique, known by the code-name "Window," of scattering tinsel strips in large quantities. This completely confused the radar aiming devices on the German anti-aircraft guns and secured freedom from interference for the pathfinding bombers which laid the flares marking the main target area and for the other bombers which followed, dropping high-explosives and incendiaries. There were four raids, nearly 800 bombers in each, and over 8000 tons of bombs were dropped, nearly half that tonnage being incendiaries. Estimates of the number of civilians killed vary, owing to difficulties of identification and other confusing elements; the most probable number is about 40,000 with nearly as many seriously injured. About 215,000 of the dwellings in the city (some 60 per cent) were rendered uninhabitable; 580 industrial plants were put out of action, many of which had been making armaments. Much shipping was sunk in the harbour. For Germany this was a great disaster, and Albert Speer, the Armaments Minister, calculated gloomily that if such devastation were visited on another six major German cities, arms production would drop disastrously. However, his prediction proved wrong; German industry showed an extraordinary capability to recover from the effects of heavy air attacks until almost the last months of the war.

A similar fire-storm was raised by the attack on Kassel on the night of 22/23 October, and proportionate damage was done to the dwellings and industrial plants of the town. Fortunately the death toll was much lower, something less than 8000.

The RAF's night-bombing offensive continued through the autumn and winter of 1943, many other large German industrial cities being subjected to heavy destruction. In August, the attacks on Berlin began, and they also continued throughout the winter. The last heavy attack of this campaign against the German homeland was made towards the end of March 1944, after which the RAF Bomber Command, together with the USAF bomber force, was switched onto tasks intended to prepare and facilitate the invasion of the Continent.

The US air forces allocated to the air war against Germany, as we have noted, adopted a different strategy: their objectives were the plants manufacturing aircraft, engines or their components. They used different techniques and tactics from the RAF, bombing by day. Covered by fighters operating from British airfields, they began in August 1942 with attacks on railway yards in Rouen. Other similar attacks were carried out during the remainder of the year, but none was made on objectives on German territory. The delay in carrying the offensive into Germany was due to the need to build up a sufficient force of Flying Fortresses (B 17's) and to train their crews in formation flying, gunnery and tactics to the degree necessary to be able to penetrate into Germany against the strong fighter defences. By the beginning of 1943 General Eaker had a force of about 500 B 17's ready to begin the campaign against the German homeland.

In March 1943 the 8th US Air Force, based in Britain, entered effectively into the bombing offensive against Germany with several successful attacks against important aircraft and engine factories. But at that time of year, with limited hours of daylight, if the targets were any distance within Germany the bombers arrived over them about the middle of the day. Cloud was, as a rule, most prevalent at this time; this hampered bomb-aiming, and of course it greatly eased the problems of the German fighter and anti-aircraft defence to know approximately when the bombing attacks could be expected. The result was that the German fighters took a heavy toll of the B 17's, especially in the well known attacks on the Messerschmitt aircraft factory at Regensburg, and the Schweinfurt ball-bearing factories. Losses rose to 20 per cent in the attack on Schweinfurt. This was prohibitively high, even though the bombing had been accurate enough to damage severely the plants attacked. It became obvious that if daylight attacks by formations of B 17's depending on their own armament for defence were continued, the results achieved would not compensate for the very great number of casualties that would be incurred.

To enable the Flying Fortresses to go on with their raids against objectives deep within Germany, it was necessary to develop a fighter with sufficient range and performance to accompany them throughout the operation. Towards the end of 1943 this requirement was met by the famous P 51 Mustang. The US 8th Air Force could now raid with fighter escort protection, and in the combats which ensued, heavy casualties were inflicted on the defending German fighters. This type of operation increased in scale during the first three months of 1944. Due to their losses the Germans were forced to concentrate on production of fighter aircraft, and as one result they began to lack enough bombers to take the offensive in the air war. In fact, they had been doing little strategic bombing for many months. They also began to run short of trained fighter pilots. The American strategy was paying off and its effect became most evident in 1944 when the Allied air forces attained almost complete control of the air space over the invading armies.

The culmination of this part of the 8th US Air Force's offensive was seen in the attacks on Berlin in early March 1944, when more than a thousand B 17's, escorted by hundreds of fighters, bombed targets in Hitler's capital, inflicting heavy loss.

From March until the late autumn of 1944 the RAF and USAF suspended their independent air warfare role, with the exception of a few forays into Germany. Instead, they concentrated on bombing targets whose destruction would be an aid to the operations of the land forces invading France over the Normandy beaches and from the Mediterranean. The chief object was to destroy the railway communications in Northern France and so to prevent the Germans from moving reinforcements to oppose the Allied advance. In this task, and in the neutralizing or destroying of certain special targets such as coastal batteries and light German naval craft in Channel and Atlantic ports, the heavy bombers were brilliantly successful. When the invasion bridgehead was established and the Allied armies broke out, the bombers were also employed to attack special targets, hard nuts such as Caen, that impeded the Allied advance. This role at times amounted to close support for which, of course, the big bombers were never intended nor their crews trained. Nevertheless, they produced the required results on many occasions. It is also to be remembered that the air war over Germany for the year from March '43 to March '44 had so weakened the Luftwaffe that the Allied armies had a very high degree of protection from air attack, while the defending Germans were subjected to constant and heavy strafing by the Allied tactical air forces.

When the USAF and RAF resumed the bombing offensive on Germany, their principal objectives were the oil-producing installations and the transportation systems, both rail and canal. Because of the reduction of the territory under Germany's control as the Russians drove ahead victoriously on the Eastern Front, Germany had become much more vulnerable to attack on these sectors, both vital to her war-making capacity. The bomber attacks gradually produced an increasing paralysis of transportation; this had become almost complete by the time the war reached its end. German production of oil had almost ceased, stocks were nearly exhausted, and if the fighting had gone on there would have been no fuel for aircraft, tanks and other military vehicles. But there was one final and shocking episode of direct attack on the civil population. In this case the slaughter and destruction of civilian dwellings could not be excused as incidental to attack on legitimate military objectives. It was, of course, the notorious assault on Dresden in the final weeks of the war. This has been impressively and minutely described in its antecedents and its horrifying actuality by David Irving in his remarkable book *The Destruction of Dresden.* Some 750 Lancaster heavy bombers of Bomber Command at-

tacked the city on the night of 13/14 February 1945, using the
techniques which had been found to be most effective for ensuring the destruction of the largest possible area of a city. A
firestorm was produced, causing far more casualties than that
of Hamburg, or indeed than any other air operation of World
War II, Hiroshima included. The estimated toll of dead was
35,600. The city was packed with refugees and prisoners of
war, swarming in to escape from the advancing Russian armies.
It was well known to the Intelligence Section of Bomber Command that Dresden harboured very little of military importance. This caused Bomber Command to query the order to
attack the city—a very rare step. The order was confirmed. The
intention behind the order and the reasons for it are not entirely clear, in spite of Mr. Irving's painstaking research. However, he clearly indicates that the political authorities must bear
the responsibility for what resulted. It seems that it was an attempt to show the Russians the might of the Anglo-American
bomber forces. By the end of 1944 the Allied advance had been
halted, and this was followed by the German counter-offensive
in the Ardennes. Meanwhile, the Russians had been surging
forward on the Eastern Front. The leaders of the Western Allies must have thought they had to do something to restore the
balance of military success between the West and the USSR, in
view of the forthcoming negotiations at Yalta.

The British bombing attack was followed the next day by a
blow by the Flying Fortresses of the 8th Air Force; over 300 of
them bombed the burning city again, and Mustangs of the
fighter escort flew over it, strafing "targets of opportunity," that
is, anything moving that caught their eye. When the crews
were briefed for this operation they were told that they were
attacking railway installations. The American Air Force commanders still seemed to pretend that such targets in the middle
of large towns could be attacked and seriously damaged without causing enormous casualties to the civil population. The
Dresden operation took place some weeks after an attack on
"railway and administrative targets" in Berlin had killed 25,000
of the city's civilian inhabitants in a single afternoon. Either the
US Air Force commanding generals did not know what was
really going on, or they had an enormous capacity for self-

deception, or they had decided that, "public-relationswise," it would be better to keep on saying that all the bombing carried out by the American Air Force was against strictly military targets.

In 1944 the new German weapons of air warfare appeared; these were the V 1 flying bomb, and the V 2 rocket. They were the forerunners of the family of rockets of all sizes and ranges which had its most spectacular flowering in the Sputnik in October 1957, and which has since multiplied and proliferated into great numbers of ICBM's, both in United States and Soviet Union arsenals. They were primarily the German answer to the bombing war against their homeland, and were intended not only to devastate British cities, as those of Germany were being devastated, but also to hamper and delay, if not prevent, the invasion of the Continent.

When put into action, these weapons were neither very accurate, nor dependable. But they would probably show about as good a pattern of placement of their explosive charges relative to the target as would the bombing of targets in Germany, for which they were retaliation. One can regard this development as steming from Big Bertha, the German long-range supergun of World War I which bombarded Paris. After all, bombardment is bombardment, whether the explosive charge is delivered by an air crew dropping it out of a bomber, by a pilotless ramjet-propelled aeroplane such as the V 1 or by a rocket. If the purpose is essentially to place a given quantity of incendiary material or high explosive within a given radius of the chosen target, the rocket would seem to be the most effective way of doing it, providing that the necessary range and accuracy can be built into the weapon. The Americans and Russians seem to have solved this problem, and incidentally, both started from the German experience, and with the aid of German technologists.

Fortunately for the Allies, and particularly for great Britain, intelligence about German preparations for the use of these weapons was obtained in advance, and counter-measures were taken by the RAF bombers. The main centre for development was Peenemünde, and in June 1943 it was attacked by nearly 600 RAF heavy bombers. The attack succeeded in destroying a great part of the experimental establishment and caused many casualties. This doubtless caused considerable delay in the development of the weapon, and the time gained was of the greatest value. The sites for launching both kinds of weapon were identified in Northern France and the Low Countries, and were attacked by both the RAF and USAF bomber forces. This succeeded in hampering and delaying the German preparations.

Over 6000 flying bombs, V 1's, were estimated to have been fired between 13 June and 3 September 1944, the period during which they were used. Nearly half of these were shot down by anti-aircraft gunfire or by fighters; about 1300 were technical failures and only 1700 reached their targets. They killed about 6000 people and injured about 17,000. Of the V 2 rockets, 1115 were fired between 8 August 1944 and 27 March 1945; they killed about 3000 people and injured over 6000. Thus the results, in terms of casualties or of real influence on the outcome of the war, were minimal compared with the destruction wrought by the British and American aircraft that bombed Germany. The importance of the V-weapons was as forerunners of today's nuclear-headed ICBM's.

It was only in 1945 that the United States captured bases in the Pacific from which a concentrated air bombing offensive against Japan could be carried out. The 21st Bomber Command, equipped with B 29's and led by General Curtis LeMay, was given this task. LeMay and his predecessor at first followed the strategy which the USAF in Europe had begun with, that is, choosing as objectives aircraft and engine factories to be destroyed by precision daylight bombing. But not many months of 1945 had passed before the policy of mass destruction of Japanese cities was adopted. Or, as it was put in a directive from General Arnold, although the primary aim was still to be the destruction of the Japanese aircraft industry, and hence their capacity to carry on the war, this was to be achieved by directing missions against "selected urban areas." This was essentially the strategy which the British adopted in 1941 for their air war against Germany, and pursued to the end. In other words, the policy was that of burning down the forest to kill the bears.

The attacks were carefully prepared in accordance with the experience of the air war against Germany. It was determined to raid mostly by night, under radar control and with incendiaries. These would be particularly effective against the Japanese dwellings, which were mainly constructed of wood. The first experimental attack on Tokyo under the new policy was successful enough to encourage the 21st Bomber Command. Then there was a pause during which all forces in the northern sector of the Pacific were concentrated on the capture of Iwo Jima. After that the air offensive resumed.

The first attack of the new series was on Tokyo, on the night of 9/10 March. This produced the largest casualty list of any city-bombing during the war: 83,793 dead and 40,918 injured, surpassing Dresden in the toll of human life. Over a quarter of a million dwellings were destroyed, and over a million people were rendered homeless. Then there was another interval during which the heavy bombing force was employed in supporting the assault on Okinawa, but by the middle of May it was released from this duty and resumed the programme of heavy incendiary attacks on the six largest industrial Japanese cities—Tokyo, Nagoya, Osaka, Kobe, Yokahama and Kawasaki. In the course of a month these were devastated in seventeen heavy attacks. Casualties were in the hundreds of thousands, and millions of Japanese people had their homes destroyed. The largest cities no longer yielding suitable targets, there followed intensive attacks, both by day and night, against many of the lesser cities and towns as well as against specifically military targets.

Japan was now practically incapable of preventing the destruction of what remained of her cities and towns, and worse, all importation of raw materials and food would soon have been cut off. In short, the country was in the position of a beleaguered and half-destroyed city in a mediaeval war, but with no hope of any rescue. It remained only for her to surrender. To hasten this, the us Government under President Truman decided that the first atom bombs would be used. It was hoped thus to avoid the desperate and prolonged fighting which invasion of the Japanese islands would have entailed.

The first atomic bomb had been exploded on the testing grounds at Alamogordo on 16 July 1945. The Allied leaders, then at the conference in Potsdam, issued a manifesto calling on the Japanese to surrender, on pain of "prompt and utter destruction." This ultimatum was refused by the Japanese Government in a public statement, but in fact they were trying to find a way to negotiate a capitulation.

Many reams have been written about the decision to use the atomic bomb, arguing that it was right, that it was wrong, that some alternative action should have been taken, that the man with the final responsibility, President Truman, is to be condemned for loosing this new terror on earth, or that his decision was entirely justifiable in the light of the situation as he knew it. Argument on this can continue endlessly. It seems to me that there are two points which should be mentioned in the context of the theme of this book. The first is that the actual destruction and loss of life at Hiroshima was less than in the attacks on Tokyo, and less than the cumulative death and suffering inflicted on civilians during the air war on Germany, and during the last half year on the Japanese. So, morally, it seems that President Truman's decision was no more reprehensible than that of the statesmen who made the decisions which initiated this kind of air warfare. Are they to be unequivocally condemned too? Perhaps if the war had gone the other way, a reversed Nuremberg tribunal would have hanged Mr. Churchill and the executive officers of Bomber Command.

The other point is that the secret of atomic explosion had been learned. If it had not been used to make a bomb in World War II, its development for use in weapons would inevitably have been carried on by the United States, by the USSR and by the other countries which have reached for nuclear war power. We should probably not be less subject today to the threat of wholesale destruction if there had been no Hiroshima. Was the production of the thermonuclear multi-megaton weapon inevitable in the current of historical development? Was it inevitable that the USA and its allies, and the USSR and its allies should have adopted the policies which have set us in the bitter opposition of the cold war? These may be questions for the research scholar, but the thermonuclear bomb and the cold war are facts. The question for today is, what are we to do to ease and then remove the threat which, in combination, the bomb and the cold war present to humanity and civilization.

# 6

## THE CONTROL OF ATOMIC ENERGY AND THE
## ATOM BOMB: 1945-1948

Even before the atomic bomb had been exploded over Hiro-shima there had been controversy over whether it should be used or not. A group of the scientists engaged in its development were appalled at what had been created. They tried to think of some way in which its enormous power could be demonstrated without slaughtering scores of thousands of civilians, yet which would convince the Japanese that they had no course but to surrender.

The first, and most notable, of the atomic scientists to act after he had realized what the discovery of how to release atomic energy implied for the world was Niels Bohr, who in 1944 was working at the research establishment at Los Alamos where the atomic bomb was made. He presented a memorandum to President Roosevelt, the main conclusions of which were as follows: Atomic energy would revolutionize industry and transport and would completely change all future conditions of warfare. Its terrible potential could only be vaguely perceived because the current research effort was continually revealing new possibilities. Any temporary advantage which the United States might have as possessor of the secret of the atomic weapon would be overbalanced by the menace to world security and, of course, to the security of the United States. To prevent secret competitive development of more and more destructive weapons would require such complete international exchange of scientific, military and industrial information as could hardly be conceived unless there were some common guarantee of security. If there were to be freedom from military and scientific secrecy in the post-war world, atomic energy must be under some form of international control.

One must admire the clarity with which the great scientist foresaw the consequences of man's new power over nature, to which his thought had so greatly contributed. It is deplorable that his wise advice was not taken and acted upon by the governments of the great powers. We are living, still, with the consequences of this failure. Who is to blame? Who would be found guilty if the case should be judged in Hell, or Purgatory, in a supernatural Nuremburg trial of the ghosts of all the statesmen, airmen, sailors, soldiers and scientists who might be accused of maintaining and building the apparatus of megamurder?

The scientists who had been working on the atomic bomb at the Metallurgical Laboratory of the University of Chicago had finished their part of the project by the autumn of 1944, and some of them, headed by James Franck and including Glenn Seaborg, Leo Szilard and Eugene Rabinowitch began to think of the implications of what they had been helping to produce. They sent several communications to the President, the most important of which came to be known as the Franck report. It argued that the primary politico-military aim of the USA in the post-war world should be the prevention of an atomic arms race, and that international control of atomic energy would be the only means of accomplishing this. It was their responsibility as scientists to educate the United States and other nations in this matter. They were convinced that adequate controls must form part of any system of international prevention of atomic armaments—a view which has prevailed in all subsequent proposals by the USA and its allies for nuclear disarmament. They reasoned that every nation, including the Soviet Union, would wish to preserve its existence, which might be threatened by an atomic arms race. Therefore agreement on international control of atomic energy would be generally desired, and only international suspicion would stand in the way. To get the desired agreement, all negotiating parties would have to be honest in their intentions and willing to sacrifice part of their national sovereignty. (Regrettably, in the negotiations since 1945, these two essential requirements for agreement have been found to be lacking.)

Dr. Franck and his associates put the point that the USA was not committed to use the bomb once it was constructed. It had been made in order to deter its use by any other nation. It was especially the fear that Germany, which would have no moral scruples about its use, might be developing such a weapon that had impelled the USA to produce it first. The Chicago scientists advised against using the bomb against Japan, proposing that its power should be demonstrated in some other way to the world and especially to the Japanese. But if the government should conclude that there was little chance of achieving agreement on international control, then it must be realized that public demonstration that the bomb was feasible would start off the atomic arms race. If the USA renounced an early use or demonstration of the atomic bomb, this might be to the country's advantage, as other countries could only come into the race gradually and without definite knowledge that the bomb would work.

Looking back, it is difficult to believe that the alternative proposed by Franck and his collaborators would have done more than retard the nuclear arms race briefly. In the conditions of United States society, the creation of a super-weapon could not long have been kept secret. How would the enormous expenditures of the Manhattan Project have been explained to Congress and the nation? Moreover, fundamental research in nuclear physics had been carried on in many advanced nations; the secret of building the atomic fission weapon could be found by scientists other than those who had been assembled in the United States. This was proved by subsequent events.

But the question was also being considered on the political plane. President Truman, shortly after he succeeded to office, appointed a committee under Secretary of War Stimson's chairmanship to advise him on whether the USA should use the atomic bomb against Japan, and also on what should be done after the war about the new atomic source of power in its military and industrial aspects. This committee included such leaders of the US wartime scientific effort as Vannevar Bush, Karl Compton and James Conant. It had on its panel of advisers Robert Oppenheimer, Arthur Compton, Ernest Lawrence and Enrico Fermi, all of whom had played important parts in the development of the atomic bomb. After much deliberation and study of alternatives, it was decided that the proper course was to use the bomb against Japan. In Mr. Stimson's words, the new weapon was to be considered as a tremendously powerful explosive, whose use would be as legitimate as use of the existing high explosives, which had already created such devastation. We see in this conclusion the natural relation between the development of air warfare, as we have followed it in the preceding chapters, and the extension of its power by the atomic bomb and later by the thermonuclear weapon.

The suggestion of the scientists who had signed the Franck report and of others who agreed with them had been rejected, because it seemed improbable that any technical demonstration would convince the Japanese that surrender was their only course. The desperation with which they had fought at Iwo Jima and Okinawa, and the heavy casualties incurred in subduing these islands, naturally led to the calculation that an invasion of Japan to gain the final and decisive victory would be immensely costly in American lives and in the lives of the other Allied troops who would participate in the invasion. To avoid these casualties by impressing the Japanese with the overpowering force they now faced seemed the reasonable thing to do in the circumstances. Although a hundred thousand Japanese non-combatants might be killed by the atomic bomb, far more Japanese lives—the lives of soldiers, sailors and airmen—would

be lost if the war had to be ended by invasion and complete
territorial conquest as the European war had been. It was not
realized that the Japanese were already on the point of surrender and that their leaders had recognized their situation as
hopeless and were looking for a suitable intermediary to negotiate capitulation.

The deliberations over whether the atomic weapon should be
used against Japan had resulted in two currents of thought.
One current set towards the necessity of abolishing or prohibiting the use of nuclear weapons in future wars; the other towards using the threat of the nuclear weapon as a means of
preventing or abolishing war altogether. This divergence of
thought has persisted until the present day. But the "peace plus
disarmament" concept which is basic to both views has been
pushed into the background, at least temporarily, by the development of nuclear weapons according to policies which stem
from traditional military thinking. This military thinking is that
the nuclear material in weapons is merely a more powerful
kind of high explosive and that wars are inevitable, especially
so a war against the USSR, the champion of the communist
cause. Therefore the only policy for the United States to follow
is to ensure that its nuclear armaments will always be greater in
mass than the enemy's, and will be deliverable by more "sophisticated" systems. To summarize roughly, since 1945 the two
differing lines of thought in the USA about the nuclear weapon
have been: (a) that it is a means of preserving the "American
way of life," the liberty of the United States and the liberties of
those nations allied with her against the deadly threat of a
communist takeover of the whole world, and (b) that the nuclear weapon, if used, will kill millions upon millions of mostly
innocent people; this is repugnant to American decency and
morality, and therefore in the long run the nuclear weapon will
not be usable as a means of protecting Western liberty and
civilization. While the weapons exist, the danger of nuclear war
will exist; therefore America should lead the way to a peaceful
and disarmed world, where there will be no nuclear weapons.
Both views are respectable, but the conclusion of those who
hold view "a" is "Arm"; while the conclusion of those who hold
view "b" is "Disarm." Both these views influence the United

States Government policies, which therefore appear to have a certain ambivalence. This has resulted, from time to time, in charges by the Russians that the Americans only talk disarmament as a screen for ever heavier arming, and in denunciations by the American extreme right of government indecision and pusillanimity.

However, once the Hiroshima and Negasaki bombs had their effect, the policy adopted by the United States Government was to propose international control of atomic energy with the purpose of preventing the use of the nuclear weapon in war. This decision was influenced by the views of the scientists quoted above, and supported by Secretary Stimson and his scientific adviser, Dr. Vannevar Bush. It was set forth in general terms in the Truman-Attlee-King declaration of 15 November 1945 as follows:

> We recognize that the application of recent scientific discoveries to the methods and practice of war has placed at the disposal of mankind means of destruction hitherto unknown, against which there can be no adequate military defence and in the employment of which no single nation can, in fact, have a monopoly.

It was further proposed that the United Nations should establish a commission to make proposals

(a) for extending between all nations the exchange of basic scientific information for peaceful ends;

(b) for control of atomic energy to the extent necessary to ensure its use only for peaceful purposes;

(c) for the elimination from national armaments of atomic weapons and all other major weapons adaptable to mass destruction;

(d) for effective safeguards by way of inspection and other means to protect complying states against the hazards of violations and evasions.

Stalin agreed with Mr. Bevin (then UK Foreign Secretary) and Mr. Byrnes (then US Secretary of State) in Moscow on 27 December 1945 that such a UN commission should be set up. This was done by the General Assembly on 24 January 1946. The commission was to consist of the members of the Security

Council plus Canada, whenever Canada was not already a member of the Security Council. Canada received this privileged place because of her contribution in uranium and research in the creation of the original atomic bombs and because of her advanced knowledge of the related science. At that time, the proposition that atomic weapons should be eliminated from national armaments was not opposed by anybody, at least not publicly.

President Truman had already set up a committee to consider how to carry out the declaration which he and the Prime Ministers of the United Kingdom and Canada had made. Mr. Dean Acheson was the chairman, and among its members were Dr. Bush, Major-General L. R. Groves, who had been in charge of the Manhattan Project, Dr. J. B. Conant, then President of Harvard, and Mr. J. J. McCloy. This committee appointed a board of consultants, which was chaired by Mr. David Lilienthal and which included Dr. Oppenheimer, and this board drafted the report which became the foundation of the plan for the control of atomic energy. These were first known as the Acheson-Lilienthal proposals, but after presentation to the United Nations Atomic Energy Commission by Mr. Bernard Baruch on behalf of the USA, they came to be generally referred to as the Baruch Plan—with the addition of various depreciatory adjectives when it is mentioned by Soviet Union spokesmen.

What was this plan, which on its presentation was hailed by the United States and friendly nations as embodying statesmanship and altruism to an extraordinary degree, and was denounced by the Soviet Union and its docile satellites as a transparent device to secure for the United States world hegemony and an effective monopoly control over the use of atomic energy in all the world? To understand its main features one must appreciate the following points peculiar to the problem of nuclear disarmament or control of the nuclear weapon:

The nuclear explosive plutonium can be said to be a byproduct of the generation of electricity by atomic energy. Some kinds of reactor use enriched uranium, though not of weapons grade. The enrichment of natural uranium to produce U-235, the other nuclear explosive, is a difficult and costly process. Research on nuclear energy for peaceful purposes can serve as a screen for research on weapons of war.

It thus appeared that, in order to ensure against clandestine production of new methods of war which could take the world by surprise, all atomic research would have to be carried out in public or under international control and, to a degree, so would all production of atomic energy. Secondly, owing to their dangerous radioactivity, all processes in making and using plutonium and uranium-235 (the nuclear explosive elements) are conducted by remote control from outside the chambers where these elements are. As a result, it is extremely difficult to tell, even when the amount of raw uranium going into a plant is known, whether all the potential explosive produced at the other end of the process is declared and to be sure that none has been diverted for secret manufacture of weapons.

A third difficulty is that the actual mass and weight of nuclear explosive required to produce these weapons of tremendous effect is surprisingly small. With modern techniques, only 7 or 8 kilograms of U-235 are needed to make an atomic bomb of the power of the Hiroshima prototype (20 kilotons). According to Sir John Cockroft, the U-235 in the Hiroshima bomb was little bigger than a cricket ball. William L. Laurence, in the *New York Times* of 22 May 1956, stated that only 25 kilograms of nuclear explosive with 200 kg of tritium and deuterium are required for a thermonuclear, or H-bomb, to produce a force of 16½ megatons—enough, if the bomb were accurately delivered and detonated, to destroy substantially any of the greatest cities in the world. So diversion of relatively small stocks of fissile material would provide enough explosive to produce a weapon of most devastating effect. The last stage of manufacture of the bomb, once the fissile material was available, could be carried out in a quite small establishment, where such activity could be easily concealed. Finally, as we look at the problem in 1966, it is realized that while inspection of a very thorough character could probably prevent illegal diversion from current production of any substantial quantity of fissile material from a plant, it would not be possible to determine whether the declared disposition of past production was accurate or not, that is, whether any of the product had been diverted and hidden. The possible error could amount to almost 20 per cent of total production. This difficulty, of course, could only be foreseen in 1945. But as long ago as 1955, the impossibility of accounting for past production and existing stocks of nuclear explosive material was recognized by disarmament negotiators.

With these special factors in mind, the authors of the Acheson-Lilienthal report concluded that a plan to make atomic energy safe for the world must embody the following conditions:

The whole process, from the extraction of the uranium and thorium ores to the production of the refined metal that could be used in the making of weapons, would have to be controlled at every stage. There was no single point in the process at which an adequate control over the whole could be exercised.

Inspection alone would be insufficient. The international authority must be given full access to all aspects of and activities in atomic research and utilization; otherwise, in the rapidly developing state of the science, new and even more dangerous methods of applying the new discoveries to war could be developed clandestinely. Inspectors, without other power than to inspect and report, would have an almost impossible task; their operation would imply a continuing suspicion of the good faith of the country whose installations they were inspecting and would create such frictions as might wreck the whole system.

If such dangerous activities as the development of atomic power (which, as we have seen, carries with it the potential to develop atomic weapons) were carried out by each nation having the technical ability and resources to do so, then rivalries would develop, with attendant fears, which would put any system of inspection of policing of atomic development under a strain which it could not support; it would break down and leave the world in a state of greater tension and greater danger.

So it was argued that the only way out of these difficulties was to create an International Atomic Development Authority (IADA) on which all nations would be represented. Contributions to the Authority and benefits drawn from it would be equitably balanced. The staff of the Authority would be internationally recruited (subject to proper standards of competence) on the same basis as the UN staff generally, and should be as free of governmental interference and have the same international loyalty as the UN secretariat personnel.

The IADA was to have a complete monopoly over the following "dangerous activities," which if not kept under international management would allow the clandestine diversion of fissile material from which atomic weapons could be built: the exploration and mining of uranium and thorium; the ownership of refineries to reduce these ores to metal; the manufacture of the metal into rods for use in reactors; the ownership of the rods; the sale of the refined metals and by-products; the construction and operation of the largest kinds of reactors and separation plants; and research on mining, power development and nuclear explosives. If any nation, or individual or group within a nation, should undertake any of these dangerous activities, it would be considered as preparing for aggression.

There would, however, be certain "safe activities" which other private or national enterprises could be licensed by the IADA to pursue, and for which the required materials could be leased from the IADA. These could comprise the construction of research reactors of limited capacity, reactors (with certain specified limitations) for the production of electric power and reactors for making radioactive materials (isotopes).

The IADA's plants would be so distributed among the nations that there would be a general balance ensuring no preponderance in atomic power capacity in the territory of any one nation. This was intended to be a safeguard against any potential violator of the treaty from seizing control of the plants in its territory. If this happened, there would be an aggregate of atomic power in the other nations sufficient to overcome the violator, if the worst came about. If any nation violated the agreement not to make atomic weapons, it would be committing an international crime, and should be subject to adequate sanctions, against which there would be no veto in the Security Council.

Looking back on this plan after twenty years of the cold war, we must regret that its breadth of vision found no response. It is not surprising that USA disarmament negotiators periodically tax their Soviet Union colleagues with the folly of rejecting it, and with all the dismal consequences which have ensued. One of the most remarkable facts about the Baruch Plan is that it was accepted by American public opinion and politicians with no dissenting voices. This shows the extent of the general American feeling at that time that peace must be assured, and especially that the new and dreadful means of making war should be prevented by international agreement from ever being used again.

The plan was presented to the UNAEC on 14 June 1946 by Mr. Baruch. Some of the language in the presentation was rather unfortunate, especially his words about sanctions: "Punishment lies at the very heart of our present security system . . ."; "There must be no veto to protect those who violate their solemn agreements not to develop atomic energy for destructive purposes," and his words to the effect that the "democracies" were not to be diverted from their plan by "mouthings about narrow sovereignty." This sort of talk is not calculated to put the Russians, or anyone else, in a good frame of mind for reaching agreements. The representatives of the USSR do not relish being treated as if they were moral outcasts, nor do they appreciate the implication that they are negotiating an agreement with the intention of violating it as soon as it is convenient to do so.

The essence of the plan was that the United States proposed to hand over to an international authority, in which all nations would have rights and shares, a source of power which probably would be as revolutionary in its effects as steam and electric power had been. The United States would not only be giving to this authority its scientific and industrial knowledge, up to this time a secret it alone possessed, but also capital assets estimated at four billion dollars; it would also agree to distribute the atomic industry installations all round the world. But what was most important, the USA was offering to divest itself of the secret of how to make the A-bomb, and the military power which the possession of that secret gave, in favour of a system of international control which would make the construction and therefore the use of the bomb by any nation in war impossible. Total nuclear disarmament was proposed, to ensure the safety of the world from the new menace, and the industrial benefits would be given as a surplus bonus.

As is well known, the USSR refused to consider the plan, and turned the full blast of their propaganda machinery against it. They denounced it as a scheme for putting the atomic industry throughout the world under the control of American "monopolistic trusts," who would through its operation possess themselves of the sources of raw materials for atomic energy throughout the world. The Baruch Plan, the Russians said, would not abolish nuclear weapons but would legalize them, so that they could still be used in US interests through the operation of the majority obedient to the USA in the control organ of the IADA.

On behalf of the USSR, Mr. Gromyko put forward alternative proposals which would have required prohibition of the production or use of nuclear weapons—the "Ban-the-Bomb" campaign which was to become so familiar in the ensuing years. All stocks of nuclear weapons were to be destroyed within three months; committees were to be set up to supervise the international exchange of scientific information and to consider how to prevent the use of atomic energy in ways harmful to humanity.

In his speech introducing these proposals, Mr. Gromyko attacked the Baruch Plan as an attempt to upset the basic principles of the UN Charter, pointing out that the powers proposed for the IADA would invade the sovereignty of states, a basic principle on which the UN was founded. There is something to be said for the Soviet Union viewpoint. They had learned by 1946 that in any conflict in the General Assembly between them and the USA, the USA could count on the support of an overwhelming majority. They were probably right in their view that, in the circumstances of the time, the IADA would be substantially under US governance—whatever gestures or pronouncements were made in the plan about international participation on an equitable basis. Stalin was in full control of the USSR at the time, and not only he, but most of the Russians in positions of any consequence in international affairs, were imbued with deep suspicion of the United States and its principal allies. This stemmed from the unhappy experiences of the years immediately preceding World War II, and also from the interventions after the 1917 revolution.

Had it not been for this suspicion and fear, foreshadowing the approaching world-wide contest between the two super-powers, the Russians might, instead of rejecting the US plan, have tried to modify it by negotiation into something which they could have accepted and which could have laid the foundation for nuclear disarmament and for the international development of the peaceful uses of atomic energy. Instead they chose to refuse it outright, and put forward alternatives that they must have known had no chance of being accepted by the USA. Meanwhile, they proceeded to develop atomic energy and the atomic weapon for themselves. They must have had sufficient assurances that their physicists, with perhaps some help from outside, could solve the problem, given enough time. They needed, in fact, only three more years, for the first atomic explosion in the USSR took place in September 1949. Incidentally, the news of this event broke during a sitting of the UN General Assembly.

So much for the the first attempt to control the menace of nuclear war. It was also the most far-reaching, at least until the proposals for general and complete disarmament were put forward in the UN General Assembly by Mr. Khrushchev in September 1959.

Meanwhile, what was the USAF thinking about the lessons of the Second World War, and particularly about the impact of atomic energy on air warfare? Naturally, they were considering what might happen in another World War, or perhaps it would be fairer to say that they were pondering on how the world position of the USA might be maintained through its air power. Probably the most authoritative statement of the ruling ideas can be found in the Third Report to the Secretary of War by General Henry H. Arnold, Commanding General of the Army Air Forces, dated 12 November 1945. The following are extracts from that report, some of them summarized:

> Today many modern war devices of great destructive power can be built piecemeal and under cover. Subassemblies might be secretly made in underground laboratories, and assembled into an annihilating war machine. War may descend upon us by thou-

sands of robots passing unannounced across our shorelines—unless we act now to prevent them.

The first target of a potential aggressor might well be our industrial system or our major centres of population. If the United States is to be secure in the future, we must never relinquish the means of preventing such a blow.

The people of the United States, peaceloving and hoping for world-wide acceptance of our concept of democracy, have never sponsored a strong peacetime military organization. History has demonstrated that we have thereby neither avoided war nor deterred others from going to war. . . . Might it not now be wise to try the alternative course of action in the hope that it will bring us what we seek—world peace and our own security?

In fact, the usa has adopted the alternative course and has built up the world's most powerful military machine. However, at the same time, the United States Government, through successive administrations, has explored the possibilities of attaining world peace—and providing for their own nation's security —through international agreement on disarmament and the development of peaceful means of settling disputes. These are the ambivalent policies previously referred to.

On the strategic theory on which future air operations should be based, General Arnold has this to say:

. . . The United States air warfare concept postulates that air attack on internal enemy vitals can so deplete specific industrial and economic resources, and on occasion the will to resist, as to make continued resistance by the enemy impossible.

The following principles should guide those who are responsible for conducting strategic air warfare:

(a) Through a world-wide intelligence system, maintain constantly up-to-date information regarding all phases of the national life, economy and philosophy of potential enemy states.

(b) Maintain an analysis, constantly revised to meet new conditions, to show the importance of all industries and other activities of potential enemies and to evaluate the relative importance of each of the units in each activity.

(c) To meet any emergency with the rapidity which survival in future wars will necessitate, prepare and maintain plans, in consonance with the latest information, to provide for the destruction of the decisive units of the key industries and other activities of each potential enemy nation.

(d) After a soundly conceived and carefully prepared strategic campaign has been launched, carry it through inexorably and without interruption.

Later, under the heading of "Intelligence," General Arnold wrote:

Our past concept of Intelligence was insufficient to cover the requirements of modern war.

Detailed and moment-by-moment knowledge of all aspects of civilian and military activity within the territory of an enemy or a potential enemy is essential to sound planning in times of peace or war. Continuous knowledge of potential enemies, covering their entire political, social, industrial, scientific and military life is also necessary to provide warning of impending danger. . . .

Strategic air warfare can neither be soundly planned nor efficiently executed without a continuous flow of detailed information of this kind.

A future Air Force developed in the light of the basic principles I have mentioned . . . together with constant supporting intelligence will enable the United States to face the future with confidence.

Whether the United States or the bulk of its citizens really face the future with confidence, now that General Arnold's recommendations have in the main been carried out, seems, at the least, pretty doubtful.

In plain language, General Arnold recommended that the United States set up an intelligence-collecting system of unprecedented scope, to serve the needs of a "strategic" air force. It was certain to inspire the liveliest apprehension among the "potential enemies" if they learned that a tremendous apparatus of spies and reconnaissance by aircraft (later by satellite) was engaged hour by hour in acquiring target information for the world's most powerful air force, equipped with atomic bombs. In such circumstances it is not surprising that the Iron Curtain dropped down and that the Russian national propensity to secrecy should have become what now seems an obsession.

On the influence of atomic energy on air power, General Arnold states simply that in his view "atomic energy . . . has made air power all-important. Air power provides not only the best present means of striking an enemy with atomic bombs, but also the best available protection against the misuse of atomic explosives."

General Arnold had the foresight to perceive that improved anti-aircraft defences, probably based on guided missiles, might greatly reduce the power of aircraft to penetrate enemy defences and deliver the atomic bomb. Against this eventuality, the USA should be provided with rockets developed from the V 2 type used by Germany for the bombardment of England, but of course greatly improved in range and precision. This has been brought about, although the Russians, as it happened, were first in this field.

He made a bow in the direction of the idea of a world authority to control the atomic bomb, but there the chief suggestion was that there would be an unceasing patrol of the whole world under the "guidance of the United Nations Organization" to prevent illegal manufacture of the weapon. Air forces used for such patrolling might be those made available to the Security Council for possible enforcement action. Presumably, as this document was made public, the USSR was soon aware of its contents, and this proposal for "unceasing aerial patrol" may have reinforced its objections to the Baruch Plan for the international control of atomic energy and prevention of the fabrication of atomic weapons.

General Arnold also appreciated the great role which research and development would have to play in the creation and maintenance of the sort of air power which he was advocating.

> The Air Force must be able to call on all talents and facilities existing in the nation and sponsor further development of the facilities and creative work of science and industry. The Air Force must also be authorized to expand existing research facilities and create and take advantage of new ones to accomplish applied research and to make such facilities available to scientists and industrial concerns working for the Air Force.

This recommendation has indeed been fulfilled to an extraordinary degree. It is estimated that 60 per cent of all research in the USA in 1963 was paid for or subsidized by the government, chiefly on behalf of the armed services.

To make sure that the American voter will understand the

need for the vast outlays which the Air Force programme would require in time of peace, General Arnold postulated that:

> Air power will always be the business of every American citizen. The Army Air Force recognizes its duty in formulating intelligent programs of education to the end that the public will understand aviation in all of its forms as well as realize the danger of unpreparedness in the air. . . . Propaganda has no place in this program.

In the US Strategic Bombing Survey, Summary Report (Pacific War) published 1 July 1946, one can read the following passage, which, as might be expected, coincides closely with the views of General Arnold:

> The prevention of war must be the ultimate end to which our best efforts are devoted. It has been suggested, and wisely so, that this objective is well served by insuring the strength and security of the United States. The United States was founded and has since lived upon principles of tolerance, freedom and goodwill at home and abroad. Strength based on these principles is no threat to world peace. Prevention of war will not be furthered by neglect of strength or lack of foresight or alertness on our part. . . . Suggestions for assuring the military strength and security of the United States are by no means intended as a recommendation for a race in arms with other nations; . . . The development of an intelligent and co-ordinated approach to American security can and should take place within the framework of the security organization of the United Nations.

I do not wish to impugn the honesty of the desire for peace of the writers of the above passages nor their conviction that the United States had the greatest responsibility of all nations to preserve peace and to be strong for that purpose. After all, no military officer in any service who had seen the results of World War II, especially in the air warfare against Germany and Japan, could wish to see a repetition of such happenings, let alone the thousand-fold worse things which the advent of the atomic bomb foreshadowed if there were ever to be a war again. But the general theme is: "If you want peace, prepare for war." This adage, ascribed to Vegetius in the fourth century AD, has not worked then or since, except for limited periods.

# 7

## COMMUNIST POWER EXTENDED OVER
## EASTERN EUROPE

It is not recorded who invented the phrase "cold war," or when, but it is certain that the cold war began as soon as the hot war in Europe ended in 1945. Even before then, Stalin had initiated the moves which put Eastern Europe under the domination of the Communist parties. For the West this expansion of communist rule over the countries occupied by the Soviet Union armies was a gross violation of the agreements reached at Yalta. In the "Declaration on Liberated Europe" the United States, the United Kingdom and the Soviet Union had pledged themselves "to act in concert in assisting the peoples liberated from the dominion of Nazi Germany and the peoples of the former Axis satellite states of Europe to create democratic institutions of their own choice." But the defect of the Yalta agreements was stated concisely by Captain Peter Thorneycroft, in a speech in the House of Commons, on 28 February 1945: "Poland . . . is occupied by a foreign, though friendly, army belonging to a country which has not quite the same interpretation of what is free, independent and democratic as ourselves." This can surely rank among masterpieces of British understatement.

However reprehensible we consider the Soviet Union policies and actions in this period to be, they are at least understandable. They were apparently based on two principles: first, that Soviet Union territory must have buffer-protection on the west by a chain of friendly states. Russia had been invaded from the west and south-west twice in the twentieth century by the Germans, whose armies had passed over the lands of allied countries or others unable to resist their passage. The second principle was that Marx and Lenin had laid down that communism should in time spread throughout all the nations of the world in accordance with an inevitable historic process; it was a tenet of communist policy to do everything possible to assist this process. The extension of communism as a national aim of the Soviet Union had been set aside by Stalin for many years prior to the Second World War. But now the Soviet Union's armies had swept forward to Berlin and the Elbe, and occupied practically every East European country. Stalin was in an unprecedentedly favourable position to carry out this operation, so virtuous by the communist ethic. Looking back, it would have been most astonishing if the USSR had not acted in the way it did. By placing communist governments in power in Poland, Bulgaria, Romania, Hungary and eventually Czechoslovakia, the Soviet Union ensured that it would have friendly states and allies between its own territory and those of defeated Germany and the Western capitalistic states, which, even when they were allies, the Russians had never ceased to hold in suspicion.

First to be engulfed by the communist boa-constrictor was Poland. In 1944 the Soviet Government set up an administration, known at first as the Lublin Committee, to which it granted legal powers to govern the Polish territory under Soviet Army occupation. In December of that year this Lublin group declared itself the lawful Government of Poland, and was recognized as such by the Soviet Government early in January 1945. This was in spite of there being a Polish Government in exile in London, which the Western Allies recognized. At Yalta, the Soviet Government undertook to establish a Polish Government on a broader basis, to include members of the resistance movement and the exile government in London. But the resistance movement leaders were speedily put out of the way, being arrested and imprisoned on charges of activity against the Soviet Union Army.

However, a coalition government was formed in Poland from elements of the London and Lublin groups. The Communists, in accordance with the tactics which were to become distressingly familiar, secured for themselves the key ministries of defence, public security and information. In May of 1946 they began to eliminate all other political parties, of which the Socialist and Peasant parties were the most important. This process continued throughout 1947 and 1948, and by 1949 all non-communist political activity had ceased, and the government was firmly in the hands of those who were obedient to the political direction of Moscow.

Romania, which had broken off its alliance with Germany in August 1944, was dealt with more speedily and ruthlessly. It was included among the satellite and liberated states whose free choice of government was supposed to have been agreed upon at Yalta. But only sixteen days after Yalta, Andrei Vishinsky, the Soviet Union Deputy Foreign Minister, arrived in Bucharest and, giving a four-and-a-half hour ultimatum, handed to the King a slate of personalities approved by Moscow for forming a new government. The King had no recourse but to yield, and a government dominated by the Communists was forthwith set up. Negotiations followed with the Western Allies, as a result of which the Soviet Union agreed to general elections, which were held in November 1946. But only the communist-dominated Coalition party was allowed to put forward candidates. Early in 1947 the Romanian Peasant party was eliminated; in December of the same year the King abdicated and in April 1948 Romania became a People's Democracy with a constitution very similar to that of the Soviet Union.

Bulgaria was treated in similar fashion. It had been occupied by the Soviet Army in September 1944, and for a while was governed by a coalition of Communist, Peasant and Republican parties with the Communists holding the key ministry of the interior, responsible for police and public order. The Communists began their programme to eliminate the other parties in 1945, and this continued through to 1947, when the leader of the Peasant party was arrested and executed for treason, and the remnants of the party were merged with the Communists. In the following year the Republican and Socialist parties were abolished, and Bulgaria also became a People's Democracy, that is, a communist dictatorship.

Hungary had been occupied by the Soviet Army in the spring of 1945, and unlike the countries above-mentioned, was allowed to have a free election in November of that year. The Communist party polled only 17 per cent of the vote. However, over the next three years the established process of subversion and trickery took place, under, of course, the *force-majeure* of the Soviet Union Army; and by 1948 the Smallholders party, which had won the 1945 elections and formed the government, was wiped out. The Communists took full control of the country and proclaimed yet another People's Democracy, with a Soviet-type constitution.

Other European countries were subjected to communist pressure, for which the Soviet Union was ultimately responsible. For the operations of the Greek communist guerillas, which began in 1946, support was furnished through Bulgaria, Albania and Yugoslavia. The United Nations Special Committee on the Balkans investigated the complaint of Greece to the Security Council concerning this interference. The results of the investigation showed clearly that direct help had been given to the Greek communist guerillas by the three communist countries, whose territories had sheltered Greek communist bands and served as a base for them, and whose armed forces had in certain instances covered their retreat. The Greek Government had received aid from Great Britain in its struggle against the communist uprising, until in 1947 the financial burden became too great, and the United States took over the responsibility. This was the occasion for the declaration of President Truman, generally known as the "Truman Doctrine," subsequently approved by Congress as a treaty between the USA and Greece. The essentials of this doctrine, which was contained in the speech of President Truman to Congress on 12 March 1947, are given in the following words:

The peoples of a number of countries of the world have recently had totalitarian regimes forced upon them against their will. The Government of the United States has made frequent protests against coercion and intimidation, in violation of the Yalta Agreement, in Poland, Romania and Bulgaria. . . .

I believe that it must be the policy of the United States to support free peoples who are resisting attempted subjugation by armed minorities or by outside pressures.

I believe that we must assist free peoples to work out their own destinies in their own way. . . .

Should we fail Greece and Turkey in this fateful hour, the effect will be far-reaching to the West as well as to the East. We must take immediate and resolute action. . . .

Turkey had also been subjected to Soviet pressure from the time when the Soviet Union armies had occupied Bulgaria and found themselves on Turkey's borders. In March 1945 the Soviet Union denounced its treaty of friendship with Turkey and demanded the transfer of territories in the east of Turkey to the Georgian Soviet Socialist Republic, and also declared that the Soviet Union should share with Turkey the responsibility of the defence of the Dardenelles and the Bosphorus, that is, that Soviet forces should be stationed in that vital strategic area. But Turkey resisted these demands. Nevertheless the pressure on Turkey and the threat to the West if the Soviet Union penetrated to the Eastern Mediterranean was sufficient to qualify her for inclusion in the terms of the Truman Doctrine.

This steady expansion westwards of the communist empire was climaxed with the takeover by a communist regime in Czechoslovakia in 1948. This event, which was not carried out in the presence of an occupying Russian army as had happened in Poland, Romania and Bulgaria, was a great shock to the Western nations. A coalition had been governing since 1946, when Communists had been elected to a considerable number of seats in the Parliament. The Prime Minister, Gottwald, was a Communist, and so was the Minister of the Interior, who controlled the police. It was the latter who precipitated the crisis in February 1948 which led to Czechoslovakia's communization, by replacing a number of the police chiefs of Prague with Communists. The non-communist members of the Cabinet demanded a reversal of the police appointments, which was of course refused by the Communists, who then armed the "Workers' Militia," called out factory workers and organized violent demonstrations in Prague and other cities. Mr. V. A. Zorin, Deputy Foreign Minister of the Soviet Union, arrived in Prague, and is generally reputed to have master-minded the Czechoslovak Communist party in its subsequent operations. Communist cabinet ministers, led by Mr. Gottwald, pressed the aged President, Mr. Benes, to accept the resignation of the non-communist ministers, while the others called on him to support them. For about a week the crisis continued, with increasing communist pressure by organized irregular forces, and the threat of civil war. Then the President let the non-communist ministers go, and turned the government over to Mr. Gottwald. Benes died on the 4th of May; the Foreign Minister, Jan Masaryk, was found dead, and many non-communist leaders fled abroad. Czechoslovakia became, as Poland, Bulgaria and Romania had before her, a communist dictatorship.

I have set down this summary of events from 1945 to 1949, known to every newspaper reader, because the actions of the USSR in this period have set the relationship between East and West in Europe up to the present day. They have resulted in the formation of two power blocks, NATO and the Warsaw Pact organization, whose influence and sphere of influence extend beyond Europe. They have left the Western democracies with deep mistrust and suspicion of the USSR, a conviction that the Soviet Union will not observe treaties and that it will use its power unscrupulously to help communist minority parties to take over democratic governments in any nation where the opportunity occurs. This picture of Soviet Union bad faith and aggression has, since 1948, inhibited all negotiations for disarmament or political measures for easing tension, and it still does. It set up the military power equation, Russian might on land versus United States air power plus the atomic bomb, and from this began the nuclear and missile arms race.

In 1948-49, the picture was of a communist drive westwards beyond the line to which they had pushed the Iron Curtain. The forces which could oppose a further surge forward of the

Soviet Union Army seemed weak. The Communist parties in France and Italy, holding a substantial number of parliamentary seats, were a divisive force in democratic Western Europe which might leave the way open for the same kind of penetration which had communized Czechoslovakia.

Soviet Union military power seemed supreme in Europe, poised on a provisional boundary, ready for another advance. While the American, British and Canadian armies and air forces in Europe were demobilized in all haste beginning in the summer of 1945, leaving only a meagre number of divisions to garrison defeated Germany, the Russians had kept a large army intact. The intelligence summaries showed nearly two hundred USSR divisions, well-equipped, and, of course, confident after their victorious drive to Berlin and beyond. What was to prevent them from overrunning the rest of Europe in a few days, in the rhythm of the armoured advances in the last weeks of the war? Very little remained in the way of military strength on the ground, or of the military or civil organization for co-ordination of the efforts of the North American and European countries which had brought about the defeat of Germany in the West.

But Stalin could see that further moves might bring the USSR into conflict with the USA in a war in which the chances for retaining early gains in Europe would be doubtful. The USSR, though victorious in its war with Germany, had incurred terrible losses, not only in manpower, but in the whole fabric of her industry. The Russian people were war-weary—as were all nations which had been belligerents. Then there was the unknown factor of the atomic bomb. The Soviet Government kept the knowledge of the effects of this new and terrific weapon from the Russian people, while at the same time propagandizing heavily in the outside world against its inhuman character and urging that it should be banned as a weapon of war. We shall never know, of course, to what extent all these various factors influenced Stalin and reinforced his native caution. What the USSR had done up to 1948 was done without the possibility of direct conflict with the forces of the United States. The risk of open war was therefore small, and the probable gains were great. Now, the game was becoming riskier, to the point that a halt had to be called.

While the Czechoslovak drama was being played out, another power struggle began on 21 June 1948; the Soviet Union blockaded Berlin. The four-power government of Germany had broken down in quarrels over reparations and currency reform, and the USSR, taking advantage of the location of Berlin, 160 kilometers within the Soviet-occupied Zone, blocked access to the city by rail, road and water, thus hoping to force the Western Allies to abandon their share in the occupation and government of Berlin, to which the Potsdam agreements had entitled them. But the Soviet Union Government had miscalculated; the astonishing success of the Berlin airlift carried out by the United States Air Force and the Royal Air Force, together with economic counter-measures against Soviet-occupied Germany, eventually brought the Russians to realize that they had made a mistake. While greatly superior in land forces, the USSR had no such superiority in air forces. And there was the atomic bomb. . . . In May 1949, after conversations which began in the United Nations, the blockade was lifted. But, as everyone knows, it was periodically threatened by Mr. Khrushchev in his last few years; and Berlin is still a very vulnerable point in the Western position, otherwise immeasurably improved since 1949.

Sir Winston Churchill, in his speech in the House of Commons, on 1 March 1955, said: "There is a widespread belief throughout the free world that, but for American nuclear superiority, Europe would already have been reduced to satellite status and the Iron Curtain would have reached the Atlantic and the Channel."

Note that Sir Winston said: "There is a widespread belief. . . ." He did not say whether he believed it himself or not. It is idle in 1965 to try to establish whether or not it was the US nuclear deterrent which preserved the freedom of Europe during the years 1945-55, or whether the other reasons Stalin had for caution were the deciding factors. The Soviet Union system of government and the mystery with which all their decisions are shrouded being what they are, it is quite likely that this question will never be decided. What is important for us to decide now is whether the US nuclear deterrent is still the best means of preserving free Europe against all stratagems and assaults, and if so, how long it will be able to do so. The alternatives to the US "nuclear umbrella" are a system of nuclear deterrence under collective control of the European NATO nations, or else national deterrents. But there are grave uncertainties and instabilities attached to each of these three systems of nuclear deterrence. Real security for Europe against nuclear devastation will only be achieved with balanced disarmament by both sides and concurrently improved political relations.

The Berlin Blockade dramatized the division of Germany into two parts: that occupied by the United States, Great Britain and France, and that occupied by the Soviet Union. As the four-power system of government agreed upon at Potsdam for the whole of Germany had broken down, the Western Allies agreed in April 1949 to the gradual transfer of governmental power to the Germans in the territory under their control; this process commenced shortly thereafter. The Russians replied by setting up a government in the part of Germany which they occupied, under the direction of the local Communist party; and Germany was effectively split into two states, one a parliamentary democracy and the other communist-authoritarian; these became the Federal German Republic and the German Democratic Republic. Thus evolved what remains the greatest political problem in Europe today, the problem that more than any other prevents peaceful settlement of the Second World War and inhibits lowering of tensions and the reduction of armed forces and armaments. In short, this is the problem that blocks real peace in Europe. It is not that a German state with a communist government is intolerable to the West; it is that this communist state, perpetrating an artificial division of the German people, should exist contrary to the will of its citizens, who have never been given the opportunity to elect a government of their free choice, and who certainly, if they had that choice, would not elect a communist government. We may deplore the case of other East European states which are ruled by communist minorities, the ultimate sanction for whose rule is the power of the Soviet Union Army. But these states and the tensions within them do not present the threat to peace that the arbitrary division of Germany does.

What effect had these events on the military policy of the United States? In particular, how did they influence the United States in determining policy on the function of air power and the use or threat of the atomic bomb in the defence of their interests throughout the world? Not only had the United States its own interests to defend, but after the war it became defender of those nations, allied and others, which desired to live in peace under institutions of their own choosing. We may find the general trend of that policy set out in the Report of the President's Air Policy Commission, dated 1 January 1948, which was entitled *Survival in the Air Age*. The Chairman of this Commission was Thomas K. Finletter who later became Secretary of the Air Force.

The first paragraphs of the report contain the following sentences:

> We believe that the United States will be secure in an absolute sense only if the institution of war is abolished under a regime of law. . . . The United Nations cannot assure a permanent peace except on a foundation of free communication throughout the world.
>
> The United States must have a double-barrelled policy abroad. It must work to achieve world peace through support and development of the United Nations. And at the same time it must prepare to defend itself for the possibility that war may come.
>
> Not being able to count on absolute security under law, it must seek the next best thing—relative security under the protection of its own arms.

We may remark, once more, that the United States still has and pursues this double-barrelled policy. Unfortunately the admirable principles enunciated in the first sentence quoted above, and the steadfast and munificent support of the United Nations by the United States, tend to be lost to sight, in many foreign countries at least, because of fears that the nuclear charge in the second "barrel" may go off. Turning to the requirements for security of the United States under the protection of its own arms, the report went on:

> We need a new strategic concept for the defense of the United States. This strategic concept must be based on air power. . . .
>
> For strategic purposes we must divide the future into two parts —the present Phase I during which we may assume that we have a monopoly on atomic weapons, and Phase II, the time when other nations will have atomic weapons in quantity and the equipment to deliver them in a sustained attack on the United States mainland.
>
> . . . A major war during Phase I is unlikely. . . . There is, however, such a thing as blundering into a war. . . . What we must have and can support in Phase II is a reasonably strong defensive establishment to minimize the enemy's blow, but above all a counter-offensive air establishment in being which will be so powerful that if an enemy does attack we will be able to retaliate with the utmost violence and to seize and hold advanced positions from which we can divert the destruction from our homeland to his.
>
> The Air Force is inadequate even for this Phase I when we are relatively free from the danger of sustained attack on our homeland. The Air Force is hopelessly wanting in respect to the future Phase II period when a serious danger of atomic attack will exist.
>
> It would be an unreasonable risk . . . to assume that other nations will not have atomic weapons in quantity . . . [and] the planes and missiles capable of delivering a sustained attack on the United States mainland by the end of 1952.

In these key extracts from the report the salient point is that after 1952 an aggressor could deliver upon the United States homeland a considerable weight of atomic bombs. And, also, it is implied that the air power which the USA should build up should be counter-offensive and retaliatory. In other words, this airborne nuclear power would come into play only if the other nation (the Soviet Union) attacked first. As an authoritative statement of strategic policy this should have been reassuring to the Soviet Union. Nevertheless, it proposed to create for the USA a force of great power able to devastate the cities of the USSR. Could the USSR really be sure that the USA would *never, never* attack first? What if politicians and military men of a different stamp to the men of 1948 should come into power? What about the theories of preventive war and preemptive strikes that had been heard of from air force officers and air war enthusiasts?

The report assumed that as the Soviet Union *could* build up an air force that could deliver atomic bombs on the USA home territory, they would do so; therefore the USA should build a bigger capacity to bomb the USSR. This is the classical pattern of the arms race.

In a speech on 30 April 1949, Lieutenant-General James H. Doolittle, a retired Air Force officer whose service in World War II is famous, expressed some ideas which would appear to have been pretty generally held. He asked the question, whether war with Russia was inevitable, and answered, No, if the USA were to follow certain principles of action. Of course, the "men in the Kremlin" were determined to impose communism on the rest of the world through deceitful propaganda, subversion, promoting revolution, and, if necessary and the conditions favoured it, by the naked use of force. But the USA should adopt a triple programme. First would be the building up of her military strength. Second, she should teach the rest of the world the rightness of the American system of government, and the fallacy and wrongness of the communist system. Thirdly, there must be a spiritualization of the American people, to be extended to the rest of the world, that is, a return to true religion, morality and decent ethics. (Some might find it a little difficult to make true Christianity square with dependence of the security of the United States on a mass slaughter weapon like the atomic bomb.)

He repeated what many have come to regard as an axiom: "Russia respects only force." He spoke also of the fear, seemingly even then exercising some Americans, that if the power of the military were greatly increased in peacetime, the United States might find itself either under a military dictatorship, or led by the military into war. However, these fears were baseless he contended; the constitution protected the country against military dictatorship, and as the Americans were not a militaristic or aggressive nation, there was no fear of their being led into war. One might remark here that the years which have intervened since 1949 do not seem to have entirely dispelled these uncomfortable ideas. One can refer to the best-selling novels of 1962-63, *Seven Days in May* and *Fail-Safe*, not to mention many more ponderous warnings that the militarization of American democracy is not impossible.

One must agree with General Doolittle when he suggested that the overall strategy for the USA should be based on keeping out of war; for no one could "win" a war in the future. All that could be provided for would be not to lose it, that is, for the USA to be able to inflict more damage on the aggressor enemy than it would itself receive. This approaches the deterrence policy, which now seems to hold the field, after various other policies, which we shall be reviewing, were for a while considered, and then discarded.

General Doolittle saw the ultimate weapon in aerial warfare as a pilotless, controlled air weapon powered by atomic energy, and carrying an atomic explosive charge which could be directed accurately from an emplacement in the United States to any point on earth. This 1949 vision has been realized, in essence. Unfortunately, the USSR has provided itself with the ultimate weapon also. Its first step in this direction was noted when on 23 September 1949 President Truman reported to the nation that within recent weeks there had been an atomic explosion in the USSR. The American atomic scientists had warned that it would only be a matter of time until the Russians discovered the secret, or the technique, of producing atomic weapons. However, they had done it in about four years—several years less than had been estimated. This was the first abrupt shock to the complacent Western assumption that superior scientific and technical ability would always keep us well ahead of the USSR in the arms race in the nuclear age.

The Soviet Union's test of an atomic device signalled the end of the United States' atomic monopoly. The US Government had not used its weapon after Nagasaki, or even threatened to use it, but it was always there. Although in the ensuing years the USA has been able to keep ahead in the quantity of its nuclear arsenal and the means of delivering it, the power of the USSR to devastate the United States homeland has kept on growing.

President Truman concluded his report by saying that the USSR atomic explosion emphasized the need for effective and enforceable international control of atomic energy, a necessity recognized by the US Government and the large majority of the members of the United Nations. But, regrettably, the UN Atomic Energy Commission had suspended its meetings, despairing of agreement. For this the Soviet Union must bear primary responsibility, as we have noted. They had determined, thinking nationally, that they must have their own nuclear weapon power, and had blocked the hope of an international solution. In 1946 an opportunity to control the danger of nuclear war was rejected because of national pride, power, greed and suspicion. Was it the same in 1963, when France and Communist China rejected the nuclear test ban, which could be the first step towards at long last bringing the nuclear arms race under control? The first opportunity to re-bottle the nuclear genie was lost in 1946; a second, perhaps, lost in 1963. How many more chances can we expect?

# 8

## FORMATION OF NATO; THE DECISION TO MAKE THE H-BOMB; THE EFFECT OF THE KOREAN WAR

We have seen in the last chapter that the first American reaction to the western-setting communist tide occurred when President Truman proclaimed that the United States would support Greece and Turkey and, by implication, any other countries which were threatened by communist armed force or subversion. The next American action to meet the challenge was of much wider scope, aimed at restoring the economies of the war-devastated countries of Europe by extending very large financial credits and other help. This plan was first announced by Secretary of State Marshall in April 1947, and began to operate within the next few months. Looking back from 1966, the generosity of the American Government and people in 1947 astonishes one. Regrettably, it seems to have earned little lasting gratitude. But its inspiration was not solely international philanthropy; at the time it was clear that if the European economies were not rehabilitated, and quickly, there would be stagnation, unemployment, and shortages of all kinds of goods. Economic misery everywhere would furnish a rich soil for the propagation of communism as a fifth column to aid the surge forward of the Empire from the East.

It is sometimes forgotten that help under the Marshall plan was offered not only to the West European democracies, but also to Eastern European countries under communist rule or influence, even to the Soviet Union itself. But the Soviet Union spurned the offer, and pressured Poland and Czechoslovakia to decline also, although they wished to grasp the helping hand. But in March of this same year of 1947 co-operation between the USSR and the Western Allies had come to an end. The conference at Moscow at that time was the last of a series of negotiations which had been going on since the war's end to decide the terms of peace for Germany and Austria. When the Moscow Conference broke up with no grounds for agreement in sight, it wrote *finis* to these negotiations, leaving Germany divided, and its division the greatest obstacle to real peace in Europe.

But to meet the threat of communist expansion, more was needed than economic help; the military weakness of the West in Europe had to be remedied; an organized alliance for defence had to be created. The decline in the military strength in Europe of the Western members of the wartime alliance against Hitler's Germany is shown by the following figures: Between May of 1945 and May of 1946 the American armed forces in Europe had declined from 3,100,000 to some 391,000; those of the United Kingdom from 1,321,000 to 488,000; those of Canada from 299,000 to nil. The Soviet Union, in contrast, kept a large proportion of its wartime divisions mobilized, and continued to produce armaments at a high rate. To quote Lord Ismay, the first Secretary-General of NATO, on the situation: "There was in fact nothing—except America's possession of the atomic bomb—to deter the Soviet from overrunning Western Europe. It was therefore necessary for the free countries of Europe to combine together for economic recovery and for defence." Massive aid both economic and military from the United States was essential if a balance was to be established in good time.

The pages that follow give in brief outline the steps towards the formation and organization of the North Atlantic Alliance. This development, and the reaction of the Soviet Union in strengthening its own military posture and organizing the Warsaw Pact as a sort of counter to what they like to call "the aggressive NATO alliance," set up the framework of the uneasy balance of power in the world today. There are, of course, conflicts and military threats outside Europe and the North Atlantic Treaty sphere, but NATO and the Warsaw Pact nations comprise the most heavily armed of the world's military powers, all the nuclear powers except China. It is recognized that if the forces which face each other across the Iron Curtain should ever come into armed conflict, there is the greatest danger that a devastating nuclear war would follow. (These points, incidentally, were reiterated almost every week in 1963 by Soviet Union spokesmen at the Eighteen-Nation Disarmament Conference in urging a non-aggression pact between NATO and the Warsaw Alliance.) Central Europe is the principal area in which the dangers of nuclear war have to be faced and where solutions must be found if the world is to see a real peace with disarmament.

The NATO idea had been in men's minds for some time. Sir Winston Churchill, who had pointed out the dangers of the Russian expansion in Europe in a letter to President Truman written on 12 May 1945, (in which he first used the expression "an Iron Curtain") broached the idea of a defensive alliance in his famous speech in March 1946 at Fulton, Missouri. However, this first call for an alliance did not have any immediate result. Mr. Louis St. Laurent, the Canadian Secretary of State for External Affairs, in a speech to the United Nations General Assembly in September 1947 said that many member nations were disturbed that the provisions of the Charter for maintaining international peace and security could not provide them a sure protection, and he added that some nations might seek greater safety in an association of democratic and peace-loving states willing to accept more specific international obligations in return for a greater measure of national security. In January 1948 Mr. Ernest Bevin, then Foreign Minister of the UK, proposed in the House of Commons a Western Union, adding the Benelux nations to Britain and France, who in March 1947 at Dunkirk had concluded a treaty for mutual assistance in defence.

The *coup d'etat* in Prague triggered action on these suggestions, and on 17 March 1948 the Brussels Treaty for a Western European Union was signed by the UK, France, the Netherlands, Belgium and Luxembourg. President Truman immediately announced that these countries having determined to help themselves, the USA was determined to help them.

On 28 April 1948 Mr. St. Laurent proposed a single mutual defence system, including Canada, which would include and supersede the Brussels Treaty system. This suggestion was welcomed by Mr. Bevin. At about the same time, Secretary of State Marshall and Secretary of Defence Lovett were holding the discussions with Senator Vandenberg and Representative Connally that led to the celebrated Vandenberg resolution. This called for the association of the United States with such regional or other collective arrangements as might affect its national security, and for the USA to contribute to maintaining peace, and to make clear its determination to exercise the right of individual or collective self-defence under Article 51 of the UN Charter, should any armed attack occur affecting its national security. This resolution was passed in the United States Senate by an overwhelming majority on 11 June 1948.

It was on 21 June 1948 that the Soviet Union initiated the blockade of West Berlin. The setting up of the Western Union Defence Organization began about 30 April, and, from July on, observers from the USA and Canada attended the sessions.

These were the preliminaries to the North Atlantic Treaty; the negotiations began on 6 July 1948. The Treaty was finally signed on 4 April 1949, in spite of the violent propaganda against it carried on by the Soviet Union, which warned various European countries that NATO was merely an instrument for furthering the imperialist aims of the Anglo-Saxon countries. Paul-Henri Spaak, the Foreign Minister of Belgium, refuted this propaganda in his courageous speech in the United Nations General Assembly in 1948, when he said, "There is but one great power which emerged from the war having conquered other territories, and that power is the USSR." Nevertheless, the Russians still think or pretend to think that the USA, in extending its military power to Europe and establishing bases there, has aggressive intentions. This notion is the theme of their interminably reiterated denunciations of "imperialist aggression."

At about this time in the United States, the military, the scientists and the politicians were discussing whether a thermonuclear, or hydrogen, bomb should be developed. Opinion among the scientists concerned was divided on this. Indeed, for some time previously scientists had held differing opinions as to what ought to be done about the nuclear weapon in the interests of the short-range or long-range security of the United States and of the world. One group felt that the only real solution was the international control of atomic energy, although they realized that the Baruch Plan was dead and that if an agreement was to be reached another approach would have to be found. Another school, observing the attitudes and actions of the Soviet Union, concluded that no worth-while and lasting agreement on the control of atomic energy and the nuclear weapon could be attained, at least not until the world outlook and policy of the Soviet Union had changed. These scientists believed that the atomic weapon would have to be developed in a range of forms which would provide powerful instruments to enable the United States armed forces to preserve peace when faced with threats of various dimensions.

The General Advisory Committee to the Atomic Energy Commission had the prime responsibility for advising the United States Administration in regard to atomic energy generally, and the scientific aspects of the development of the nuclear weapon in particular. The scientists composing this advisory committee, the leading members of which were Robert Oppenheimer and James Conant, were disturbed because American military and political thinking seemed to be coming to the belief that the United States could depend almost exclusively on strategic bombing, with the atomic bomb, of course, for its security and to protect its interests. The scientists felt that this was not a policy on which the USA could rely indefinitely. For one thing, they knew that the Soviet Union would produce its own atomic bomb sooner or later. However, their estimate of the time the Russians would require for their breakthrough was too long by about four years.

At this time, also, certain politicians and senior USAF officers began to think in terms of a new isolationism. Their basic idea was that the USA should depend only on itself, with as little reliance on and as few commitments to allies as possible. The USA would ensure respect for its interests and preserve its security by possessing a very powerful air force based solely on USA territory, and capable of delivering the atomic weapon to the Soviet Union heartland or to any point of conflict. Such an idea had been expounded at various times in the past by Alexander de Seversky and others. It is a curious comment on this theory that this withdrawal of United States military power from "foreign bases" has for many years been one of the principal objects of the Soviet Union, and still is, as set out in their plans for general and complete disarmament and in multitudinous propaganda statements.

Neo-isolationists thought the bomb secret was possessed by the USA alone and had to be preserved by the most drastic security measures. It was indeed argued that the control of the whole atomic energy programme should revert to the military. The scientists were naturally alarmed by these suggestions for more security and greater military control, as a threat to their independence and indeed to the eventual progress of American science in basic research. They didn't like the idea, and who can blame them, of being periodically investigated and perhaps kept under surveillance by the FBI. Fortunately, the scientists were not alone in opposition. For example, such a respected military commentator as Mr. Hanson Baldwin warned against the danger of the new isolationist, or Fortress America, ideas, writing "The bomb has become, unfortunately, our psychological Maginot Line."

Another idea, which reinforced the new isolationism, was that it was the Soviet Union strategy to bleed America white, that is, to destroy her economy and render her unable to help the rest of the free world while still maintaining the American way of life. This was to be done by obliging America to intervene with costly conventional forces when communist subversion threatened to take over governments of countries which previously had been in the sphere of influence of the USA or its allies. As Vice-President Nixon said in a radio address of 13

March 1954: "Rather than let the Communists nibble us to death all over the world in little wars, we would rely in the future primarily on our massive mobile retaliatory power . . . against the major source of aggression."

When the first Soviet Union atomic explosion was detected in September 1949, it became vital and urgent to decide whether the USA should construct the hydrogen bomb, or superbomb, as it had been called. On 5 October 1949 Admiral Lewis Strauss, at that time head of AEC, proposed that studies should be started at once on how to make it. It was reasoned that as it was possible that the Soviet Union would produce an H-bomb in the course of time, the USA must build one first. Led by Dr. Lawrence, some of the scientists in the Berkeley California Radiation Laboratories decided, after consulting Dr. Teller, then employed at Los Alamos, to press the General Advisory Committee and other persons in key positions to develop an H-bomb with all speed.

Another view was held by Drs. Conant and Oppenheimer and others. They felt that those who relied so heavily on strategic bombing failed to appreciate the power and flexibility of action which the Soviet Union possessed in its conventional forces. This would be a more serious threat when the Russians would be able to deliver nuclear weapons in numbers. It would enable them to impose caution on the United States in the use of its nuclear power; that is, there would be a nuclear stalemate to a greater or lesser degree. The rightness of these scientists' views has come to be appreciated in the 1960's.

In an article in the *Saturday Evening Post* dated 15 October 1949 General Omar Bradley advocated arming the NATO forces in Europe with tactical atomic weapons. Such weapons had been developed by the AEC and were nearly ready for production. (See page 118.) But because fissile material was still scarce, its diversion to the making of small weapons for use by other services was strongly opposed by USAF officers, who felt that all available supplies should be reserved for strategic bombing.

The General Advisory Committee at its meeting in October decided not to recommend development of the hydrogen bomb, although they estimated that there was a better than even chance that it could be made. They thought it would be wrong to commit great resources to a crash programme on the H-bomb, but recommended expansion of the production of other nuclear weapons. In their recommendations they made the following points: first, that there would be a dangerous imbalance of the American military power if total reliance were placed on the strategic employment of nuclear weapons; second, that nuclear weapons in the long term would be a threat to United States security; and third, that the President should inform the American people of the dangers to the USA and to world security of an unlimited nuclear arms race. These recommendations were before their time, but they are seen now to have been wise, and are generally accepted as bases for current American defence and disarmament policies.

This debate on whether to produce the thermonuclear weapon was conducted in deep secrecy, although there were occasional leaks, and the American public had only a vague idea of what the controversy was about. At this time, late in 1949, influential people in Washington were worried about many events and situations: the scares about atomic spying; the final triumph of the Communists over Chiang Kai-shek in China, regarded as a grave defeat for the United States; the controversy between the Navy and the Air Force over the value of the B 36 bomber; and, generally, the strategic concepts central to the organization, armament and employment of the United States armed services. But most agitating of all were the repercussions of the Soviet Union's explosion of an atomic device.

About this time, too, another school of thought developed, of which Dr. Teller was the most notable exponent. (Incidentally, his testimony before the Senate Committees in 1963 on the nuclear test ban treaty showed that his ideas have not altered.) This school held the view that the Soviet Union must be contained, that an arms race would necessarily continue until the political differences between the contestants in it were settled, and that the only alternative to security through armaments would be a completely "open" world. But then the problem becomes: How does one persuade the Soviet Union to become completely open? Are they likely to abandon their policy of secrecy while the USA adds daily to its stock of ICBM's and discusses a policy for their use which the Soviet Union interprets as a pre-emptive strike policy? How long is the world likely to have to wait for the Soviet Union to become an open democracy like the United States? Are Dr. Teller and those who agree with his views willing to have the arms race go on indefinitely, in spite of its admitted economic waste and dangers?

On 31 January 1950 President Truman handed down a decision that the AEC should continue work on all forms of atomic weapons, including the hydrogen bomb. This, in itself, did not settle the controversy whether the H-bomb should be produced or not, but the issue was practically decided when on 10 March the President approved the Secretary for Defense's recommendation for providing the necessary facilities for quantity production of fissile material for all types of nuclear armaments, and other requirements, such as tritium, for the construction of a hydrogen weapon.

The Korean War, which broke out in June 1950, had most important influences on armaments policy and on the thinking about how, when and where nuclear weapons could be used. Its effects took two forms which relate to the subject of this book. The first was the effect which this aggression, carried out by a satellite of the Soviet Union, had on the build-up of NATO forces in Western Europe. The second effect was to show that there were limitations on strategic bombing with nuclear weapons. This led American political and military leaders to reconsider *in extenso* the strategic concepts governing the worldwide conflict with the Soviet Union.

It was on 25 June 1950 that the North Korean forces, which had been indoctrinated, trained and provided with armaments by the Soviet Union, crossed the border between North and South Korea, and advanced on Seoul. On 26 June the Security Council of the United Nations called for a cease-fire. On the next day it denounced North Korea as an aggressor and decided on economic and military sanctions, as provided in the Charter. It was possible to do this because the Soviet Union was not sitting in Security Council meetings at that time, in protest against Nationalist China (Formosa) instead of the

People's Republic (Peking) representing China at the UN. If the Soviet Union had been present, it could have vetoed this decision, in which case the United States and other participating nations intervening in Korea would not have been in the legal position of carrying out a peace-keeping task under the Charter. Also on 27 June, President Truman ordered US air and naval forces in the Far East to go to the aid of the South Koreans. Other nations supported the action of the United States and in due course furnished armed forces and other assistance.

The European powers of NATO were alarmed by this communist aggression, which could be repeated elsewhere, even in Western Europe. So they began urgently to rearm and reorganize their military forces. In May of 1950 the Western Allies had only 14 divisions in Europe, supported by about 1000 aircraft. There was no central command organization to co-ordinate the efforts of these national forces, which were designed primarily for the occupation of Western Germany. On the other hand, the Soviet Union had 25 divisions in East Germany and other East European countries and these were supported by an estimated 6000 aircraft, all under centralized command. Besides these forces, the Soviet Union had many more divisions inside their own boundaries which could be deployed rapidly along the Iron Curtain.

When the North Atlantic Council met at New York on 15 September 1950, the problem of how to defend the NATO area from a Korean-type aggression was debated. It was decided that a forward strategy should be adopted. This meant that the foremost line of defence should be on the borders of Western Germany and of other European countries of NATO contiguous to countries in which the Soviet Union held power. It was also decided that NATO defence must be integrated under a Supreme Commander.

About this time, Secretary of State Dean Acheson, in view of the need to defend West German territory, proposed that German troops should be brought into the NATO forces, although not in any formation larger than a division. This, of course, was a reversal of the Allied policy of disarmament and demilitarization of Germany. However, by this time the Soviet Union had encouraged East Germany to raise a "People's Police," which was about 50,000 strong, and heavily armed. Chancellor Adenauer on 15 August 1950 declared that he favoured the formation of a unified West European army, and said that West Germany would supply a contingent to it if asked to do so. However, no such action ensued, owing to objections raised by France. These were the immediate effects on the NATO posture of the threat made manifest by the communist aggression in Korea.

When the Chinese communist armies intervened, the UN Command considered air attack on their bases in China, and even the carrying of the land war into Chinese territory. But the European NATO allies feared that if the war were extended beyond the borders of Korea, the Soviet Union would be bound to intervene in turn, and the most probable area for that intervention would be in Europe. If this happened, the United States, with the bulk of its forces engaged in a Korean-Chinese war, would not have much left with which to support its European allies if the feared Russian drive towards the west should take place. There was also the fear that if nuclear warfare were started in the Far East, the Soviet Union might have the means to extend it to Europe. Another reason may have been that there were not enough nuclear weapons to use them effectively in the Far East theatre while retaining a sufficient reserve against the possibility of the Soviet Union's extending the war into other areas.

For these reasons, the political authorities controlling the operations in Korea (that is to say, the United States Government in consultation with the other governments that had forces engaged) limited the area over which bombing could be carried out. The USAF and the UN Command (staffed mostly by Americans) felt very frustrated.

In spite of not being allowed a free hand in "strategic" bombing or in the use of nuclear weapons, the USAF operated extremely effectively in Korea, using high-explosive and napalm bombs, rockets and machine-gun fire. Supported by naval aviation, the USAF maintained a clear superiority throughout, and was able to give support to the sometimes very hard-pressed land forces by direct tactical action such as attacks on enemy communications, the "interdicting" of the supply routes which slowed or brought to a halt the offensive operations of first the North Korean communist forces and later the Chinese communist forces.

After varying fortunes, the front lines were stabilized near the 38th Parallel, which had been the pre-war boundary between North and South Korea, and negotiations for an armistice began in June 1951. These dragged on for three years before a settlement could be reached, although there were no important changes in the situation during this period.

Even before the armistice, an extensive debate began in the United States on the conduct of the war and its lessons in relation to future strategic policy. Mr. Thomas K. Finletter, who had been Secretary of the Air Force from 1950 to 1953, in an article published in May of 1955 pointed out that the Korean war was a special case and that the experience gained in it could not be applied in a general way in determining the future role of United States air power in support of United States policy in the Far East. The Korean war was a United Nations operation and had to be carried out under the principles of the UN Charter. This meant that if the communist forces were pushed back to beyond the pre-war boundary, the 38th Parallel, the political object of the war was attained. "Total victory" —the unconditional surrender of Communist China—was not in question. These political conditions limited the use of air power. It was not its function to enforce surrender by destroying the communist cities and economy. (Mr. Finletter explained the danger of extending bombing into Chinese territory in the same general terms as given on page 109.) He further remarked that the American people strongly resented the heavy casualties that had been suffered in Korea, and that the conduct of the war had become a subject of controversy in United States politics. (This doubtless precluded a calm and constructive assessment of the lessons.) Mr. Finletter believed it very unlikely that a limited war in the Far East under the UN Charter rules would take place in future, or, at any rate, that the United States would willingly participate in such an operation.

The Korean war experience stimulated the debate about tactical nuclear weapons and made it more urgent to decide

whether they should be produced, how they could be fitted
into the weaponry of the US armed services and whether they
would increase US fighting power and flexibility of response to
aggressions. "Project Vista," an extensive study of the problem
of reducing the strategic nuclear weapon to tactical size, was
embarked upon after the report of the General Advisory Committee in October 1949 called for a review of US strategic policy. (See page 105.) The scientists who favoured developing
tactical nuclear weapons thought that they would enable the
United States to develop policies for meeting war threats, other
than by the nuclear bombing of the enemy homeland. One objection raised at that time against spreading nuclear weapons
in small sizes throughout all the US armed services was that if
conventional weapons were replaced or largely supplemented
by nuclear weapons, the problem of getting rid of the tactical
nuclear arms, or subjecting them to "arms control," would become much more complicated than if it were only a question of
limiting the use and numbers of the larger "strategic" weapons.
Now, in 1966, the United States has in its forces a great deal
of nuclear weaponry in many sizes and for many tactical functions. Arrangements have been made with some of its allies
which would allow them to use tactical nuclear weapons if war
should break out; but meanwhile they are kept under strict USA
control. The early objection to this "proliferation" of nuclear
weapons was well founded from the viewpoint of those seeking
to limit armaments and avoid the danger of nuclear war.

# 9

## MASSIVE RETALIATION; PREVENTIVE WAR; PRE-EMPTIVE ATTACK

Although, as we have noted, "tactical" atomic weapons had been under development for the United States forces since about 1948, no general doctrine for their use was brought into the open for some years. Or at any rate, it did not become the subject of public debate. Attention was fixed, instead, on the policy of "massive retaliation," generally associated with the name of the late John Foster Dulles. The idea certainly was no new one, having been expounded by USAF generals as far back as 1947. Doubtless, also, Mr. Dulles based his defence policy statements on advice tendered by professional military men. In his speech before the Council of Foreign Relations in New York on 12 January 1954, which is regarded as the first definitive announcement of the massive retaliation policy, he said it was based on important decisions of the National Security Council, that is, presumably, on a consensus of the highest level of professional advisers.

Calling attention to the danger of a deployment of us forces which would try to cover defensively every area where communist aggression or infiltration was to be feared (that is, a failure to observe the classic military principle of concentration, with resultant weakness everywhere), he said that local defences must be reinforced by the further deterrent of massive retaliatory power, and that the way for the free world to deter aggression was to be willing and able to respond to it vigorously at places and with means of its own choosing. American military establishments could be given the necessary great retaliatory force and be designed to fit such a policy, instead of leaving the initiative to the enemy, and trying to build up US forces of all sorts, strong enough to counter all his possible moves. The new policy, Dulles claimed, could provide more security at less cost, not only for the USA but for its allies.

Those who developed this policy probably were inspired, in part, by a desire to avoid any repetition of the frustrating experience of the Korean war, where, many Americans thought, total victory had not been won because the Administration had not allowed use of nuclear weapons. And the Administration had not done so, it was also thought, mainly in deference to the fears of allies. This sort of block could be avoided for the future by announcing, before any crisis arose, a firm policy to use the big nuclear weapons. It was hoped to gain the general assent of allies by this procedure, but in the event, the allies never did accept the massive retaliation policy very enthusiastically, and it was also criticized at home. Mr. Dulles had to soften his position in various later utterances. Nevertheless, over the next few years the budget allocations showed that preparing for massive retaliation was the military policy being pursued.

In theory, the threat of massive retaliation could prevent the USSR from following a course of action dangerous to US interests in any part of the world. There is little doubt that the existence of this unvoiced threat did impose caution on the USSR in certain areas during the period in which the United States' superiority in the means of waging nuclear war was greatest. The USSR was careful not to let the Berlin blockade escalate into open hostilities, and in the Korean war, took care not to become directly involved.

The framers of the massive retaliation policy were seemingly not greatly concerned by the facts that the USSR had exploded an atomic bomb in 1949 and a thermonuclear device in 1953.

That is, they did not seem to consider the possibility that the Soviet Union would be able to build up a force for the delivery of nuclear weapons which would be able to inflict unacceptable devastation on the USA. In other words, the nuclear stalemate was not foreseen in working out this policy. Perhaps this was because most Americans easily assumed that they could keep far in advance of the Soviet Union in scientific and technical development—a conceit which was finally shattered by the launching of Sputnik I in 1957.

About the time that it was decided to adopt the policy of massive retaliation, there was an idea current that it would be necessary for the USA to make a choice between two alternative systems for organizing and arming its defence forces: either to continue to build up conventional as well as nuclear armaments, or to depend primarily on nuclear armaments to meet all contingencies wherever military force would have to be used. Having in mind the balance of power between the USSR and the USA as it then appeared to be and the estimated capacity of the Soviet Union to arm itself with nuclear weapons, it was reasonable to believe that nuclear weapons would be used in many possible theatres of war. Therefore it would be necessary for the USA, in order to be superior everywhere in nuclear weapons, to spend so much money on them that it would leave little for conventional armaments. The Eisenhower Administration attached great importance to balancing the national budget; hence the total amount of money available for the forces and their armament was limited. So nuclear armaments and air force requirements had priority, and the massive retaliation policy fitted in with this state of affairs. This was in spite of the fact that most people then thought that the use of nuclear weapons implied all-out war.

It was basic that the United States should be able to retaliate with devastating force if the Soviet Union attacked its homeland. Also, as we have seen, the NATO alliance depended at that time on the threat of retaliation by the Strategic Air Command to deter an invasion of Europe by superior Russian conventional forces. Even now, most of the European members of NATO show the greatest alarm if anyone suggests that the

United States is not still completely committed to respond to any Soviet Union aggression in Europe by engaging its full nuclear power.

When, however, strategists and policy-makers began to examine the general concept of massive retaliation in relation to specific situations which might arise in parts of the world other than Western Europe, for example the Far East or the Middle East, they perceived that massive retaliation was not the absolute answer to the problems of defending United States interests. Suppose the Korean situation which led to war in 1950 recurred and South Korea was in danger of being overrun? Could nuclear weapons, whether labelled tactical or strategical, be used against the North Koreans and not against the Chinese forces? Once Chinese forces were engaged in the war, would not the massive retaliation principle have required massive attack on Chinese cities? Could such punishment have been meted out to the Chinese wthout previously neutralizing the Soviet Union? Mr. Khrushchev explicitly stated, in a letter to President Eisenhower dated 7 September 1958, that an attack on Communist China would be taken as an attack on the USSR itself and that an attack with nuclear weapons would be responded to with nuclear weapons. The Soviet Union maintained this commitment after the first break with China in 1963; whether it still does is very doubtful. But if Vietnam is substituted for Korea, the dangers of a massive retaliation policy in this part of the world are seen still to exist. This matter will be discussed briefly in Chapter 15.

But let us look at the problem as it probably appeared to strategists in the late 1950's. To control China in the hypothetical Korean situation by threat of massive retaliation it would first be necessary to ensure that the USSR would not intervene. A first strike or preventive war against the Soviet Union would be ruled out by general United States policy. So it would have been necessary to present ultimata to both China and the USSR. If such ultimata had been presented, the People's Republic of China might have ignored them, while they would have been given a political and strategic advantage. Of course the Russians might have backed down and told the Chinese that they would not support them if they defied the US ultimatum, although it is difficult to believe that the Russians would have submitted in such a tame way, with the loss of face entailed. But the point is that whatever the Russians did, the application of the massive retaliation principle in this imagined Korean situation would have resulted in an immediate confrontation between the USA and the USSR, with the imminent danger of all-out nuclear war. So the question arises, in how many areas in the world would the USA be willing to risk all-out nuclear war to protect allies or clients, or even friendly neutrals, from communist pressure? In 1954 Indo-China was on the verge of being entirely taken over by the Communists, and the use of nuclear weapons in that theatre was debated and rejected. In the Lebanon-Jordan crisis of 1958, American support against subversion was given by landing marines and soldiers, not by threatening anyone with massive punishment by nuclear weapons.

There seem still to be some men, who, while intellectually aware of the consequences of a nuclear war for all belligerents, somehow shut their minds to the real and terrible facts. Perhaps the prospect of a communist-dominated world is so abhorrent to some people that it obscures the horror of the possible extinction of scores of millions of human beings and the accompanying destruction of most of the values of civilization. "Better Dead than Red" is the extreme statement of this blinkered-mind thinking. In 1964 fire-eaters said that the United States Government was pursuing a "No-win" policy. They apparently believed that no military policy should be adopted which did not aim at total victory—forcing the unconditional surrender of the enemy. It was perhaps the uneasy feeling that there may be some military men of this stamp of mind in a position to influence decisions on peace and war that inspired such fantasies as the film *Dr. Strangelove*. Whatever grounds past military leadership may have given for such apprehensions, surely they are no longer valid today. It is to be hoped that the myth-figure of the mad general will presently fade out of the public mind.

The doctrine of massive retaliation which Mr. Dulles announced to the world was modified, in due course, following public debate. But Americans must suspect that there are other doctrines concocted in secret, or plans made for action in specific eventualities, which are dangerous to their lives and also to their liberties. The concern of Americans over these possibilities was illustrated by the great success attained in 1962-63 by the novels *Fail-Safe* and *Seven Days in May*, dealing in different ways with the theme of what the concentration in a few hands of the power to set the nuclear apparatus in motion could imply for life and liberty in the USA.

In an article published in October 1957 (the month of Sputnik I) Mr. Dulles showed how the policy of massive retaliation had been toned down in the four years since he had first announced it. He wrote:

> The United States has not been content to rely on a peace which could be preserved only by a capacity to destroy vast segments of the human race. . . . The resourcefulness of those who serve our nation in the field of science and weapon engineering now shows that it is possible to alter the character of nuclear weapons. It seems now that their use need not involve vast destruction and widespread harm to humanity.

In other words, the nuclear weapon had now become "tactical" and was to confer a great advantage on the USA and the allies under American protection. As we shall see, this belief was in error, because it was assumed that the USSR would lag far behind the United States in the development of so-called "tactical" nuclear weapons. The policy also ignored the very great probability of escalation of the nuclear conflict. The facts about weapon development cited by Mr. Dulles in his 1957 article were known, as we have seen, when he announced the massive retaliation policy. The true reason for the change in doctrine was probably that he and his colleagues responsible for United States foreign and military policy had learned through experience and reflection that to rely on massive retaliation to defend American interests in areas of secondary importance was too dangerous. It was comparable to using dynamite to exterminate rats in the cellar.

Before we go on to discuss the development of thought about tactical nuclear weapons, especially as armament for NATO forces in Europe, we should take a look at some other strategies which have been proposed for the use of nuclear weapons, namely, preventive war and pre-emptive attack. While massive retaliation was for a while the accepted policy of the United States Government, preventive war and pre-emptive attack were only subjects for somewhat trigger-happy theorizing, and never became official doctrines, much less government policy.

In the days when the USA had a monopoly of the atomic weapon, and for a while after the first USSR atomic explosion, some bellicose Americans thought that the United States should attack the Soviet Union and stop its development of nuclear weapons before it was too late, and in the process destroy its capacity to extend communism further. This was a special application of the general idea of preventive war, which can be defined as a war initiated by one nation to forestall the assumed or believed intention of another nation to attack it at some later time. Some German militarists paraded this notion before World War I; it is supposed to have influenced Hitler to attack the USSR when he did. To cite a more recent and localized example, a few Israeli extremists in the 1950's advocated attacking Egypt, because they thought it was clear that Egypt intended to attack Israel. In neither the first nor the third instance I have cited did the responsible government entertain any such aggressive intention; nevertheless, when theories of this sort are publicly aired, the nation labelled as the enemy must feel uneasy, and even threatened. It creates an atmosphere in which war seems the normal and reasonable response to a minor provocation or act of hostility.

The first argument advanced by those who in the early and euphoric days of the nuclear age advocated a preventive war was that nuclear war would inevitably come about some day, just as wars had periodically erupted throughout the ages in spite of secular vows of permanent abstinence made by military powers. Also, it appeared certain, in the circumstances of those days, that in a war waged with nuclear weapons, the country which struck first would have a far better chance of winning, that is, of escaping the most disastrous consequences. This assumed that the country launching the preventive war would have fairly accurate information about the location of the airfields on which the aircraft the enemy could use for retaliation were stationed. (Of course, the appearance of ICBM's has radically altered the equation.) Surprise would have to be achieved, and in passing one may remark that this would be difficult, if not impossible, in the American "open" society. In the first place, little goes on in the United States, even in sectors of the national defence which in other countries would be highly secret, which does not soon become public knowledge. When there is little interference with the free movement of individuals over practically all of the country, and few or no prohibitions on what may be printed in the newspapers or broadcast on the radio, this must be so. Furthermore, Congress, which is jealous of its prerogative to declare war, finds out about what goes on through its close contacts with the military services, even if it should not be informed by the Executive. If the pressing of the button were all that had to be done, the secret might conceivably be kept among a small group of men in power. But it would seem impossible to conceal for long the preparations and planning necessary to begin a war against the Soviet Union by a surprise attack and bring it to a successful conclusion.

On the other hand, we must keep in mind the experience of the Cuban crisis of the autumn of 1962, when the action to deal with the build-up of Soviet Union missiles in Cuba was decided upon by a small group of the Executive and the armed services, and only became known to the public when the President informed them by television broadcast. If Mr. Khrushchev had miscalculated, and refused the United States' demand for withdrawal, war could have come to the USA with practically no warning.

It is quite possible, although there is now no evidence to prove or disprove it, that the USA had a greater relative advantage over the Soviet Union in the late 1950's than earlier, and might then have been better able to accomplish the aims of preventive war than in the early days when it possessed the monopoly of nuclear weapons, but relatively few of them. An unfortunate result of the visions of the enthusiasts for a preventive war is that with the roles of the United States and the Soviet Union reversed, they have come back as nightmares to haunt the less warlike majority of Americans. If the USSR should become sufficiently confident that their powerful ICBM's with warheads of thirty megatons or more could destroy most of the United States' intercontinental striking power, and should decide on a preventive war, they *could* probably effect surprise, owing to the rigid security behind the Iron Curtain. (I do not suggest, however, that the Soviet Union nowadays is any more likely to launch a preventive war than the United States.)

It was also argued by the extremists that if nuclear war were inevitable, the longer it was postponed, the more destructive it would be, for the Russians could be expected to achieve a rapid build-up of nuclear weapons and the means to deliver them. Therefore the USA should not wait to be overtaken but use its quantitative advantage in nuclear weapons and long-range aircraft while it lasted. The strength of this argument diminished as the 1950's progresssed and the estimates of Russian "nuclear capability" grew, to the point at which it was obvious that unacceptable damage to the USA could be caused by a Soviet retaliatory strike.

Some optimists now (1966) think that nuclear war is impossible. This is merely wishful thinking; nuclear war is possible so long as nuclear weapons exist. But it is not inevitable, specifically not inevitable as between the USA and the USSR, and their respective allies. But although nuclear war is not inevitable, the threat will not disappear of itself, and if the arms race continues it cannot grow less. The threat will only be reduced to the point where people will not be more afraid of perishing in a nuclear holocaust than they are, say, of being struck by lightning, if the great nuclear powers definitely change their policies. They must cease to seek security through piling up nuclear armaments, and find it instead through agreements to disarm and settle international disputes peacefully.

By the end of the 1950's new factors had to be taken into account in the theorizings about preventive war. These factors were the coming of the ICBM, the lack of any means to prevent its arrival over the target area, the fact that its launching pad could be more easily concealed than bases for bombing aircraft and the further consideration that the installations necessary for its launching can be "hardened," that is, placed underground with concrete and armour-plate protection to ensure that they could not be destroyed by the explosion of even a heavy nuclear weapon more than a mile or so distant. In short it appeared that there would soon be both Russian and American invulnerable retaliatory forces. So the arguments in favour of a preventive war disappeared.

The theoretical advantages of a preventive war have been briefly sketched above, ignoring the moral issue, which is, in fact, decisive even in the world of the nuclear age. It is almost impossible to imagine the American people concurring in the proposition that it is of no consequence how many millions of Russians are killed without warning, provided that this would ensure the future safety of the United States. The bombing of Hiroshima and Nagasaki has created widespread feelings of guilt among Americans. Would they be happy living in a world "made safe for democracy" by Hiroshimas multiplied several thousand times? Would the surviving nations be happy living in a world with such an America? The fact is that a preventive war would be so repugnant to the moral sense of the American people (Birchists and other neo-Neanderthals excepted) that it is impossible. And this has been consecrated in the official policy of successive US administrations and in public declarations by the highest authority. Even such a believer in the unrestricted continuance of the arms race as Dr. Edward Teller explicitly rejects the idea in his book *The Legacy of Hiroshima*, and in 1950, a high-ranking Air Force officer was removed from his appointment after he had publicly argued for preventive war. This dampened enthusiasm for the theory in the armed services, or at least for its open advocacy.

A study of the reactions of the American people in the period preceding the Civil War, and before both world wars, shows that a prolonged period of conditioning to the idea of war is necessary before they will actually pick up the gauntlet. This is not purely a moral attitude. Americans—like the majority of mankind everywhere—fear war, which they know will bring them sacrifice and deep anxieties, even if not death and the destruction of their wealth. Moral scruples are reinforced by the fact that the Russians have developed thermonuclear weapons and can effectively strike the United States homeland with them. When the Soviet Union exploded its atomic and thermonuclear bombs the American public was not greatly excited; certainly there was no demand for preventive war to scotch the threat. The impact of the launching of Sputnik in October 1957 was greater. It was soon realized that the Russians could hit American cities with thermonuclear weapons and that there would be no defence, no means of preventing this.

From preventive war, let us pass on to its little cousin in nuclear strategies, pre-emptive attack. It can be defined as a strike by US nuclear-weapon-carrying forces against the similar forces of the Soviet Union when the latter are about to be launched in an attack on the USA. In theory, it escapes the moral objections to preventive war which we have just cited. It is a spoiling attack, a seizing of the initiative just before the enemy's offensive is begun; the purpose is to put out of action as many as possible of the enemy's intercontinental ballistic missiles and aircraft, and thus lessen the effect of his nuclear attack on the USA. If it is certain that the enemy is indeed going to attack, there can be no moral objection to defending oneself by hitting the engines that are preparing one's destruction. The catch, of course, lies in knowing with absolute certainty that the enemy is going to attack. If, in fact, the enemy has no firm immediate intention to attack, then a pre-emptive strike becomes preventive war.

Nowadays, if a surprise attack on the homeland of the USA should ever be launched, the ICBM would be the principal means of delivery of the nuclear weapons. Under these conditions it would be very difficult to determine the time chosen by the enemy for zero hour. His intention might be given away by other actions, such as a general mobilization of his armies or moves of aircraft and surface vessels. But ballistic missiles are either in a constant state of readiness to be fired or can be made ready in secrecy. We can be sure that if the Soviet Union should ever prepare a surprise attack on the United States, they would take every precaution to achieve secrecy, and take every advantage of the possibilities for the concealment of intentions which their society affords.

It has been made clear that neither great nuclear power

wants to initiate nuclear war by mistake, nor to incur the odium of being the first to unleash nuclear war. This is a serious consideration indeed. But it could happen through an error in interpreting intelligence data if a policy of pre-emptive attack, making sure of getting in the first nuclear blow, had previously been adopted. This is what strategists mean when they speak of fearing the outbreak of nuclear war through miscalculation or misunderstanding. A number of measures to stop this happening were discussed at the abortive conference on measures to prevent surprise attack at Geneva, in 1958, and one has actually been put into effect, the direct telegraph-telephone line between Washington and Moscow. If another crisis like the Cuba affair should arise, explanations could be exchanged in a matter of minutes. Other measures for the prevention of surprise attack are sporadically discussed and could be made operative prior to a disarmament agreement.

If a pre-emptive strike policy for the United States nuclear forces is to be feasible and is to promise a real advantage, very accurate information on the location of the Soviet Union's ICBM's would be needed. We do not know how much the US Intelligence Services really know about this; such information obviously must be kept highly secret. How quickly would US Intelligence learn about changes in the state of readiness of the Soviet Union's intercontinental missiles? When the Soviet Union force for carrying nuclear bombs to the USA consisted of bombers, grouped on relatively few specialized air bases, the pre-emptive attack theory may have had a certain attraction, and possibly it would again if the information about ICBM's could be as complete as it was about the aircraft dispositions. But this is not likely, and furthermore, the "hardening" of the ICBM bases reduces the possibility of knocking out a proportion of the missiles high enough to make a pre-emptive attack a reasonable war policy.

Responsible United States authorities tell us in public statements that the Strategic Air Command exists to deter attack, not to initiate it. The theory of deterrence of different degrees and against various kinds of threat has been discussed exhaustively by Mr. Herman Kahn in *On Thermonuclear War*, and we shall be examining some of his views later. While the plans for pre-emptive attack have presumably been put away in the dead files of the Pentagon, the average layman may still conceive it as one of the modes in which the United States, or the Soviet Union, could use its nuclear power. The strategy of counterforce, of which a good deal has been heard in the last few years, has some points of resemblance with pre-emptive attack and we shall be discussing this later also.

Dr. Henry A. Kissinger, in his notable book *Nuclear Weapons and Foreign Policy,* tells us that nuclear weapons, which a decade earlier had been few in number and difficult to produce, had become plentiful by 1957, the year his book was published. All sizes of them were in production, from tactical weapons of as little as 0.1 kilotons, or $\frac{1}{200}$ the explosive power of the Hiroshima bomb, up to the thermonuclear weapons of 20 megatons, or a thousand times the power of the proto-bomb. The part of his book which interests us here is that in which he develops a theory of limited war with nuclear weapons. Could the lesser nuclear weapons be used in such a way as to give the United States a decisive advantage in war, without entailing the drastic choices of the massive retaliation policy? Could military tactics and strategy be devised for the use of the lower range of nuclear weapons which could validate American foreign policy, yet which would not visit unlimited destruction on the enemy, and risk the same kind of destruction and death for Americans? These were the questions which he proceeded to examine, after a searching critique of previous United States policies for the employment of the nuclear weapon, dealt with in more summary fashion in the preceding pages here.

It is to be borne in mind in reading what follows that Dr. Kissinger later changed the views which he set forth in *Nuclear Weapons and Foreign Policy,* and we shall be referring to his later opinions in due course. But for the purpose of this book, which is to exhibit how military thinking about the waging of war with nuclear weapons developed, it is useful to explore his earlier thinking.

It will be best first to look at some of Dr. Kissinger's ideas about the defence of NATO Europe and how nuclear weapons could be related to it. We will thus have the advantage of examining his theory of the way tactical nuclear weapons could be used in application to a real case, in which we more or less know the geography, the numbers and armament of the opposing forces, political factors and all the other matters which have to be taken into account in the estimate or appreciation of a military situation. Far too much theorizing about nuclear weapons and their employment in war is conducted in purely abstract terms; that is, the public is being invited to accept a number of generalizations about the probable nature and practice of nuclear war, without being given studies in detail of specific possible war situations in which nuclear arms might be employed and from which generalizations might be derived. What science there is about the conduct of war is empirical, which is to say that its general principles are derived inductively from experience. It may be objected (as pointed out in earlier pages) that there is no body of experience of war in which nuclear weapons have been used. That is true. How, then, are we to assess the changes which the new weapons will make in the practice of war? The power and effect of the new weapons is one of the factors in any given war situation; other factors are geography, strength and armament of opposing forces, time and space, and the rest. So, the best and most realistic way for us to determine what nuclear war will be like, or whether limited war with tactical nuclear weapons will be possible, is painstakingly to study the possible use of nuclear weapons in a series of hypothetical war situations (but the most probable ones), bringing into the studies as many real and known factors as exist, including the experimentally established physical effects of nuclear explosions. Such map exercises should be supplemented by as realistic as possible exercises with troops on the ground, although of course, the actual exploding of nuclear devices will not be practicable. The conclusions reached from such a series of studies will, or should, furnish the closest approximation to true knowledge about the way in which nuclear weapons could be used in war. Even so, such conclusions could only be a probable guide to action. In the catastrophic event, things would probably turn out quite differently to the predictions arrived at by the most sophisticated methods.

Doubtless the general staffs and the war colleges of the nuclear powers, assisted by auxiliary corps of tame scientists and academic strategists, have been carrying out a series of such studies for the past fifteen years or so. But if they have, the product of their labours has not been made available to the public, except in a few instances of rather spectacular exercises, which have penetrated the publicity media. From this it results that when a private student of war, for example Dr. Kissinger, sets forth certain ideas in general terms on how tactical nuclear weapons could be used, if he does not refer to detailed studies, exercises and experiments from which he draws his conclusions, one has to assume that he is concocting his ideas without a sufficient base of experimental data, and that no matter how brilliant and powerful his intellect may be, his conclusions may end up a long way from reality.

However, in *Nuclear Weapons and Foreign Policy*, written in 1957 (and based on material accumulated by a panel of military and foreign policy experts who commenced work in 1953), Dr. Kissinger has given a very good statement of the difficulties which have afflicted the North Atlantic Alliance from a lack of an agreed defensive strategy. While there have been several successive agreements on the overall defensive plan and on the contributions in military forces which each ally should make, no final and satisfactory answer has been found to the basic question: If the assurance against Soviet Union invasion of NATO Europe is provided by the United States Strategic Air Command, what precisely is the purpose and function of the conventional forces provided by the European allies, and dependent on this function, what should be the size and armament of these forces?

We have seen that in the early days of NATO it was the general view that only the threat of retaliation by United States nuclear airpower stood in the way of Russian power to push the Iron Curtain further to the west. Once it was generally accepted that ultimately the defence of Europe rested on the power of the US Strategic Air Command, it proved very difficult to prevent a corollary idea from being generally accepted also; namely, that it didn't matter so very much what the European members of NATO did in the way of providing conventional forces for the defence of their own territory. These ideas stood (and still stand) in the way of the build-up of NATO conventional forces capable of repelling Russian forces deployed close to the Iron Curtain.

From the American viewpoint this was naturally far from satisfactory. In the days before the implications of Sputnik had sunk into the American military and political consciousness, they were confident in their power to take the necessary action if the necessity should ever arise. Furthermore, the need to prevent Western Europe from falling under communist domination, as Eastern Europe had, seemed a justification for American commitments to defend Europeans against this threat. In the early days of NATO, European nations were slowly rebuilding their war-ravaged economies, and could with difficulty sustain the additional burden of rearming their defence forces and allocating additional manpower to military service. But an alliance cannot depend on the military power of one of its members alone; otherwise, as Dr. Kissinger remarked, it becomes not an alliance but a series of protectorates.

Some of the American concepts of the role of conventional forces in NATO did not encourage the European partners to make an effective contribution to the military strength of the alliance. Metaphors such as "trip-wire" and "plate-glass window" indicated that the purpose of the conventional NATO forces was to be able to repel a minor incursion of Soviet Union forces; if the incursion were by a larger force, then when the NATO conventional forces were no longer capable of resisting the Russian advance, the SAC would be unleashed. If this was to be the way it would go, why should the European nations cramp their economic recovery by heavier taxation, and their governments incur political odium by extending the terms of conscript service just to furnish another division or two to the "trip-wire" or "plate-glass window" whose only function would be to be snapped, or smashed?

It will be seen that the defence of Europe against invasion by the superior Russian conventional forces rested, really, on the threat of massive retaliation by the United States. As we have seen (page 116), American politicians and military staffs began to calculate the possible cost of massive retaliation to the

United States if the threat alone should be insufficient and if the bombs should actually have to be dropped. The lack of proportion between likely types of provocation or minor hostilities and a reply by all-out nuclear war became apparent. The most important calculation of this kind was, of course, that which related to Western Europe. As the mid-fifties wore on into the later fifties, the threat of Soviet Union response to American massive retaliation became greater and more alarming, partly because of the furore about the bomber gap. The bomber gap was the difference between the bombers which the USA was actually building, and those which the Air Force intelligence estimated that the Soviet Union was building. It was represented, at one time, that the Soviet Union would be able to catch up with and surpass American strength in the air. It turned out, once the compensatory American bomber production programme got under way, that there had been errors in evaluating the evidence about the Russian aircraft construction programme, and that, in fact, they were not building so very many. American supremacy in the global bombing business seemed assured again; the aircraft industry was prospering, and the public would doubtless have been relieved of much anxiety if Sputnik I had not flashed across the sky, soon to be followed by apprehensions of a missile gap. However, this gets us ahead of our history.

Even after the original estimates of Russian intercontinental bombing capability had been scaled down, they remained serious; the Soviet Union had greatly increased its power to deliver nuclear weapons over the North American continent. The invulnerability of the United States homeland was disappearing, and with it the attractiveness of the policy of mass retaliation.

Dr. Kissinger makes the point that the refusal of the United States to share information about nuclear weapons with its allies left them with only vague and generally exaggerated ideas of the effects of these weapons if used in war. The refusal to share the information could be justified by those American military and political authorities who placed a very high value upon secrecy about the nuclear weapons. The revelations in several notorious cases of spying and defections of scientists engaged in the nuclear weapon production programmes seemed to point up the need for more rigid security. It is clear that military plans for the use of nuclear weapons in the case of an assault upon Europe, the number and power available, how they could be delivered and what targets they would be directed against, were in the Top Secret category. American military men had a poor opinion of the security of information entrusted to some of the allies, especially in those countries where Communist and Socialist parties were an important political factor. This mistrust was doubtless justified. But the end result of the secrecy about nuclear weapons was that the European allies had an insufficient idea of their powers and limitations, with a consequent failure to develop a good policy for the integrated defence of Europe with conventional and nuclear armament. The fact that control of SAC was outside the purview of the NATO command was another reason why the allies were unable to understand all the implications of nuclear war. (In May 1963 something was done to remedy this lack of understanding by the decisions taken at the Ottawa North Atlantic Council conference on the control of nuclear weapons in NATO. Officers of the European allies were to be associated with the planning carried out at SAC headquarters in the western United States.)

One sometimes wonders what would have happened if the USA had not had the atomic bomb in 1945. The general opinion as cited in previous pages was that it was only the fear of this weapon that deterred the USSR from invading Western Europe in the years that followed World War II. Perhaps it is not a very useful exercise to look back at this hypothetical case. However, one may surmise that if in a nuclear-weaponless world the threat of the Russians' large conventional forces still in being had made itself felt in 1946 and thereafter, there would still have been a NATO alliance, and the European members would, willy-nilly, have had to furnish enough conventional force, together with the contributions by America and Canada, to defend their territories. War-ravaged they may have been, but so was the Soviet Union. Perhaps the considerable forces which the Soviet Union retained under arms were calculated as being necessary to garrison the countries on which communist regimes had been imposed, and to guard against the possibility of a resurgent Germany. In other words, large as they seemed to the West, they may have been calculated by the Soviet Union on the basis of a defensive, rather than a potential offensive policy. The point of this argument is that now, when to most observers the efficacy of the threat of nuclear attack on the Soviet Union homeland by the sac has been diminished to the point of stalemate, are we not in about the same position as we should have been in in 1946 if there had been no atom bomb? But, of course, the Western European countries are now economically much better able to sustain the burden of the conventional armament and forces needed to stand against the Soviet Union threat.

# 10

## TACTICAL NUCLEAR WEAPONS AND LIMITED WAR

A new phase in the search for a strategy for the defence of NATO Europe began when the North Atlantic Council decided on 17 December 1954 that tactical nuclear weapons would be made available to the NATO forces. The principal reason for this decision was that it was believed that a numerically smaller force which had tactical nuclear weapons could defeat larger forces which had only conventional armament. Put in the European context: the exiguous forces of NATO, if armed with tactical nuclear weapons and trained and organized for their use, would be able to defeat the "Russian hordes," the 175 Soviet Union divisions that for years had been the bogey of Western strategists, and which were assumed to be ready at a moment's notice to roll across the territory of NATO Europe to the Atlantic coast.

Germany was, and still is, the country most deeply concerned with NATO defence strategy, for it this land which would be the first to be invaded if the Soviet Union should really attack. Until it was decided to employ tactical nuclear weapons, the German writers about defence matters, and presumably the German military staffs, had been mainly concerned as to how the conventional forces which they were committed to furnish to NATO would be used. They generally argued for a strategy of forward defence, that is, holding the limited West German ter-: ritory right up to the Elbe, instead of the flexible defence concept which seems to have ruled previously. Under the flexible defence strategy, the forward formations of the NATO forces would withdraw before the invading Soviet Union armies, eventually to make a stand on the Rhine, or thereabouts. Meanwhile the SAC, by bombing critical points on the invaders' lines of communication, and other strategic objectives in the Soviet Union homeland, could greatly reduce the offensive power of the invading armies, leaving them open to counter-attack by reinforced NATO formations. Naturally, such a strategy, under which all Western Germany would be a battleground open to temporary Soviet Union occupation, aroused less than no enthusiasm among Germans. If this was what would happen if war broke out, what would be the use of their providing a large number of conventionally armed divisions to the NATO forces?

After considerable debate, the thesis of a forward defence urged by the Germans and others of like mind was accepted. Dr. Kissinger in *Nuclear Weapons and Foreign Policy* expresses some unhappiness that German military men insisted that nuclear weapons had not changed the basic principles of strategy or tactics. Presumably Dr. Kissinger did not agree that the development of these arts had been continuous, and that in spite of the colossal increase of explosive power conferred by the atomic and thermonuclear weapons, there was no abrupt chasm marked by the month of August 1945 between pre-Hiroshima and post-Hiroshima thinking about the interrelation of strategy and policy, and about the tactical employment of weapons.

Let us digress for a moment to discuss this question of the continuity of the development of strategy and tactics. We have seen that the pre-1945 concept of strategic air warfare was that the way to defeat the enemy was to concentrate on destroying his means of production and his economy generally, to visit such death and destruction on his homeland that the enemy government would be unable to carry on the war and would be forced to capitulate. Now, in the era of ICBM's, *Polaris* submarines and multi-megaton warheads, there is no change in this basic concept. Of course, it is hoped that the menace of this incommensurable destructive power will deter any enemy from doing anything contrary to the vital interests of its proprietor. But that does not alter the strategic concept of all-out air warfare.

It is more difficult to judge definitely whether tactical theory must change now that there are tactical nuclear weapons. So far as I am aware, no positive, precise doctrine has been settled for the employment of these weapons, the consequent changes in the employment of retained conventional armaments and the roles of the several fighting arms and auxiliary services under the assumed new conditions. Of course, there have been several theories that have been tried out on an experimental basis, with accompanying experimental changes in army organization. As only the United States forces have had full information on the kinds of tactical nuclear weapons available, their physical effect, and the means of delivering them to target, plus all the logistic and other problems related to their employment, and as experiments have been conducted for the most part in secrecy, it is difficult to know how far tactics for the employment of smaller-yield nuclear weapons have been developed. However, the essential feature of nuclear weapons is that they pack enormous explosive power and multiply the destructive effect of chemical high explosives by a thousand or a million times. Their effect on various kinds of targets can be assessed by the knowledge we have of the effect of chemical high explosives, the Hiroshima and Nagasaki bombings, and subsequent experimental explosions. The essential factor is that destruction of area targets can be accomplished practically instantaneously, the zone of destruction corresponding to the power of the weapon. The "Davy Crockett" nuclear warhead, which is probably the smallest in service, is said to have a yield of ¼-kiloton, that is, equal to 250 tons of trinitrotoluol, while the warhead of the US Army's new Pershing missile is reported (in *Time*, 23 August 1962) to have a yield of approximately a megaton. As the area of destruction and other effects on the ground are roughly proportional to the cube root of the power of the explosive, the ratio between ground effects of a Hiroshima-size bomb and those of the ¼-kiloton Davy Crockett warhead would be as the cube roots of 20,000 and 250, or roughly 4.3 to 1.

In Hiroshima, there was practically total destruction of buildings over a radius of 1½ miles from "ground zero," and severe burns were inflicted on people up to 3½ miles distant. So a ¼-kiloton warhead could, on this rough calculation, destroy all except very strong concrete buildings within a radius of about 600 yards from the point of burst, and inflict severe burns on persons within a radius of about three quarters of a mile. This gives an approximate notion of what small tactical nuclear weapons might do. Starting from the Davy Crockett, there is a whole range of tactical nuclear weapons, increasing in power up to the Pershing. If the Pershing's warhead is indeed one megaton, its effect on the ground would be about sixteen times that of a Hiroshima type bomb. So it can be seen that the commanders in a war in which tactical nuclear weapons were used would have quite an extensive choice of destructive instruments with which to play the escalatory game.

It seems to be the general idea that producing such effects, these weapons could be used to smash up troop concentrations, centres of resistance, or vital points on lines of communication. The threat which they would pose would oblige all troops in the theatre of operations to disperse widely, consequently nullifying superiority of numbers of a conventionally-equipped army; for if the conventional troops could not concentrate to attack, they could not overcome the resistance of a nuclear-armed defending force, relatively small in numbers.

Some six months after the decision to arm NATO forces with nuclear weapons had been taken, a tactical exercise was carried out by the allied air forces in Western Europe, under the enigmatic code-name of "Carte Blanche." The general purpose was to study what might happen if command of the air over a theatre of operations were fought for by hitting opposing airfields with nuclear weapons. The war was fought in a north-south direction, and the area covered was Western Germany, the Low Countries and eastern France. Three hundred and thirty-five notional bombs were dropped within 48 hours, about evenly divided between targets in the areas of the "Northland"

and that of "Southland." The German journalists, who were given exceptional facilities to observe the exercise, concluded that the area between Heligoland and Salzburg, Dunkirk and Dijon would have been almost completely devastated. Which of the two air forces was held to be the winner was not disclosed, but it was abundantly clear that the population of the area fought over would be the losers. For them, victory or defeat would be meaningless words; death and destruction would be the universal realities.

Exercise "Sage-brush," carried out over a comparable area in the southern United States a few months before, had led to the same conclusions about the effects on the population of the territory over which this kind of nuclear war should be waged.

As Dr. Kissinger sums it up in *Nuclear Weapons and Foreign Policy*, the "Carte Blanche" exercise had been designed to reassure the Germans that the NATO forces would be able to protect German territory by using tactical nuclear weapons. In fact it showed that the power of nuclear weapons is so great that to employ them in the defence of Germany (or any other European territory) would be to ensure that the country, instead of being protected would, in fact, be destroyed. But Dr. Kissinger then seems to suggest that a doctrine for the use of tactical nuclear weapons could be devised which would not entail "total devastation." Before examining Dr. Kissinger's suggestions as to the elements of such a doctrine, we might briefly consider the reactions of the German Government and public to the lessons of "Carte Blanche." The Germans were not very sure of what useful purpose conventional forces could serve if it were probable that any Soviet Union invasion of Western Europe would set off a nuclear war. They did not find satisfactory answers to the questions of whether local defence of Europe is possible, or whether it is possible to conduct a limited war, using nuclear weapons. These questions have not been answered, so far as I have been able to learn, up until the time of writing, in 1966. They are not very well defined questions. As for the first, does it mean defence of Europe by European, American, British and Canadian forces all using conventional weapons? This question can only be answered in reference to defence against what? Against a sudden dash by the Soviet

Union forces now deployed near the Iron Curtain, to seize some important strategical objective? Against invasion by all Warsaw Pact forces after a general mobilization? Against USSR forces with only conventional arms, or with nuclear weapons?

As for the second question: What is meant by limited war? It can be limited as to theatre of operation or in the extent to which the belligerents commit their resources; and it can be limited in its objective. As we have seen, the war in Korea was limited in accordance with all these criteria. If asked whether it would be possible to conduct a limited war in Western Europe, say in the area roughly corresponding to that covered by "Carte Blanche," using tactical nuclear weapons, we should run into many additional questions which would have to be answered before we could return an answer to the prime question.

Before leaving "Carte Blanche" and its repercussions, I should like to hark back to the comment on page 126 to the effect that one can come much closer to realistic conclusions about the effects of nuclear weapons on tactics and strategy if one studies them in the framework of an exercise in a terrain likely to be a theatre of war, with all assumed factors as close as possible to reality. It seems clear that whatever the other benefits of "Carte Blanche," it clarified the thinking of a great many people who had been considering nuclear war more or less in the abstract.

In Chapter 6 of *Nuclear Weapons and Foreign Policy* Dr. Kissinger gives an outline of tactics and organization deemed suitable for fighting a nuclear war. I should remind the reader again that most provisions of the policy or strategy he recommends in this Chapter 6 are revised or abandoned in his later book, *A Necessity for Choice.* Therefore the criticisms which follow should be construed as of a tentative doctrine which represents a phase in the development of ideas about how nuclear weapons should be used in war—or about how they should not be used. It seems to me that the ideas expressed in the earlier book must have originated with some of the military members of the panel whose conclusions on foreign policy and defence Dr. Kissinger was employed to put into book form.

When I say originated, perhaps transmitted would be a better term, for no doubt much study had been given in the US Army and Air Force to developing a doctrine for the use of nuclear weapons in war, not entailing all-out or "strategic" warfare involving the massive bombing of the enemy's homeland.

The first of the principles of limited war waged with tactical nuclear weapons, as formulated by Dr. Kissinger, is that the idea of a continuous front should be abandoned. Instead, extremely mobile operations would be carried out in a large area or zone. This would be rather like naval warfare where the units (ships) are self-contained, so far as supplies are concerned. (It may be remarked here that those who developed theories of tank warfare between World War I and World War II envisioned a similar kind of area warfare, but with the tank force as the mobile, self-contained unit or formation. However, a tank force, or indeed a naval force, can only continue to operate in an area so long as its fuel holds out. The deep, armoured drives of World War II could only go far and fast if their supporting fuelling echelons could keep up with them and if their lines of communication could be kept free of serious interruption. Dr. Kissinger notes this, referring to German experience during the Russian campaign.)

Dr. Kissinger proposes "small, highly mobile, self-contained units, relying largely on air transport" in the fighting zone. The tactical nuclear weapons (nuclear warheads) and the rockets or other means of projecting them would be very light compared with conventional weapons and ammunition. The units would presumably depend for their high mobility on cross-country vehicles, that is to say, tracked vehicles, which are notoriously great consumers of fuel. So, gasoline supply by air would be no easy matter in any case, but what is more important is that supply by air transport of fighting troops is only feasible if one has very substantial control of the air space through which these supply and transport operations are to be carried out, as experience of paratroop operations in World War II showed. This implies the need for a powerful tactical air force, with its airfields and other base installations, and if two nearly equal opponents are fighting for air superiority over the zone of operations, these bases will be attacked. So this kind of warfare would approximate the situation postulated in exercise "Carte Blanche," and would have the same results.

Dr. Kissinger explains that the reason why the small units for this imagined sort of nuclear war tactics would have to be very mobile is that if they were detected they could be destroyed, presumably by enemy nuclear weapons. So they must be able to shift position constantly. However, it is not quite as easy to play such hide-and-go-seek games as it is to write about them. Concealing a unit with cross-country vehicles in Central Europe would not be like hiding guerillas in the wilder parts of Yugoslavia or in Vietnam.

It is suggested that with units so organized it would be possible to defeat an aggressor by preventing him from controlling territory. The small, mobile, nuclear-armed units would do this by "defeating their enemy counterparts" and destroying important objectives. But what if the enemy counterparts were similar highly mobile units equipped with nuclear weapons? When Dr. Kissinger wrote his book, the Soviet Union had large-yield nuclear weapons, and could be expected to develop tactical versions; these, in fact, they now have. And what "important objectives" would be destroyed? According to Dr. Kissinger, "cities, communication centres and industrial installations" would be ruled out as targets, since attacks on them would cause "appalling casualties," and presumably would cause an escalation of the nuclear war so that it would no longer be limited. Thus the enemy forces would have a sanctuary in these places.

There is one more point which Dr. Kissinger puts forward in *Nuclear Weapons and Foreign Policy* as being necessary if nuclear war is to be limited, avoiding the catastrophe of an all-out nuclear war. This is that "diplomacy" should give the allies of the USA—and, more important, the potential enemy—a clear understanding of the nature of limited nuclear war. As to this, one can only say that if any American diplomat has a clear understanding of the nature of limited nuclear war, he has not yet given it to the allies in NATO. And as for giving Russian diplomats a clear understanding of it, and persuading them and the government they represent to agree in advance to a set of ground rules for conflicts in various parts of the world—Bernard Shaw might have made a play out of this fantasy.

But Dr. Kissinger changed his view about the possibility of limited nuclear war in his later book, *The Necessity for Choice,* as I mentioned previously. He briefly rehearses the arguments in favour of a limited war fought with tactical nuclear weapons given in *Nuclear Weapons and Foreign Policy* and then states the counter-arguments of those whom he calls the advocates of a conventional strategy.

The first argument against the feasibility of limited nuclear war is that any use of nuclear weapons is inconsistent with the concept of limitation. Once they were used, all restraints would disappear. The reason is, as we have seen, that there is a continuous spectrum, as the jargon has it, of nuclear weapons of power rising from sub-Hiroshima to multi-megaton, and there is no clear point of demarcation between the several classes. So how can any limit based on explosive power be set? How could belligerents trust in any agreements not to hit certain classes of objectives (for example, cities) with nuclear weapons? It has not been possible to make and keep such agreements when only conventional weapons and chemical explosives were in question, as the history of the development of air warfare showed in the earlier chapters of this book. How much harder would it be to make an agreement to limit the use of nuclear weapons, knowledge of whose power and effect rests on very limited experience and which could be used to deal a shattering and conclusive blow if the agreement were not kept? The opponents of the idea of limited nuclear war cite the conclusions of "Sage-brush" and "Carte Blanche," in which some limitation of nuclear warfare had been postulated. These conclusions, as we have seen, were that the zone of operations would be devastated, that its population would suffer enormous casualties, and that, at such a cost, no country would buy this kind of defence.

About the tactics proposed, the opponents of the limited nuclear war theory argue that small detachments depending on nuclear weapons would be very vulnerable to being tracked down and destroyed by numerically stronger opponents, even if they had only conventional arms; while if the enemy had both conventional and nuclear arms, the small detachments would face certain defeat. Nuclear weapons would be more suited to offensive tactics than to defence. (They would be capable of obliterating resistance in fortified defensive positions far more quickly than could artillery, mortars or aircraft using high explosive.) As NATO is committed to a defensive strategy it would not seem consistent to encourage a form of warfare favouring the offensive, that is, the aggressor.

Dr. Kissinger reaches no firm conclusion on the merits of the controversy, but he states that within the US armed services, and within the NATO alliance, there is no agreed doctrine on what limited nuclear war should be, and how it could be fought. This makes it very doubtful that nuclear war could, in fact, be limited. Furthermore, the Soviet Union's stockpile of nuclear weapons is constantly growing, and so are the numbers of its intercontinental and intermediate-range rockets. This means that limited nuclear warfare, if there could be such a thing, would have to be fought against an opponent who would have the same kind of weapons. Between equally-armed and equally-motivated opponents, the side with the larger forces would win. Thus the notion that nuclear arms could offset the numerical inferiority of the NATO forces can no longer be considered valid. In 1960 missiles of various ranges began to replace aircraft as the principal means of delivering nuclear weapons. This means that the struggle for air supremacy—an essential element of strategy when the aeroplane was the means of delivering the nuclear weapon—would be replaced by a battle of opposing missilery. It would be World War I counter-battery or artillery duels raised to the range and height of destructiveness of the nuclear-missile age. Obviously, the contest, even if it began with an exchange of relatively short-range rockets, would spread farther and farther back towards the homeland on each side; it would soon become unlimited nuclear war. Indeed, many who think about this subject would conclude that any nuclear war would start with an exchange between the "strategic" nuclear weapon delivery forces—long-range aircraft and intercontinental missiles.

Dr. Kissinger also held that disarmament negotiations would

make it harder to establish a satisfactory or tenable doctrine of limited nuclear war. The idea of totally eliminating nuclear weapons, which the Russians have urged since 1946, is attractive to nearly all nations which don't have them. The first horror felt by the prospective victims of nuclear warfare in communist countries spread to neutrals, when they saw that the effects of nuclear warfare would not be confined to the countries of the belligerents alone. Finally it reached the intelligent minority of American citizens when they began to realize that in a nuclear war they too would be vulnerable to the terrible destructive power with which the arsenals of the potential enemy had been endowed as a result of technological developments in warfare for which their own nation was primarily responsible.

Another opinion which Dr. Kissinger expresses in *The Necessity for Choice* is that the conventional forces in NATO should be considerably strengthened so that they could repulse aggressions of enemy conventional forces without recourse to tactical nuclear weapons, thus lessening the risk of escalation into unlimited nuclear war. At the same time it must be recognized that since the enemy has and could use tactical nuclear weapons, then obviously to counter their use by the enemy, the NATO forces could not be left without them. However, tactical nuclear weapons in NATO forces should be organized in units which would come under the control of higher echelons of command than the division. If the division and the units within it were so organized that their fighting power depended on nuclear weapons, or if organized and armed so as to have a dual capability (as the expression is), the divisional and subordinate commanders, if they had begun fighting with conventional weapons and seemed likely to be defeated, would be under almost irresistible pressure to use nuclear weapons. At some stage, if the defence depends on tactical nuclear weapons, authority to use those weapons must be delegated by the President of the United States to the Supreme Allied Commander in Europe (SACEUR), and he must in turn delegate the authority down to the officer immediately in command of the unit which has the guns or rockets to project the nuclear weapon. That would mean it would be a lieutenant-colonel, probably, who would be given the authority to fire a nuclear weapon and who might be the one to fire the first shot in a nuclear war. (The process of arming lower echelons of military formations with nuclear weapons and creating the danger of being unable to control the outbreak of nuclear war has been named "diffusion downwards." The more generally recognized dangerous diffusion, or "dissemination," is the handing over of nuclear weapons to countries not previously possessing them.)

These general conclusions, set out by Dr. Kissinger in his 1961 book, appear to coincide with the policy of the US Department of Defense, which doubtless worked out the same conclusions for itself. The policy outlined has been urged on NATO European allies since early 1962. The European allies have shown themselves very reluctant to increase the numbers of their forces and modernize their conventional armaments to the degree necessary to enable them to face the deployed forces of the USSR and its Warsaw Pact allies with a good prospect of containing any attack without resorting to tactical nuclear weapons. Indeed one hears the theory advanced that the only real safety for Western Europe lies in having the Russians believe that nuclear weapons would be used to repulse *any* aggression, that is, that any aggression would mean a nuclear war. In other words, this theory would, in an indirect way, put the sanction of the SAC against any minor military incursions. Thus it is almost indistinguishable from the discarded policy of massive retaliation and would constitute a kind of built-in brinkmanship.

# 11

## NATO AND NUCLEAR WEAPONS

Armaments are the tools of war. Like other tools they have evolved gradually, through long experience, with occasional great accelerations due to some invention or improvement in technique. To find so abrupt and significant a change in the tools of war, such an increase in the potential of slaughter, as has been effected by the discovery of how to release atomic energy explosively, we have to look as far back as the day when men first began to use gunpowder to project missiles. And as we compare the explosive force of atomic fission with that of gunpowder, the changes in warfare they have wrought hardly seem commensurable; the order of comparison is as between an elephant and a flea.

It took a very long time for soldiers to understand the changes in warfare which gunpowder had brought about. It is, therefore, not surprising that it is taking a long time for the modern directors of war to discover that it is not possible to establish a positive and clear doctrine as to how the nuclear weapons should be used, and to understand that if there is to be any defence in the nuclear age, it is essential to find a means of ensuring that these weapons will *not* be used. The penalty for failing to find such a means will be the destruction of civilized life on a major portion of the earth.

We can best see how hard it is to adapt the enormous power of atomic energy to the requirements of warfare by studying the varying concepts of the use of nuclear weapons as they were applied to the strategic problems of NATO. It is along the Iron Curtain that the frontiers of Soviet Union and United States power impinge; it is across the Iron Curtain that the nuclear powers eye one another most directly, at short range. In other parts of the world, in the Middle East and in South-East Asia, there are conflicts and a potential engagement of force, but these are collateral. The line of force from Washington to Moscow passes through the territories of the European NATO states.

We have seen that when NATO was first organized it was thought that the United States' monopoly of the atom bomb prevented the Soviet Union from continuing the process of extending its power to the west, from subjugating yet more of the nations of Europe by subversion and intrigue by the native Communist parties supported by the overpowering presence, within or just beyond the border, of Russian armies.

In the 1960's there began a debate, still unresolved, on how nuclear weapons for the defence of Europe should be controlled. Who is to give the order to fire the nuclear weapons, and under what circumstances? The European powers no longer feel entirely sure that the United States will loose its nuclear striking power if there is a major aggression against European territory. Successive American administrations have given repeated assurances, and these are accepted—on the situation as it now is. But will the situation be the same five, ten, twenty years hence? The Europeans reflect on certain facts, and cannot repress all doubts.

These facts, which are known to anyone who reads the newspapers, have already been stated in this book. To recapitulate, they are the Soviet Union's production of an atomic explosion in 1949 and a thermonuclear explosion in 1953, and their orbiting of Sputnik I in October 1957, proving that they possessed an intercontinental ballistic missile. These events, taken together and reinforced subsequently by the numerous feats of

Soviet Union "cosmonauts," by the successful space probes and by the test explosions of many thermonuclear weapons, culminating in the 60-megaton blast of November 1961, all demonstrate that in a war in which thermonuclear weapons were exchanged, the Soviet Union could inflict devastating damage on the United States, even though greater damage would be visited on the USSR. In view of this the Europeans had to ask themselves whether the Americans would, in every case, use their nuclear power to protect European territory and interests. (In his book *On Thermonuclear War* Mr. Kahn has discussed with scientific detachment the problem of how many million American lives the President might be prepared to sacrifice in order to meet this commitment. We shall be examining his argument presently.)

A more precise warning than Mr. Kahn's was given by Mr. McNamara in his statement to the House of Representatives Armed Services Committee on 18 February 1965. This was based presumably on the latest and best calculations of Pentagon staffs and strategic analysts. He said that in the event of "general war," that is, all-out nuclear war, no defensive measures could reduce American fatalities much below eighty million. In Chapter 14 we shall be examining in more detail some of the points that Mr. McNamara made in this important address.

One historic sequence of events must be present in the minds of Europeans, or at least in the minds of the British and the French, when they ponder on whether the Americans will automatically respond to any threat by the USSR to employ its nuclear arsenal against Europe. This historic sequence is, of course, what happened at the time of the Suez adventure in November 1956.

On 5 November, when the United Nations was near to finding a formula to repair the consequences of the invasion of the Sinai and Port Said, and when the Soviet Union had practically completed the suppression of the revolt in Hungary, Marshal Bulganin sent a note to Prime Minister Eden, in which the following passages occurred:

> . . . two great powers have attacked a very weak country. In what position would Britain have found herself if attacked by

more powerful states possessing every kind of modern destructive weapon?

And there are countries now which need not have sent a navy or air force . . . but could have used other means, such as rocket technique. . . . If rocket weapons had been used against Britain or France, they would probably have called this a barbarous action . . . in what way does attack made by armed forces on the nearly disarmed Egypt differ from this?

A similar letter was also addressed to M. Guy Mollet, Prime Minister of France, and Mr. Ben Gurion was treated to a severe lecture, accompanied by vague menaces, on the wickedness and folly of acting as cat's paw for the imperialists.

Perhaps some readers, who recall this history, may think to themselves that Britain and France were then aggressors. Furthermore, they had failed to consult their partner in NATO, who held the main responsibility in the alliance for the protection of Europe. In the end, too, that partner made it clear to the Soviet Union that if they fired any rockets, retaliation would be instant.

Many British and French doubtless prefer not to think of this episode, and hope that it will never again happen that they or other European nations could be threatened because they had done something considered wrong by both the Soviet Union and the United States, and by the majority of other nations. But can such an eventuality be dismissed from the minds of European statesmen, military advisers or any other European responsible for or concerned with the defence of his country? Is it impossible to imagine a future situation involving a threat to interests which Europeans consider vital, but which Americans do not, when Europeans would think they must use force to protect those interests, and when the Soviet Union, knowing that the Americans did not support the European action, could threaten to use their nuclear weapons to counter the European use of force? Without producing a whole scenario to justify the argument that such a contingency is possible, we can think of threats, arising in the Middle East again and extending into the Mediterranean, to interfere with the supply of oil vital to the European economy.

So far as I am aware, neither the British nor the French have ever publicly argued that the events of November 1956 have had anything to do with their determination to possess a nuclear deterrent, which, without rivalling the nuclear force of the superpowers, would ensure that the Soviet Union would have to pay a heavy price for using nuclear weapons against them—such a price as the destruction of one or more great Russian cities. General Pierre Gallois has set forth the theory of such limited national deterrents, and he and others who favour them argue that any nation which aspires to have an independent foreign policy in matters of peace and war, and perhaps disarmament, which will be attended to and respected, must first possess nuclear weapons and effective means of delivering them.

In his notable press conference of 14 January 1963, President de Gaulle answered questions about France's position on nuclear armaments, particularly in relation to the agreement which had been reached between President Kennedy and Prime Minister Macmillan at Nassau, in December. The following passages occur in the report of his speech in *Figaro* of 15 January 1963. (Author's translation.)

> For a great people, to possess freedom of action is a categorical imperative; for alliances have no immutable quality, whatever sentiments they may be based upon. And if one loses, even for a while, freedom of action, one risks never regaining it. . . .
>
> Above all, it is a fact that in case of a general atomic war between the Soviet Union and the Americans there would inevitably be frightful destruction, perhaps fatal to both countries. Under these conditions, no one in the world can say, and in particular no one in America can say where, when, how and in what degree American nuclear armaments would be used to defend Europe.

After referring to President Kennedy's determined action in the Cuba crisis, President de Gaulle went on:

> But the fact remains that the American nuclear power does not necessarily and immediately provide the answer in all eventualities affecting Europe and France. Thus, principles, conditions and circumstances have determined us to provide ourselves with an atomic force to meet our needs.

The directors of the defence and foreign policy of the United States seem to regard the British nuclear deterrent force, and the emerging French *force de frappe,* either with impatience or with rather scornful amusement. They point out the enormous disparity between the power of the British force as it is (and the French as it will some day be) and that of the SAC, in terms of the megatonnage they can deliver on the territory of the USSR. The Americans argue that it would be far more effective in the combined defence of NATO if Britain and France would abandon the expensive and too difficult task of building up a "credible" nuclear deterrent, and devote their manpower and money to making their conventional forces strong enough to be able to repulse a Russian invasion of NATO Europe without recourse to nuclear weapons.

The British deterrent force consists of some 180 medium-range bombers of the Vulcan and Victor classes, which can carry at least one, and possibly more, thermonuclear bombs of 10-megaton capacity. Putting it at only one bomb, this gives a total capacity for the force of 1800 megatons. This is compared with the total megatonnage which the US strategic bombers and missiles are capable of delivering. Taking the figures given in the article in *Time* of 23 August 1963, which were based on public statements by Mr. McNamara and on other nonclassi-fied information, we find that approximately 36,000 megatons of bombs could be delivered. So the British deterrent force's capacity to deliver nuclear weapons is only 5 per cent of that of the United States Strategic Air Command. In the last months of 1963, the French *force de frappe* began to be equipped with Mirage IV, an aircraft with a considerably shorter range and carrying less warload than the British V-bombers. Conse-quently, it will be some years before the French force reaches the capacity of the British. The French plans include the pro-duction of a medium-range ballistic missile, capable of reach-ing targets in the Soviet Union, but at the most favourable es-timate it will be several years more before this can be operational.

Making these comparisons, Americans responsible for de-fence policy point out that the increase in deterrent force for NATO as a whole produced by the British and French nuclear deterrent forces is really negligible. At the same time, it is very expensive and prevents the British and French from contributing the divisions with fully modern armament which could bring the land forces of NATO to the level adequate to repulse an attack by the Soviet forces deployed in East Germany and the East European socialist countries. The American strategists and policy-makers would much prefer that all nuclear weapons should be under American control. They would be willing to give (and in some cases have given) their allies the means of delivery of tactical nuclear weapons, and lay down the warheads close at hand (but still under American guard) ready to hand over if war broke out and they had to be used. But there would be an American veto over the use of any nuclear weapon. The desirability of such a policy from the American viewpoint, in view of what has been said above about the vulnerability of the USA, needs no explanation. It is hardly more necessary either to explain why nuclear armament for NATO, but under American veto, is unacceptable to the French now, and can hardly be contemplated by Britain and other European countries as a satisfactory long-term solution to the nuclear arms control problem. Before leaving the subject, another weakness of the British and French deterrent nuclear forces should be mentioned. This is the fact that, at present, their only means of delivering their nuclear weapons is medium-range bombing aircraft.

The piloted bomber is vulnerable to attack by defending fighters as it traverses the hostile territory on its way to its target. Bombers from Britain would have to cross at least 700 miles of the Soviet Union to reach Moscow. The modern surface-to-air missile (SAM) is a greater danger to the bomber than the piloted fighter is. The anti-aircraft artillery of World War II was limited in its accuracy, although when concentrated in defence of an important target it could down a considerable percentage of the attacking force. But the SAM is equipped with sensing devices that enable it to "home" on its bomber target after it has been directed on its first intercept path by the indications of radar. The Soviet Union is known to have devoted great resources to developing radar and missile systems of air defence. They are estimated to be very effective, capable of bringing down a high proportion of attacking bombers. Exact information about the capability of the Russian air defence is not available to the public, if indeed to the NATO military, but there is a general assumption, in assessing the results obtainable from piloted bomber aircraft in a strategic offensive, that losses among them would greatly exceed the percentage losses in bomber aircraft during World War II, even during the periods when the air defences of Germany were strongest. Of course, only a very few of the large thermonuclear bombs which the attacking forces are capable of carrying would have to be exploded over the targets to cause the most terrible devastation, and everybody knows this. Nevertheless, it would be an unpleasant prospect for the air force generals or marshals to order nuclear bombing attacks from which only a half or a quarter of the crews could be expected to return. We need hardly mention the effect on the morale and nerves of the crews.

To counter the threat to the long-range piloted bomber, "stand-off" air-to-ground missiles have been developed. These are guided missiles carrying a nuclear warhead which can be discharged from the bombers in flight at a considerable distance from the target. Thus the bomber does not have to run the gauntlet of the enemy anti-aircraft, or surface-air missiles and get right over its target. The United States air-surface missile is called the "Hound-dog," and it is said to be able to find its target with the necessary accuracy when discharged from 200 miles away. The RAF has a similar missile, "Blue Steel." The United States was developing a missile called "Skybolt" with a projected range of 1000 miles. The RAF was counting on obtaining this missile, which would have prolonged the effective power, or postponed the obsolescence, of the V-bomber force. But late in 1962, the US Administration decided to cancel the development programme, on the grounds that it would be extremely difficult and expensive to develop and produce a missile with this range and other technical requirements, and that it would be a superfluous addition to the power of the Strategic Air Command. This decision caused consternation in the RAF and the British Government, and Mr. Macmillan hurried to meet Mr. Kennedy in Nassau. After a day or so of hasty and intense discussion, the so-called Nassau Agreement, providing for future American co-operation in the modernization of the British nuclear deterrent force, was hammered out.

The USAF, as well as the RAF were taken aback by the cancellation of the Skybolt programme, one of Mr. McNamara's decisions aimed at eliminating unnecessary military expenditure, including projects of research and development which were not likely to be productive or which would tend to duplicate offensive or defensive weapons. Here, obviously, the duplication was between the power of the long-range aircraft to deliver bombs on Soviet targets, and the power of the rapidly-increasing American rocketry. Not only the USAF was disturbed over the cancellation of the Skybolt programme, but the contractor also, and the communities where the hardware was to be built. There was considerable discussion of this decision to cancel in the various committees of Congress dealing with the allocation of funds for defence, but in spite of opposed viewpoints, the decision stuck.

We can hardly accuse Europeans of being irrational when they doubt that in every possible case of aggression or threat by the Soviet Union against their territory or interests, the United States would intervene, regardless of the devastation their homelands would suffer in the event of a thermonuclear war. Put another way, can Europeans expect that United States nuclear power, which at present appears to be many times greater than that of the Soviet Union, will deter the Soviet Union from all overt aggression against European countries?

This problem has been discussed from the American viewpoint by Mr. Herman Kahn, in a way that should show the vital necessity for all Americans—not just Mr. Kahn and his fellow-oracles and the cadres that operate the government machinery—to think about this problem. They must do so if they believe that theirs is a real democracy and that the ordinary citizen has the power to influence his fate. In this case, his fate can be seen in terms of whether he will live out his days to the end of his natural span, or whether he is to expect a 1 in 2, or 1 in 10 probability of being barbecued on a nuclear judgement day. Mr. Kahn calls his second volume *Thinking About the Un-*

*thinkable.* Perhaps he might have named it *Thinking About What Americans Don't Want to Think About.*

Mr. Kahn writes about three categories of deterrence, I, II and III. He discusses the ways in which the United States nuclear power can, or should be able to, deter the Soviet Union (and possibly other nations regarded as potentially hostile) from broad classes of actions contrary to the vital interests of the USA. Of these three categories, or types of deterrence, Type II would include an attack by Soviet Union forces on European NATO allies. Can the threat of large-scale attack with nuclear weapons by the United States positively deter the Soviet Union from any such action? Can it, for example, deter them from using force to put an end to the existing status of Berlin, and incorporate it into the so-called German Democratic Republic?

Before attempting to answer this question, we should look at the position as to the Type I deterrent, which means the capacity of the United States nuclear forces to deter the Soviet Union from initiating a large-scale attack with nuclear weapons on the home territory of the USA on so-called strategic targets such as the elements of military force stationed there, the cities and the centres of production.

Here the situation seems to be fairly reassuring, for the time being at any rate. As a result of the great expenditures and enormous efforts deployed in the construction of ICBM's and auxiliary hardware of great technical complexity since Sputnik I revealed the vulnerability of the USA, the United States now has, according to public statements of Mr. McNamara, a many times greater capacity to hit the Soviet Union with nuclear weapons, measured in the tens of thousands of megatons, than the Soviet Union has to hit the USA. The Soviet Union Government knows this, and as it would clearly suffer the greater damage if it came to a thermonuclear exchange with each super-power attacking the home territory of the other, it would not initiate that kind of a war. The deterrent has been made stronger since the United States has widely dispersed its ICBM's and has provided many of them with fortified emplacements capable of protecting the missile against anything but a direct hit by another thermonuclear bomb. The long-range bombing aircraft, previously very vulnerable because of their concentration on relatively few bases in the USA, have also been dispersed, and placed on alert schedules which would ensure that even in a Soviet surprise attack, large numbers of them would survive for retaliatory action. The nuclear-powered submarines armed with *Polaris* missiles are a further element of almost invulnerable retaliatory capacity.

All this makes a direct attack on the United States by Soviet Union nuclear forces seem highly improbable. But, and this is a very important but, the United States, even with the great advantage in quantity of nuclear weapons and means of delivery that it appears to have at present, cannot be sure that by attacking first in a preventive war, or by pre-emptive attack, it could deprive the Soviet Union of a remaining retaliatory capacity which could kill tens of millions of Americans and inflict immense devastation.

Put it another way. If the Americans strike first at the Soviet homeland with their nuclear weapons, they will do so knowing that the Soviet Union has the retaliatory power to kill tens of millions of Americans. So we must consider this fact, in assessing the extent to which United States nuclear power protects Europe against Soviet aggression, that is, the extent to which it is capable of Type II deterrence. Mr. Khan, in his first book, *On Thermonuclear War,* showed the horrid dimensions of the problem which would face the President of the United States if he had to decide whether to initiate thermonuclear war in order to honour the commitments made by the United States under the North Atlantic Treaty. The specific commitment is that an attack on the territory of any member will be considered as an attack upon all, that is to say, that the USA would be in honour bound to respond to an attack on part of Germany as an attack on part of the continental United States. This is the obligation, but would the President really act in the same way if the Soviet Union say, should land troops west of Hamburg, as if they had landed in Alaska? Or would he even act as Mr. Kennedy did in the Cuba crisis?

Mr. Kahn invites us to consider a "scenario" in which the Soviet Union has dropped bombs on the capitals of the principal European members of NATO, but show no signs of preparing to attack the United States. The USA nuclear forces seem strong enough to deter the Soviet Union from doing so, unless the USA itself begins hostilities against the Soviet Union. The President is inclined, and is advised, to order the SAC to strike at the Soviet Union in order to fulfil US obligations. He then asks for an estimate of the damage the Soviet Union forces could do to the United States, particularly of the number of casualties they could cause. Mr. Kahn then goes on to consider what the decision of the President would be—to strike or not to strike—in a range of possible casualties among Americans, starting with 100 per cent (when he naturally would conclude, according to Mr. Kahn and everybody else, that it would not be worth while to have 190 million Americans dead to prevent, conjecturally, Europe from becoming Red). As the hypothetical casualties become lower in the scale of tens of millions, the problem for the President would become more agonizing. Mr. Kahn reports that he has conducted a sort of informal poll among Americans, as to what number of American citizens the President should, or would, be prepared to sacrifice in order that the USA should honourably keep its engagements. He said that their estimates of an acceptable price fell between ten and sixty millions "clustering toward the upper number." (This particular passage was one which was heavily attacked by reviewers, who could not believe that it represented a common viewpoint among Americans.)

Mr. Kahn also put the same question to Europeans, and was not very surprised when their answers came out between two and twenty millions, "clustering towards the lower numbers." We may consider the "acceptable megadeaths" in both of them to be very inflated. What is significant about these two sets of answers is the difference between the European and the American estimates. Many times more Americans were convinced the USA would honour its commitments than were the Europeans.

One should devoutly hope that no President of the USA will ever really have to make such a decision. But it is more than clear that the President's advisers—and doubtless the President himself—have been thinking very hard about how the probability of his having to take such a decision can be reduced to the minimum. One evidence of this is the emphasis placed by the United States representatives at successive NATO ministerial meetings on the need for the European nations to strengthen their conventional forces. There have been many public statements by responsible spokesmen of the United States Administration to the same effect. The Americans would like the NATO land forces to be able to repulse any attack by Soviet Union conventional forces now deployed outside the USSR, without having to use nuclear weapons and without having to depend on the threat of nuclear intervention by the SAC. But the Europeans have shown no desire to call up the men and spend the money necessary for this, and seem to prefer to shelter under the most inappropriately named "nuclear umbrella." If they would think of the US President's problem, as posed by Mr. Kahn, they would perceive that the nuclear umbrella has many weak patches in it.

On page 154 we mentioned Mr. Kahn's classification of three types of deterrence, I, II and III. As we have discussed Types I and II briefly, the reader may wish to know something about Type III, which Mr. Kahn describes as graduated, or controlled deterrence. This would operate against aggressive acts, or "provocations" as Mr. Kahn terms them, of less scope than, for example, extensive invasion of NATO Europe. This kind of deterrence would exist when a potential enemy feared that if he committed a "provocation," his opponent would be able to respond by counter-action, which, while limited, would make the aggression dangerous, or at least unprofitable.

The above definition, one sees, does not require that nuclear weapons be used in the counter-actions, or reprisals, but neither does it exclude their use. Mr. Kahn suggests that an international code might be formulated, to govern the use of force in reprisal for "provocations," but he does not pursue this idea very far, and I think with good reason. We have seen, in the last chapter, the difficulty of limiting the scope of war if nuclear weapons are employed. The counterforce strategy is basically one of controlled reprisals, though not restricted to reprisals against minor "provocations." We shall be examining the limitations of this proposed strategy in Chapter 14.

When the problem of deterrence of hostile acts, particularly deterrence by threat of massive employment of nuclear weapons, is talked or written about, inevitably the question of "cred-ibility" is examined. Will the enemy believe that if he acts in a certain way inimical to important interests of the USA (or another nuclear power) he will be hit by nuclear forces? This problem can hardly be dealt with in accordance with any rigorous scientific technique. The evolving science of psychology is as yet unable to cope with the inordinately complicated and heterogeneous factors that come into play, such as the emotions, the prejudices, characters of the rulers or decision-takers and of all the subordinate echelons of advisers and executants in the armed services and other state apparatus who may be involved. The proceedings of governments endeavouring to enforce their will, or protect their interests, by the threat of the use of the nuclear forces of which they are the proprietors have been compared to bluffing in poker, to playing Russian roulette and to the hare-brained juvenile jousting called "playing chicken." As the world is today, it does not seem likely that suspected bluffs will be called, or the trigger pulled, or the car held on the line until the collision point. But there is always the possibility that it is not a bluff, that the loaded chamber is opposite the firing pin, that the adversary will not flip the wheel in time. And if the guess is wrong, the consequences will be catastrophic. But how long can this sort of game go on before someone does the wrong thing, and the contestants will pay in multi-megadeaths? We may credit the deterrent effect of American nuclear armament with having preserved NATO Europe since World War II against military aggression by the Soviet Union. The fear of the catastrophic consequences which would ensue if the enormous nuclear power now possessed by both the United States and the Soviet Union were unleashed is a deterrent against any military adventure today. But can a peace kept under threat of armaments last forever? There is a danger that such a precarious peace may not last very long, if the armaments race continues. Deterrence as it exists today is preventing war, but a stable and lasting peace can only come through harmonization of the international policies of the great nations, accompanied by disarmament.

Why are the United States and the Soviet Union brandishing their nuclear rockets and bombs at one another across the Iron

Curtain? To be more specific, what is the political question in
Europe which all this armament might conceivably be used to
resolve in favour of one party or the other? To put it in the way
more favoured in government explanations, what is the interest
which this armament is to defend against the aggressive de-
signs of the other party?

Nowadays, whatever may have been the case in the early
1950's, few people really believe that the Soviet Union has any
intention of invading Western Europe and of communizing it by
force of arms. The unresolved question which stands in the way
of peace and armaments reduction is the partition of Germany,
and the related dangerous and anomalous position of Berlin.
The conditions of the problem are generally so well known that
it is unnecessary to detail them here. But the NATO allies are at
a serious strategic disadvantage; they have engaged their prestige in the maintenance of their rights in the city, as set out in
the Potsdam agreements with the Soviet Union. The Soviet
Union can apply pressures on the Berlin enclave and has done
so frequently, whenever it has suited her fluctuating policies.
But it is a little like putting pressure on a fulminate of mercury
detonator. One day the whole charge, thermonuclear warfare,
may be exploded.

At this point we shall leave the problems of using nuclear
weapons to defend the territories of NATO in Europe. The
reader may feel somewhat frustrated, because there are very
serious objections to each proposed strategy or policy. We
shall, however, continue the discussion of these problems in
Chapter 14 in the context of more recent events. But before
doing so we shall look at the other major policy for finding
security in the nuclear age—the policy of disarmament. We
shall briefly examine the positions taken by the major participants in the disarmament negotiations of the last few years,
and discuss some of the blocks in the way of progress towards a
peaceful world free from the menace of nuclear holocaust.

# 12

## DISARMAMENT NEGOTIATIONS: 1960-1964

Since the nuclear weapon was used to end the war with Japan, successive American administrations have worried about how to find a way to eliminate the threat to the world created by the tremendous power of the bomb. But not finding any formula to accomplish this to which the USSR would assent, the governments of the United States have also been preparing, in varying rhythms, the most colossal apparatus for destruction which the world has ever seen. These two objects have been pursued more or less concurrently. One might say that the United States has been trying to move in two directions at once. But while disarmament for the most part has so far only been talk, though very serious talk with all the solemn paraphernalia of diplomatic negotiation and international conferences, in the sphere of armament there has been action—the continuous build-up of tremendous nuclear-weapon power in the Strategic Air Command and other branches of the American armed services.

This does not mean that the United States Government is insincere in its professed concern for disarmament, as the Soviet Union representatives have the habit of saying at the disarmament conference table. (They blandly ignore the Soviet

Union's own enormous contributions to the arms race—ICBM's, 50-megaton bombs, huge submarine fleets, and so on.) It is merely saying that the USA, like other nations, finds it easier to react to the new nuclear threat to national existence by the way in which nations have always reacted to external threat. That way was to arm themselves as best they could against the menace. But the world requires another reaction in the thermonuclear age, the reaction of reason, represented by the drive to find a way in which the nations can agree never to use this weapon that has the power practically to destroy each or all of them.

Since 1946 the USA, in consultation with its allies, has been trying to find that way out, through negotiations with the USSR. It is not necessary to trace the course of these discussions from 1946 to 1960. That would be a chronicle of the exploration of various paths to disarmament and peace, and the finding of blocks on each of them. However, these seemingly fruitless parleys helped to clear ideas on what the nations would have to do if they wanted to find security and relief from the dangers and burdens of the arms race. The early disarmament negotiations might also be metaphorically described as a clearing away of the brushwood. For our purpose, it will be enough to outline where the USA and the USSR now stand on disarmament. Their allies generally take the same line as they do, and the neutral, or non-aligned, nations are all fervently in favour of the disarmament of the great powers, though not very aware that they have any disarming to do themselves or that they have other sacrifices to make in the interests of peace.

There are several reasons why the disarmament negotiations so far have failed, and these have been set down in numerous books and articles. These reasons for failure can be looked on as obstacles to be overcome if we are to reach a stable *pax mundi,* and their nature will appear when we examine the contrasted positions of the two sides on the principal subjects of negotiation at the Eighteen-Nation Disarmament Conference in Geneva, and elsewhere.

At this point it may be useful to define what is meant by disarmament in this book. The prime sense is simple: it is the opposite of armament. And as armament is a series of acts which takes time, so will disarmament take time. In my view, it should always be understood as a process, not as a state. Perhaps considering disarmament as a process might obliterate the dispute, which diverts a number of students of the subject, as to whether "arms control" is a more practical object than disarmament. The meaning of words and their implications are important in this, as in any other political question. The definition of "Arms Control" given in a booklet of the US Arms Control and Disarmament Agency is as follows: "It is . . . important that the major powers *do something now* to cut the risk of war, while at the same time working for agreement on arms reduction plans. So the concept of 'arms control'—controlling, in the sense of calming, the military situation—was evolved. Arms control means measures, other then arms reduction itself, which lessen the risk of war." By excluding *reduction* of armaments this constitutes a somewhat narrower definition of arms control than that given on page 7. (It is perhaps worth noting that the title originally proposed for the Agency in the bill put before Congress did not have "Arms Control" in it. But Congress insisted on the amendment, maybe because they equated disarmament with surrender.) Perhaps a good many of those who favour the term "arms control" do so because it sounds better, and because they think that it will be less likely to arouse hostility and determined opposition. "Arms control" as a phrase might be assimilated to "birth control," which has become a respectable and inoffensive way of referring to what used to be a delicate subject, while "disarmament" has a drastic and disagreeably final connotation like "sterilization" or "castration."

Without entering into the context of the many proposals for "arms control" one may point out that a difficulty in using the term is that it does not translate very well from English into other languages. The Russians are constantly declaiming against American proposals for disarmament measures as being only "control over armaments." By this they mean control in the French, or scientific, sense—checking, verifying, validating. But they are completely opposed to applying this kind of control—or verification, as the West now prefers to term it—unless there have been concrete acts of disarmament. Otherwise, the

Russians say, when you apply these measures of "control," you are merely collecting information for military intelligence purposes. It would seem well not to add to the already heavy difficulties of negotiating with the Russians. Let us use the term "disarmament" to signify the process of reducing all kinds of armaments, and eventually doing away with all of them except limited numbers of those of minimum lethal powers, necessary for police-type forces to keep order within nations and internationally. It is only by working for the abolition of international war, as the world has known it, and the monstrous armament of the nuclear-missile age that the world can be released from the fear of imminent nuclear war.

There are only two roads the world can take. One is to continue the armaments race, which is preparation for World War III on the nuclear scale, that is to say, an unimaginable disaster to civilization. The other is to disarm, reversing the process, reducing and finally eliminating the most dangerous weapons, and developing at the same time means of settling disputes between nations peacefully and of preserving the peace through international organization. There is no middle way the world can go. Men can only make the danger of nuclear war greater or less; and as long as armaments are increased, as long as scientists and engineers are racking their brains to improve the apparatus of mass slaughter, the danger will grow. While these efforts go on, deterrence cannot be stable. The policy of deterrence should be looked on as an interim stage, of limited duration, on the road to real safety, when there would be no missiles ready to fly at a minute's notice, and no "fail-safe" squadrons of intercontinental bombers hovering over the Arctic wastes.

A new phrase, or era, in disarmament negotiations opened when Mr. Khrushchev presented his plan for general and complete disarmament to the United Nations General Assembly on 18 September 1959. The adjective "general" meant that all nations of the world had to disarm; "complete" meant that all armaments would be destroyed or dismantled, except small arms required by the remaining police (or militia, as the Russians prefer to call their minions of the law) who would provide for the internal security of states. All armed forces in excess of such police (militia) would be disbanded; all war departments, general staffs and apparatus for military training and mobilization were to be swept away. All this was to be accomplished in three stages, within a period of four years.

In presenting the plan Mr. Khrushchev put the main emphasis on getting away from the danger of nuclear war, which would require the abolition of nuclear weapons and the means of delivering or projecting them. But the plan took account of the fact that it will never be safe to do away with the specialized apparatus of nuclear warfare if conventional armaments and forces are left under national control. For if war ever breaks out between major powers, it will inevitably become a nuclear war—even if all nuclear weapons should have been abolished when it started. Nuclear weapons would be put together as quickly as the scientists and engineers could manage. Nuclear weapons can be destroyed under a programme of disarmament—but not the knowledge of how they are made. Therefore, to prevent nuclear war requires the prevention of all war; or perhaps it would be more scientific to say it requires the reducing of the probability of the outbreak of war between major powers to a minimum.

It is interesting that in this first formulation of the Soviet Union plan for general and complete disarmament, the destruction of nuclear, chemical and biological weapons and their means of delivery was left to the last stage. ICBM's had only recently been added to the USSR arsenal, and they set great store by them as a means of offsetting the general superiority of the USA in means of delivering the nuclear weapon. The Soviet Union position on when the means of delivery, or vehicles, would be destroyed has since undergone several changes.

As this is not a treatise on the development of disarmament concepts during the long and generally dreary negotiations, there is no need to give in detail the Soviet Union plan, nor the competing plan that the USA, supported by her allies, laid before the Ten-Nation Committee on Disarmament in March 1960. It will be enough to note the opposed, or in some cases coincident, positions of the USA and the USSR in the more important categories of disarmament measures. Among these the most important problem, indeed the crucial problem, is how to get rid of the nuclear weapons.

It will be recalled that Mr. Khrushchev's drastic disarmament plan had a precedent (as he reminded the General Assembly) in the proposals for complete disarmament presented in 1927 by Litvinov on behalf of the Soviet Union in the League of Nations preliminary disarmament commission. This revolutionary approach to the problem was little appreciated by the other great powers either in 1927 or in 1959. They regarded it very suspiciously as a somewhat transparent scheme to disarm the Western nations, to nullify their superior technical defensive capabilities and to leave them vulnerable to the onrush of the "communist hordes." Timorous right-wingers croaked that the communist nations with their very large populations could retain large numbers of "police-militia." These internal security forces would be organized in military formations, as they now are, under a central command, and therefore would be able to intervene in an irresistible mass if there were communist-promoted insurrections in the nations to the west of the Iron Curtain.

These shivery viewers-with-alarm seem to think that the Western governments would be stupid enough to agree to a plan which would leave the USSR and the "socialist" states with what would amount to greatly superior military forces, even if they were called police-militia and carried only small arms. They also appear to believe that the danger of communist takeover in Western European states (and presumably elsewhere) can only be met by organized military force. That is to say, there must be armies, navies and air forces equipped with every kind of armament from sub machine-guns to ICBM's in order to stand against the spread of communism. In other words, those who object to disarmament because of the fear of what lightly-armed Communists could do, are saying, in effect, that communism is a stronger political and social system than parliamentary democracy and free enterprise, and that unless non-communist nations are ready to wage international war with every weapon including the thermonuclear bomb, the Communists will take over the world. They could hardly go further in agreeing with Mr. Khrushchev's notorious remark, "We shall bury you," meaning that the communist system will survive and thrive, while the capitalist system will wither and die.

An important feature of the Khrushchev plan, in its original and later editions, is that it required that all "foreign" troops should be repatriated and all foreign bases should be dismantled in the early stages of disarmament. This obviously would have the result of disrupting the NATO alliance and making combined defence impossible for the Western nations. The provision might well have been written into the Soviet Union plan by their General Staff. Later in the negotiations, the Soviet Union delegates expended much verbiage arguing that in fact their proposals were not one-sided and disadvantageous to the West; but of course they convinced nobody.

The day before Mr. Khrushchev expounded his celebrated thesis, Mr. Selwyn Lloyd, then UK Foreign Secretary, had given the General Assembly outlines of a British disarmament plan based mainly on earlier British-French proposals. Later, in the First Committee, M. Jules Moch, who for years had led the French disarmament delegations, gave a French view that the only feasible way to effect nuclear disarmament was to concentrate on eliminating the means of delivery of the nuclear weapons. These are the "vehicles," namely, the rockets, long-range bomber aircraft and submarines adapted for discharging nuclear-headed rockets. The reasons for this were that nuclear warheads had been produced in such great numbers that it would be impossible to account for them all, and they were of such small dimensions that they could easily be hidden. Thus it would be impossible to verify, or control, fulfilment of an obligation to destroy all nuclear bombs and warheads. This fact had been realized and acknowledged by both sides since 1955. But on the other hand, ICBM's, aircraft and submarines are big things, and neither they nor the records of their construction can easily be hidden. Hence the obligation to do away with them could be controlled.

These proposals by the three nations created much stir in the 14th United Nations General Assembly, and eventually a resolution (No. 1378) was passed which in the preamble stated that progress towards the goal of general and complete disarmament would contribute to saving succeeding generations from the danger of a new and destructive war, by putting an end to the arms race. It called on the governments of the nations concerned to achieve constructive solutions to the question of general and complete disarmament, which was the most important facing the world. The final operative clause in the resolution expressed the hope that measures leading towards the goal of general and complete disarmament under effective international control would be worked out in detail and agreed upon in the shortest possible time.

This was the task that the General Assembly proposed for the Ten-Nation Disarmament Committee, which, in August 1959, had been set up by agreement between the foreign ministers of the USA, the UK, France and the USSR. The members of the Committee were the USA, the UK, Italy, France and Canada for the NATO side, and the USSR, Romania, Poland, Czechoslovakia and Bulgaria for the Warsaw Pact—a "parity" distribution which the USSR had insisted upon, as they were tired of being in a minority as they had been in the UN disarmament sub-committees. It was decided that the Ten-Nation Disarmament Committee should begin negotiations in Geneva on 15 March 1960, having before it for "thorough consideration" the Khrushchev, Selwyn Lloyd (UK) and Moch (French) proposals which had been laid before the United Nations General Assembly.

In February the five NATO members of the Committee met in Washington to decide what they would put forward as an alternative to Khrushchev's general and complete disarmament. After some negotiation a plan was got together, mainly based on the British proposals which had been presented in the UN General Assembly. There were divergencies of views between the allies, as is normal, and these persisted until a few days before the Geneva Conference was due to begin. The Western plan, as finally stitched together, was designed to be carried out in three stages as Khrushchev's was, but the first stage did not contain any actual disarmament, no dismantling of hardware, no disbandment of troops. It represented a stage prior to disarmament and contained a number of provisions for joint studies of some of the more difficult problems, such as the stopping of manufacture of fissile material and the transfer of existing stocks to peaceful uses, the structure of a peace-keeping authority, and so forth.

One important difference between the Soviet Union general and complete disarmament plan and the Western plan was that the former was to be negotiated and agreed upon in all its three stages, and consolidated in a treaty before disarmament began. The Western approach was gradual. We wanted to agree upon and put into effect the first stage, which, as mentioned, did not contain real disarmament measures, and hence would have avoided the difficult subject of control, or verification. The negotiation of the final and more difficult stages of disarmament would only be completed when the earlier stages were in progress, and it would be possible to check theoretical disarmament propositions in the light of experience gained. While Western governments and disarmament experts still prefer the gradual approach, they found during the negotiations that it had become necessary to adopt a disarmament plan, or programme, which is laid out in stages in a sort of draft treaty, beginning from the present galloping arms race, and ending at the final goal of general and complete disarmament.

The West was pushed away from the gradualist concept because of the effective way the Soviet Union representatives attacked the Western plan of March 1960. They said there was no definite commitment to go on from any one of the three stages to the next, and this proved that the West wanted to evade committing itself to complete disarmament. The Soviet Union representative (Mr. Zorin) also tried to argue that Resolution No. 1378 of the UN General Assembly had called on the Conference to negotiate a treaty on general and complete disarmament, which, of course, it had not, as the final clause of Resolution No. 1378 shows. Nevertheless, the Soviet Union line of argument proved effective in the long run. After all, the Western nations had voted for Resolution No. 1378 XIV, which endorsed general and complete disarmament as a goal. But it did not say the Khrushchev plan was the way by which it must be reached; in fact the resolution invited the Ten-Nation Disarmament Committee also to consider thoroughly the British and other proposals which had been laid before the 14th General Assembly. But the West eventually became committed to negotiating an integral programme of general and complete disarmament by subscribing to the Joint Statement of Agreed Principles, negotiated in 1961, of which more details will be given later.

The Ten-Nation Committee duly met on 15 March 1960 and went on meeting until about the middle of May, when it adjourned because of the summit conference which was planned for the latter end of that month in Paris. The discussion only served to define more sharply the differences between the two sides. It became clear to the Western delegates, however, that in order to be convincing in our protestations that we believed in disarmament just as much as the Russians, we should have to infuse a good deal more customer-appeal into our plan. This meant that the USA, as principal owner of the military hardware in the alliance, would have to change its stance.

Who were the customers to whom the disarmament plan had to appeal? Liberal opinion in most of the Western countries favours disarmament as a way out of the danger to which the nuclear armaments race subjects their nations, and is a factor with which political leaders have to reckon. Also, the great powers carry on the disarmament dialogue with much concern for its effect on the neutral, or uncommitted, or non-aligned, nations as they variously describe themselves. The contest between the communist world, under the leadership of the USSR, and the free enterprise world, under US leadership, to capture the allegiance of non-aligned nations, or at least to influence their development, is one of the most important elements of the cold war. More than that, it will be a determinant of the future social and economic development of the world. In this contest, disarmament policy is an element of the highest importance.

The non-aligned states are all in favour of disarmament, particularly nuclear disarmament. One fairly obvious reason for this is because they don't themselves have nuclear armaments and the power they confer or symbolize. If the armaments were done away with, one of the principal differences between great powers and lesser nations would disappear. After all, when we speak of "The Powers," what we have in mind are military powers, although nowadays, of course, there can be no real military power which is not based on great economic power.

Another reason why the "less-developed countries" among the non-aligned want disarmament is that they are revolted by the immense spending on armaments by the "advanced" nations; $120 billion per annum is the often-quoted figure, and they groan when they think of how much economic aid could be given to them if this sterile—worse than sterile, potentially catastrophic—expenditure could be stopped.

Furthermore, they fear the results of nuclear war. They see that a war between the NATO and the Warsaw Pact powers would result in enormous devastation, if not a breakdown of Western civilization—a disaster of an unheard-of scale for humanity, and a setback of decades or centuries to their hopes of attaining the economic and social goods of the developed countries which they so envy.

Most readers will remember the dramatic shooting down of the American U 2 photographic reconnaissance aircraft over Sverdlovsk just before the Paris Summit Conference was to begin, Mr. Khrushchev's unacceptable demands for apologies and guarantees against repetition of such intelligence-gathering operations before he would meet President Eisenhower, and the consequent abandonment of the meeting. All this naturally affected the course of disarmament negotiations.

When the Ten-Nation Disarmament Committee reassembled on 7 June 1960, the Soviet Union tabled amendments to Mr. Khrushchev's original plan. These had been published on 2 June, and evidently it had been intended to offer them as a new position at the aborted Summit meeting. In some of its provisions, the Soviet Union plan was brought rather closer to that of the Western nations. The most important new provision was that all nuclear weapon vehicles should be destroyed in the first stage of disarmament. The Soviet Union claimed that this would eliminate the danger of nuclear war two years after the treaty for general and complete disarmament should be signed. Mr. Zorin, the USSR delegate, asserted that this idea was really the French proposal put forward at the 14th UN General Assembly. M. Jules Moch, however, firmly denied paternity. The French idea had been for a staged reduction and final abolition of nuclear weapon vehicles, not a complete extirpation in the first stage.

The Western delegations quickly pointed out that the Soviet Union was proposing to get rid of, in the first stage, those armaments on which NATO chiefly relied for its defence, namely, the means of delivering the nuclear weapons. This, combined with the Soviet requirement for the withdrawal of all foreign troops and military bases from Europe, would have resulted in leaving the USSR conventionally-armed force substantially superior in Europe, and capable of overwhelming the armed forces of the European NATO partners.

Nevertheless, following consultation between the Western nations at the Ten-Nation Disarmament Committee on the need of strengthening the provisions of our plan, Mr. Frederic Eaton, the leader of the American delegation, went to Washington to consult the President and the appropriate departments of the United States Government about amending the plan. He returned about 26 June with what was called a "Programme for General and Complete Disarmament under Effective International Control" which was a considerable improvement over the March 1960 Western position. It still did not call for any reduction of nuclear weapon vehicles in the first stage. But it did provide for the armed forces of all states to be reduced in the final stage to what would be needed to maintain internal order, and to provide contingents to the international peace force. All other armaments would be destroyed and manufacture would be stopped. This was to state the final goal as complete disarmament, as the Soviet Union plan did. There were other changes which brought the Western plan a little closer to that of the Soviet Union.

But on the day after Mr. Eaton had returned with the new, more forthcoming proposals in his briefcase, the delegations of the Warsaw Pact countries, led by the USSR, walked out of the Ten-Nation Disarmament Conference under the pretext that the West had no real intention to disarm, and was using the Geneva negotiations as a screen for a further heavy arms buildup. It was true enough that the USA was continuing to accumulate armaments and, in particular, was pressing on with a vast ICBM programme to overcome the apprehended missile gap.

But the Soviet Union had not suspended manufacture of armaments either and never claimed that they were doing so. It is true that Mr. Khrushchev had announced in January 1960 that 1.2 million of the 3.6 million men in the USSR armed forces were to be disbanded. But this reduction was never carried out, perhaps mainly because of opposition in the Soviet Union armed forces for whom the U 2 incident must have been quite a piece of luck.

The real reasons for the Soviet Union's withdrawal from the Ten-Nation Conference have yet to be explained. It is quite clear that the decision was a sudden one and as much a surprise to the Soviet delegation as to the Western representatives. Mr. Zorin had been to East Berlin to meet Mr. Khrushchev over the weekend (the 27th was a Monday) and had evidently got his instructions then. The Soviet delegation, we heard later, had been up throughout the night of Sunday-Monday writing their withdrawal speech, and perhaps the speeches for their Warsaw Pact partners. Mr. Khrushchev had just come to East Berlin from the Bucharest conference of Communist parties at which, as we now know, the bitter dispute between the Soviet Union and the Chinese Communist parties came into the open—or rather became open to the communist leaders of the world. This uproar, in which Marxist-Leninist doctrinal polemics masked a national power-struggle, and the consequent disorder in the communist world, may have been one of the factors which influenced Mr. Khrushchev to break off the talks. The Russians at Geneva had privately been hinting at another possible reason, their view that the 1960 presidential election campaign in the USA was about to get into orbit and that during it, and until there should be a new administration in the following spring, no serious developments in the USA disarmament position were to be expected.

The break in negotiations lasted until 1961, when the new Democratic administration under Mr. Kennedy took over. The United States Arms Control and Disarmament Agency was established, with William C. Foster as Director. ACDA's first task was to prepare a new position on a treaty banning nuclear testing. A committee had been hammering and chiselling at this problem since 1958, and continued its work at a slow pace in spite of the breaking off of the Ten-Nation Disarmament Conference. In March 1961 the USSR and the USA agreed that another conference on general disarmament should be organized, but this time the Soviet Union insisted that the negotiating body should contain representatives of the neutral nations as well as representatives of NATO and the Warsaw Pact. At this time, Mr. Khrushchev was trying to sell the conception of a world divided into three parts—the Socialist Camp, the Capitalist Camp and the Neutral Camp. The USSR insisted that the disarmament negotiating body should be representative of all three groups. Agreement was eventually reached, and eight neutrals—Brazil, Mexico, Sweden, India, Burma, the UAR, Ethiopia and Nigeria—were added to the Ten Nations of the previous committee. These nations were, in the USA formulation, representatives of the principal geographical divisions of the world. This negotiating committee was endorsed by the 16th General Assembly of the United Nations.

As well as agreeing upon the negotiating body, the USA and the USSR representatives, Mr. John McCloy and Mr. Valerian Zorin, had agreed on a set of principles under which the conference would operate. These principles were also endorsed by the United Nations General Assembly. The most important of them are given in the following paragraphs.

The object of the negotiations was to agree on a programme to achieve general and complete disarmament and to ensure that nations would no longer resort to war to resolve internation disputes, but instead would settle them by peaceful methods. This would require the creation of effective arrangements to maintain peace in accordance with the principles of the United Nations. General and complete disarmament would mean that at the end of the process the nations would have only such non-nuclear armaments and armed forces as would be necessary to maintain internal order and provide manpower for a United Nations peace force. All other armed forces would be disbanded; military training would cease and all institutions for conducting it, together with general staffs and war departments of governments, would be abolished. Existing stocks of nuclear, chemical, biological and other such weapons would be destroyed, their manufacture would cease, and all means for delivering them, such as rockets, aircraft, artillery and submarines, would be scrapped. A limited number of rockets for space exploration and other scientific purposes could be kept.

The programme of measures to reach this goal would be carried out in stages, within specified time-limits. All measures would be balanced so that no state or group of states could gain military advantages at any stage. All disarmament measures would be carried out under strict international control to ensure that all parties honoured their obligations. This would be done under the supervision of an International Disarmament Organization, which would have all the powers required for it to meet its responsibilities.

Finally, there was a provision that the negotiating parties should try to reach and implement the widest possible agreement at the earliest possible date. This rather ambiguous language—the result of compromise—was meant to cover the Western contention that the conference should deal with, and if possible agree upon, some steps in the direction of disarmament, prior to agreement on the whole programme. Such measures included the cessation of nuclear testing, precautions against surprise attack, and other steps, which while not actually being disarmament, would lessen tension, tend to check the arms race and facilitate the way to the hoped-for disarming. They would thus come within the American definition of "Arms Control" (see page 163). Real disarmament would of course be constituted by such concrete measures as the destruction or conversion of armaments, and disbanding of elements of the armed forces.

The Eighteen-Nation Disarmament Committee began its sessions at Geneva on 14 March 1962, and these have continued on through 1966, except for recesses during the United Nations General Assemblies and at other times to allow the principal parties to take stock of their negotiating positions and sometimes to revise them. Up to 25 August 1966 the Committee had met 286 times. The results of all these meetings and the hundreds of thousands of words placed on the record are not very impressive. But in 1963, three agreements had been reached: the direct communication link between Washington and Moscow, so that urgent consultations could be rapidly and effectively carried out if such a crisis as that of Cuba in October 1962 should again occur; the Moscow Nuclear Test Cessation Treaty, signed 5 August 1963, which prohibits all testing of nuclear weapons except underground; and finally the agreement by the USA and the USSR that they would not put weapons of mass destruction into orbiting satellites, nor into outer space in any other manner.

No one pretends that these agreements have stopped the arms race, although the nuclear test ban has to some extent checked the development of new weapons. But the combined effect of the three agreements has been to encourage hopes for further advances, and to ease tensions between the nations of the NATO alliance and those of the Warsaw Pact, in order to create a *détente*, "the spirit of Moscow" as the Russians express it, acknowledged by most observers though denied by a few hardliners. The problem facing the disarmament negotiators and those people in all countries who want more progress towards a stable peace is how to make the next moves towards the goal—agreed to by both sides, as noted above—of general and complete disarmament. At this point it may be useful to set out the standpoints of the two sides on the principal elements of the disarmament programme.

The most important question is, as I have stressed already, how to reduce and finally get rid of the means of delivering nuclear weapons, especially those which can deliver them at very long ranges. The United States' position is very simple: reduce them by 30 per cent, like all other armaments, in the first stage, by a further 35 per cent in the second stage, and get rid of the remainder in the third stage. By this stage, peaceful means of settling international disputes must have been agreed upon, and there must be peace-keeping machinery established under the United Nations on which all nations can rely to protect their independence and vital interests.

The Soviet Union position, from June 1960, has been that all vehicles for the nuclear weapon should be destroyed or converted to peaceful use in the first stage. After this proposition had been battered by arguments of the Western delegations at Geneva during most of 1962, Mr. Gromyko announced a change at the 17th UN General Assembly: the Soviet Union would agree to the USA and the USSR retaining a limited number of ICBM's until the end of the second stage of disarmament. During the 1963 sessions of the Eighteen-Nation Disarmament Committee the Western side tried to get the Soviet Union representatives to explain such essential features of the Gromyko proposal as the approximate number of ICBM's to be retained, the order and timing of reducing the present large numbers of nuclear weapon vehicles to the "strictly limited number," and especially the method of demonstrating to those concerned that all nuclear vehicles had been destroyed that were supposed to be destroyed. The West got no answers to these probings, except to be told that the USA and its partners must accept the Gromyko proposal "in principle," after which explanations and clarifications would be forthcoming. Of course the United States and its allies could not possibly commit themselves to accepting such a vague and potentially dangerous proposition.

Among the reasons Mr. Gromyko had given for this change of position were the following: that the Western members of the Eighteen-Nation Disarmament Committee had argued that the former Russian proposal to abolish all means of delivering the nuclear weapon vehicles in the first stage would leave it possible for some to be concealed by nations or elements in them determined to cheat and so gain a great advantage in a nuclear-disarmed world; that even if specialized means of delivering the nuclear weapons were destroyed, other improvised means—such as converted civil air liners—could be used for the purpose; and, a more remote possibility, that if the great nuclear powers disarmed themselves, some smaller, irresponsible or malevolent nation might build nuclear weapons and the means of delivering them and so hold the world to ransom, or at least create considerable trouble. Keeping a limited number of ICBM's would, the Russian argument ran, overcome these difficulties. To an extent, this is so. In fact, the Soviet Union proposal is essentially the same idea as a minimum stable nuclear deterrent, which had been discussed extensively by several Western academic strategists. But when this last point was put to the Soviet Union delegation at Geneva they scornfully rejected the suggestion that their idea had anything in common with the vapourings of the Pentagon's academic hired men.

The 1962 Gromyko proposal had been for a "strictly limited number" of ICBM's, anti-missile missiles, and so on to be retained until the second stage of disarmament. At the 1963 UN General Assembly, Mr. Gromyko changed the Soviet position further, and proposed that ICBM's and lesser weapons previously stipulated could be retained until the third stage, thus bringing the Soviet Union proposal nearer to the US position that a proportion of nuclear weapon vehicles should be retained until the last stage of disarmament. But he did not clarify in any way how the reduction should be executed and verified—questions which the Western delegations in Geneva had been asking during the previous year's negotiations. The subject was discussed throughout the 1964 sessions of the disarmament committee, but the Russians gave out no more information than they had in 1963. They did propose to set up a working group to study how the programme could be executed and verified, but made this contingent on the prior acceptance "in principle" of their proposal, and would not agree that the USA plan for reduction of nuclear weapon vehicles should be discussed in the working group. Prolonged efforts of the non-aligned members of the committee to find terms of reference for the working group acceptable to both the USA and the USSR were fruitless.

As it looks in 1966, the great obstacle to agreement on disarmament is the disparity between the power of the United States and that of the Soviet Union to deliver nuclear weapons. Mr. McNamara summarized it thus, in his speech to the Economic Club of New York, on 18 November 1963:

> The US force now contains more than 500 operational long-range ballistic missiles . . . and is planned to increase to over 1700 by 1966 . . . the Soviets are estimated to have today only a fraction as many intercontinental missiles as we do. . . . In addition the US has Strategic Air Command bombers on air alert and over 500 bombers on quick reaction ground alert. By comparison, the consensus is that today the Soviets could only place about half as many bombers over North America on a first strike. Furthermore, their submarine-launched ballistic missiles are of short range and generally are not comparable to those of our *Polaris* force. The Soviets pose a very large threat against Europe,

including hundreds of intermediate and medium range ballistic missiles . . . but given the kind of force that the Soviets are building, including submarine-launched missiles beyond the reach of our offensive forces, the damage which the Soviets could inflict on us and our allies, no matter what we do to limit it, remains extremely high. . . . This has been true for our allies ever since the middle and late fifties.

Mr. McNamara's statement is so important and so closely reasoned that I hesitated to quote extracts from it, for fear of omitting qualifications and balancing statements. But the point is that the USA believes it is greatly superior to the USSR in the long-range vehicles, namely rockets and bombers, and further believes that the USSR is unlikely to be able to overtake its lead in this armament. Having this superiority, which the US Government must feel safeguards it and its allies from nuclear aggression and massive invasion by the Soviet Union, would the USA, now or in the foreseeable future, give up this superiority in nuclear weapon delivery power, and reduce itself to mere equality in deterrent power with the Soviet Union? President Johnson, in his message to the Eighteen-Nation Disarmament Committee on 21 January 1964, proposed a freeze on the present situation. And the present United States proposal for disarmament in nuclear weapon vehicles is for a proportional reduction. But can the Russians accept either of these ways to deal with the problem? So far, they have opposed the idea of proportional reductions, attacking it as leaving the world under the threat of nuclear war throughout most of the disarmament process.

In some other important aspects of disarmament, covered both in the US and the USSR plans, there is not very serious disagreement. The Soviet Union has agreed to the proposals of the USA for reduction on non-nuclear, or conventional armaments on an across-the-board percentage basis; 30 per cent of them to be done away with in the first stage and 35 per cent in each of the two following stages.

The American disarmament plan, with the rather verbose title of "An Outline of Basic Provisions of a Treaty on General and Complete Disarmament in a Peaceful World," calls for a reduction of numbers of men in the American and Russian armed forces to 2,100,000 each in the first stage, the forces of other nations to be reduced proportionately. The Soviet Union plan would make the number 1,900,000. In the second stage the numbers are even closer together: 1,100,000 for the USA and 1,000,000 for the USSR. Of course, the positions are not really as close as the raw figures would imply; there still remains the problem of defining exactly what is to be included in these numbers: what about civilian employees and para-military forces? There is also the question of reservists, and so on. But these matters would be relatively easy to negotiate, if the political decision to reach a compromise were made. Another point is that in modern war, the numbers of men are far less important than the quantity and power of the armament they have to operate.

There is also the question of stopping production of fissile material for weapons use. The American plan proposes to do so in the first stage—or even before the first stage. During 1963 several spokesmen announced cautiously that the USA now has enough nuclear explosive for any foreseeable requirement of its armed forces. Consequently it could well afford to stop production, if the USSR would do likewise, with sufficient measures of inspection. But the USSR so far has rejected the proposal to stop producing nuclear explosives, presumably having considerably less than the USA in stock, and anyway not enough to satisfy the demands of its military staffs. It is possible, but not probable, that agreement could be reached on the stopping of production of fissile material, and the conversion of part of existing stocks to peaceful uses before the problem of reduction of nuclear weapon vehicles is solved. The Soviet Union plan for disarmament leaves the stopping of production and disposal of stocks of fissile material until the second stage, that is, until after nearly all of the nuclear weapon vehicles will have been liquidated.

Both the USA and USSR disarmament plans provide for the setting up of an international organization for the overseeing and verification (or "control") of disarmament. The two proposed organizations are pretty similar except for the top direction where the Soviet Union still calls for a triumvirate—representatives of the Communist, the Capitalist and the non-aligned worlds; this is the famous troika idea which they have tried, so far unsuccessfully, to get the United Nations to adopt to replace the office of the Secretary-General. The United States plan is for a single administrator, in accordance with the principles of good business or administrative organization. This difference of approach could probably be overcome by negotiation, if the more difficult problems of disarmament were solved. The Soviet Union has not made much lately of its troika proposals.

The only move in the direction of disarmament which occurred during the 1964 sessions of the Eighteen-Nation Disarmament Committee was of the "mutual example" type. President Johnson announced that American production of U-235 would be reduced by 40 per cent over a period of four years. Production of plutonium would be further reduced by 20 per cent. Mr. Khrushchev responded by announcing that the USSR would not proceed with the construction of two large reactors, intended for the production of plutonium. These steps in the direction of cessation of the production of nuclear explosive, though not very big ones, were welcomed.

It is when we come to the measures for ensuring that the nations shall settle their differences peacefully after the third stage of disarmament has been reached that another serious— perhaps the most serious—difference between the American and Soviet plans appears. The Soviet Union plan is practically nothing more than a reaffirmation that the provisions of the UN Charter for the peaceful settlement of disputes shall be observed, and that international forces for dealing with breaches of the peace or the security of nations shall be organized and controlled as laid down in Chapter 7 of the Charter. The key to this position is that the Soviet Union and the other permanent members of the UN Security Council would retain their right of veto over the creation and operation of any peace-keeping force. This, as regards keeping the peace by international action under the United Nations, would leave the world exactly as it has been since 1945. The existing provisions of the UN Charter are unsatisfactory and will continue so while the USA and the USSR and their allies on either side disagree so fundamentally as to how the world should be organized, politically, economically and socially. In most conceivable future clashes of nationalities and in situations of revolutionary change, it is un-likely that the permanent members of the Security Council will very often find themselves in agreement on the peace-keeping action which should be taken. And under the existing provisions of the UN Charter, if one side or the other applies a veto, no action can be taken. So the American plan, while stating that peace-keeping procedures, including the use of international armed force, should be established within the framework of the United Nations, calls also for strengthening the organization. This can hardly be done without amending the Charter—a task for which the prospects do not seem hopeful for some time to come.

The problem of how peacekeeping operations by the United Nations should be authorized and financed became acute in the autumn of 1964, as the 19th UN General Assembly was about to convene. This was immediately due to disagreements over payment for the United Nations Emergency Force (Suez-Sinai) and ONUC (Congo). The Soviet Union, its communist bloc allies, France and some other nations held that these operations were not legally authorized, and that they were not obliged to pay for them. The United States, the United Kingdom, most Western countries and a majority of other member states maintained the contrary. Efforts over the preceding eighteen months to reach a compromise had failed. The contingency of a procedural motion to deprive the delinquents of their vote under the provisions of Article 19 of the Charter greatly perturbed the non-aligned nations. It was agreed to avoid voting on the issue, which might have disrupted the United Nations entirely. By ingenious procedural devices, decisions were taken which enabled the established functions of the United Nations to be carried on until it would be time for the next General Assembly to meet.

One specific decision was to set up a committee of thirty-three members, whose task it would be to find agreement on the question of the authorization and payment for future peacekeeping operations. The committee had also to find a compromise financing plan which would dissipate the threat of UN bankruptcy. In the five months it had to work in, it was impossible for the committee to resolve the conflict as to how the United Nations should go about its peacekeeping functions and achieve a workable reconciliation of the views of the communist countries and those of the free democracies. Yet this is a problem which must be solved if the world is to be able to deal with situations such as Suez, the Congo and Vietnam without incurring the danger of involvement of the major powers in a general nuclear war.

It is generally known that one of the main difficulties in trying to reach agreement with the USSR on the various sectors of the disarmament complex has been the reluctance of the Russians to define adequately what sort of control over disarmament or verification of measures of disarmament they are prepared to accept. However, they protest that they are as much in favour of adequate control over actual disarmament as the Western negotiators are, and there have been improvements in their stated positions from time to time. But there is still a wide gap between what the West think necessary to provide "effective international control" and what the Soviet Union is prepared to agree to. We can only hope that this difficulty will yield to patient negotiation, as we deal with concrete measures of disarmament.

# 13

## THE MILITARY-INDUSTRIAL COMPLEX, USA

President Johnson, in his television address to the nation on 21 January 1964, when the Eighteen-Nation Disarmament Committee reassembled at Geneva, said: "Disarmament is not merely the Government's business, but everybody's business." Attending to disarmament for the Government are the US Arms Control and Disarmament Agency, the State Department, the Department of Defense and the Atomic Energy Agency. The heads of all these branches of the US Government meet together in a group called the Committee of Principals, to decide on US disarmament policy and how it is to be negotiated with the Soviet Union and explained to allies. But how much concerned with disarmament is "everybody"? One hopes that this is not another case of "What is everybody's business is nobody's business." Of course, all of us should be concerned about disarmament, since the policies adopted by the Government may determine whether we will live out our natural lives or be burned up, buried under rubble, radio-activated, or perish in some of the other horrid eventualities that will arise if the arms race runs on uncontrolled and the nations continue to rely on ever-increasing armed force for security.

In the autumn of 1963 Philip Noel-Baker asked in a pamphlet, "Who wants disarmament?" and Harold Wilson, a year later to be Prime Minister, answered, "With the exception of a few who are wedded to the concept of a power-dominated world, or who reap financial rewards from the arms industry, there is no one who does not passionately want disarmament."

It is not easy to identify the "few" positively, least of all those most influential. If we ask, "Who does not want disarmament?" we shall not find many who denounce the idea absolutely and finally, and who are reported in the public press as doing so, but there are multitudes of "well-yes-but'ers." That is to say, there is no one in favour of having a nuclear war and blowing the most civilized and productive parts of the northern hemisphere to smithereens. Equally, there are few who would not admit that the world would be more secure if there were some means of getting rid altogether of nuclear weapons and the means of delivering them. But they think it is impossible in the world we live in, humanity being what it is and especially the Russians being what they are, to achieve the sort of worldwide agreements that would be necessary to make disarmament effective. These people express themselves mainly by *clichés:* "There have always been wars, and there always will be"; "You can't change human nature"; "You can't trust the Soviets"; and so forth. So they offer no alternative to letting the armaments race run on, and hold out no hope that it will not in the end come to a nuclear war.

There is another method nowadays of finding out who is in favour of what, and that of course is to take public opinion polls. We shall be examining presently what evidence the pollsters produce about public attitudes to disarmament in the USA and Canada. One thing that the polls have proved over the years, if it needed proving, is that what the public thinks today is very likely to be quite different, in quantitative terms, from what it thought six months ago, or what it will think six months hence. It should also be noted, of course, that the public takes its opinions mainly from politicians, editorialists, commentators in press and radio, professors and scientists, the last-named being listened to with undue respect when pontificating outside the sphere of their special competence.

If a Gallup pollster should ask a civilian whether he thought that military officers were in favour of disarmament, he would probably just laugh and come back with "Like distillers are in favour of prohibition," or some such quip. If one were to ask a selection of the military officers themselves, their answers would probably fall into the "well-yes-but" category, partly because their government is on record as favouring disarmament under specified conditions. No other attitude is to be expected of military officers in the climate of the cold war and in the present circumstances of military life. After all, one would not buy a watch-dog who was never suspicious of the intentions of strangers or who lacked confidence in the idea that a good set of teeth and jaws are the best things to keep his master's household from harm.

The first chapter mentioned how the threat to the security of their employment that disarmament poses can influence the thinking of the military and of the scientists who gain their livelihood by doing the military's scientific chores. The emotions aroused by a feeling of personal insecurity may have more to say than cold reason when they think about disarmament or the threats to their nation's safety which armaments are supposed to avert. Military officers in the United States or any other country have engaged in a service in which they are presumably prepared to lay down their life in defence of others. No one should suggest that they would be so selfish as to think consciously to themselves: "Whether disarmament would be better for the country and make the lives of all its inhabitants safer or not, it would mean that I would be out of a job, and therefore I am against it." But every serving officer might well examine his conscience in this particular and ask himself the question, "Can my attitude to disarmament be affected, unconsciously, by my personal interest?"

Ex-President Eisenhower, recognizing the potential conflict between the interests of the armed forces and the armament industry, and those of the nation as a whole, sounded the alarm in his valedictory message, 17 January 1961. The most pertinent passages are the following:

> . . . this conjunction of an immense military establishment and a large arms industry is new in the American experience. The

total influence—economic, political, even spiritual—is felt in every state house, every office of the Federal Government. . . .

In the councils of Government, we must guard against the acquisition of unwarranted influence, whether sought or unsought, by the military-industrial complex. The potential for the disastrous rise of misplaced power exists and will persist.

It is certainly to be expected that the total influence of the military-industrial complex would be against disarmament. We have examined briefly why military men are, and traditionally have been, against disarmament. The reason why the military industrialists, including all gaining their living from the making of armaments and military equipment, would be against disarmament is very clear also; they might lose their livelihood. Workmen and employees and also managers and executives would see their jobs disappear, while the investors and capitalists would lose money. It is obvious that many or most of such people would see disarmament as something very bad for the country and would be disposed to use their influence (which President Eisenhower said is great) to prevent any disarming.

The importance of the armaments industry in the economy of the United States during the years since the Korean war has been set out in many articles in the periodical press, in books and through other media. No long argument as to this is needed in the present book. However, it would be incomplete if the main facts about the power of the military-industrial complex were not summarized, together with some of the facts which indicate that the danger to the American democratic process might have been a real one if it had been allowed to develop. The Kennedy Administration, it is true, greatly increased military spending, but at the same time took measures and instituted policies which largely eliminated the dangers of "unwarranted influence" which had exercised General Eisenhower. These policies have been carried on under President Johnson. A distinct change of viewpoint is discernible; very few now accept the cold war and the arms race as an essential component of the American way of life.

In assessing the importance of military spending in the United States economy, we can start from the fact that in the defence message President Johnson presented to the Congress for the year 1966 it is estimated that spending on defence during the current financial year will be $52.5 billion. Of this, $24.2 billion will be spent on procurement of armament and equipment, research and development, atomic energy (mainly production of nuclear explosive) and military aid to allies (mainly in the supply of arms). The total defence expenditure will be 42 per cent of all budget expenditure for the year. The Gross National Product of the USA for the year 1966 is estimated at $667 billion in the message. We can say that the defence expenditures for 1966 are estimated at 8 per cent of the GNP, and expenditures on armaments 3.6 per cent.

Looking at these figures crudely presented, one might say that it should not create more than a very temporary dislocation of the American economy if all expenditure on armaments and defence should cease abruptly. Hence this factor should not be decisive in influencing the policy of the United States Government on whether to disarm or not, or how fast to disarm. But 3.6 per cent of the GNP does not represent 3.6 per cent of the pressures on the various branches of the government, especially on the Executive and Congress. What produces strong pressures is that the armaments industry is largely concentrated in relatively few states.

According to *U.S. News and World Report* of 28 August 1963, the total of defence contracts in all states was $25.2 billion. California held 25 per cent of the total, and other states the following percentages: Connecticut 4 per cent; Massachusetts 4 per cent; New Jersey 5 per cent; New York 10 per cent; Ohio 5 per cent; Pennsylvania 3 per cent; Texas 5 per cent; and Washington 4 per cent. That is, nine states out of the fifty held 65 per cent of the defence contracts.

What is perhaps more important as an index of the dependence of states on the armaments industry and defence generally is the relation between employment in defence industries, and total employment in manufacturing. In Kansas, Washington, New Mexico, California, Connecticut, Arizona and Utah, more than 20 per cent of manufacturing employment was in defence industries, while in five more states it was more than 10 per cent. These data are taken from "The Economic Impact of Disarmament in the United States" in the volume *Disarmament: its Politics and Economics,* published by the American Academy of Arts and Sciences. The author of the article is Professor Emile Benoit, chairman of the panel which produced a report on the same subject for the Arms Control and Disarmament Agency. Professor Benoit also observes that the ratio of defence business to total business is very high in certain industries: 95 per cent in the aircraft and missile industry, 60 per cent in ship and boat building, and 40 per cent in radio and communications equipment.

It will readily be seen that these concentrations of interest in keeping the production of armaments and military equipment going at a high level will create more pressures on politicians than if the same total amount of business were spread uniformly all over the country and through all the manufacturing working force. Seymour Melman, in his book *The Peace Race* quotes Representative J. L. Whitten, a member of the Defense Appropriations Committee, as declaring:

> . . . Just about every district and every state and every labor union and every store owner is getting a cut out of present expenditures in the name of "defense," and it makes it extremely difficult for the Congress or the services to hold down these things in line with what it really needs.

It is well known that labour unions in industries affected or threatened with loss of jobs owing to reduced production or cancellation of armament or military equipment items are usually the first to protest against any decisions of this nature. As they speak for a large number of voters, their protests naturally command immediate attention from their representatives in the Congress. Certainly the labour unions cannot be blamed for doing their best to keep their membership in employment when loss of jobs is threatened by the shifting tides of defence expenditure. But it is to be hoped that the line taken in the current struggles to maintain employment will not harden into a rooted fear of and opposition to any United States Government policy of extensive disarmament.

It would be very wrong to conclude that politicians who seek to win defence contracts for industries located in their constituencies, or who try to protect their constituents against loss of employment consequent on reduction of defence spending are cynically acquiescing in the arms race for their political advantage. They no doubt are convinced that the security of the United States requires armaments to be manufactured, and that if this is so, then the people they represent should have a share in the employment and emoluments distributed as a result of the production of those armaments. There are undoubtedly material advantages to their constituents, and hence political advantages to themselves in the continuing production of armaments. Therefore their judgement on whether disarmament will make for a safer world, or the reverse, will not be unbiased. Policies that call for building ever greater masses of military equipment may seem more reasonable to them than if they were the representatives of simple agricultural communities, who had nothing to contribute to the arms build-up except their taxes.

Another important factor determining the attitude of politicians to the arms race, and conversely to disarmament, is the way they, and the country generally, view communism, and Soviet Russia. To be against communism, as everyone who believes in parliamentary democracy has to be, leads to the view that one must necessarily be against the Soviet Union; to be against the Soviet Union, which has great military power, leads to the conclusion that the USA must have greater military power in order to preserve its freedom and institutions, the American way of life, from overthrow by aggressive communism led and directed by the men in the Kremlin. All this sounds simple, terribly simple. Such a chain of emotional reasoning could lead to the conviction that in resisting the evil aggression of communist-led Soviet Russia, any military means are justifiable, including the use of multi-megaton nuclear weapons to incinerate whole populations.

It is, of course, the prerogative, and perhaps the duty of a politician, to alert the people against communism, or any other threat to their liberty, whether it comes from abroad or from elements within the nation. But it is generally thought not to be good democratic practice for politicians and military together to propagandize the people in favour of some specifically political line of action. The danger to be apprehended is that the military, starting as allies of the politicians, may become the senior partners in the business, and take over its direction, and even the direction of the country.

In 1958 it was decided by the US National Security Council that the military could and should consider it a part of their duty to indoctrinate the civilian population as well as military personnel against the dangers of communism. The result, not surprisingly, was that military men willing or ordered to take on this duty of demonstrating the evils of communism usually found that their audiences consisted of people who wanted to have their flesh made to creep, or who had a predisposition to be roused to a good comfortable red-heat by denunciations of communism. These were the elements of the people whose political thinking was far to the right. They were not necessarily those who subsequently have been identified as John Birchers or other elements of the right-wing lunatic fringe. But the participation of the military in the anti-communist propaganda campaign obviously was tending to identify them with the right wing in politics, and the far right at that.

The dangerous possibilities of indiscriminately assigning military officers to carry out political indoctrination were forcibly brought to public attention by the unhappy story of Major-General Edwin A. Walker, who was relieved of his divisional command, and subsequently became involved in right-wing activities which brought him into conflict with the law. The Walker case, and some indiscreet public statements of a number of other senior military officers, decided the Kennedy Administration in its early days to take firm action to check the tendency for generals and admirals to make pronouncements not only on defence policy but on foreign policy; to tend to usurp the proper function of elected representatives. So the Pentagon laid down stringent rules that before delivery all speeches of military officers had to be cleared by the proper authority in the Defense Department; that meant by the civil authority. In the final result, the Secretary of Defense would decide what the military officers, who are responsible through him to their Commander-in-Chief, should be permitted to say or write in public. This action was taken following a memorandum to the President and the Secretary of Defense by Senator J. W. Fulbright, Chairman of the Senate Foreign Relations

Committee. That there should have been any questioning of the rightness of the action taken by the Administration in this matter is somewhat astonishing to one brought up in the old-style British military tradition, as the present writer was. That tradition, supported by regulations, is that the military should take no part in politics, and that they are obliged to get authority to publish anything they write, and that they are responsible for not saying anything in public contrary to government policy. The writer understands that this is, or was, until after World War II at any rate, also the tradition of United States military officers.

However, the Pentagon directive was violently attacked by some senators. Finally a senate committee chaired by Senator J. C. Stennis was set up to inquire into the matter. After long hearings, covering nearly a year, the committee issued its report, on 25 October 1962. (But on this date the attention of the nation was focused on a real situation in Cuba which might have led to war. Naturally there was not much interest in the precise conditions under which military officers should be allowed to talk to the public about war, or about foreign policies which might lead to war or peace.) According to the report by Cabell Phillips in the *New York Times,* 26 October 1962, the committee agreed that the doctrine of civil superiority over the military in government affairs should be held inviolable. The Executive had the inherent power of requiring military officers to submit any public statements for review prior to delivery. As to military participation in "cold war seminars," the committee said that "More harm than good can result from these programs unless there is complete co-operation by local persons of sound judgment and discretion."

It would seem that before the policy change referred to, there was a danger that the public, hearing stories of how some military officers co-operated with right-wing groups, would get the impression that all military officers were equally far-right in their views, hating not only communism, but also some aspects of current United States Government policy, especially social legislation. In short, there was a danger that military officers might be thought to be incipient fascists.

Another development in the usa after World War II may

have cast doubt in the mind of the public as to whether senior officers in the military service were always selfless guardians of the peace and security of the American people. This phenomenon, now fortunately brought under control, was the extensive employment of retired officers, frequently of the highest rank, by those corporations that are big contractors for armaments.

Of course, the employment of retired senior officers in armaments firms is not an exclusively American practice. One recalls precedents in Great Britain, going back many years. But before World War II, the armaments business did not involve such vast sums, nor the production of the weapons for nuclear war.

The report of Representative Hebert's committee, set up to investigate this matter, listed 762 retired officers who had found employment in armaments-producing firms (*New York Times*, 18 January 1960). They ranged in rank from four-star generals and admirals down to colonels and naval captains, and their remunerations varied from $84,000 to $5000 per annum. In total it was a formidable list, and after the facts had been allowed to sink in, it was clear to everybody that there was a conflict of interest which ought to be removed for the country's good. That is to say, if the senior officers of the armed services who were responsible for advising on how the taxpayer's money should be spent for armaments had expectations of very substantial advantages to come from some of the firms hoping for defence contracts, it was to be feared that their judgement would not be as impartial as it should be. The committee recommended legislation providing that for two years after retirement, officers should not be allowed to accept from armaments firms, jobs having anything to do with sales to the Department of Defense. While this does not seem to be a very drastic remedy, no doubt it has had the necessary effect. In any case, it was a definite acknowledgement that the previous state of affairs was not consonant with the public interest.

The honourable and devoted majority of the military profession in the United States must be grieved that the actions of a few of their members have caused some publicists to call into question the disinterestedness of the profession as a whole. If there are American officers who are political fanatics, or who seek personal aggrandizement or financial advantages in the service, their number must be infinitesimal. But this chapter began with the question, "Who doesn't want disarmament?" It was necessary to mention some of the facts which tended to associate the military, in the public mind, with armament industrialists. Such a coalition could exercise the "unwarranted influence" on the decisions of the US Government which President Eisenhower warned against. There is a presumption that the "unwarranted influence" could be exerted against policies directed towards lessening of tensions, agreements with the opponents in the cold war, and eventually towards the twin objectives of a peaceful world and disarmament.

I think that most military officers would claim that peace in security for their nation is the eventual object to which they consecrate their endeavours. If that is true, then officers, and especially those of high rank, should think seriously whether in the discharge of their responsibilities they are helping or hindering the long-term object of a stable peace. We refer again to Mr. Thomas Finletter's image of the United States' "double-barrelled policy" abroad (p. 94). Military officers naturally tend to fix their attention on the "Preparation for Defence" barrel, while more or less ignoring the other (and longer-range) barrel of the abolition under a regime of law of the institution of war.

In a television address on 7 November 1957 which dealt with Science in National Security, President Eisenhower had this to say at the close of his remarks:

> What the world needs today even more than a giant leap into outer space, is a giant step toward peace. Time and again we have demonstrated our eagerness to take such a step.
>
> As a start in this direction, I urge the Soviet now to align themselves with the practical and workable disarmament proposals, approved yesterday by a large majority in the United Nations.
>
> Never shall we cease to hope and work for the coming of the day when enduring peace will take these military burdens from the back of mankind, and when the scientist can give his full attention, not to human destruction, but to human happiness and fulfillment.

In an address to a joint session of the Congress of the Republic of the Philippines, the late General MacArthur said:

> The Great Question is: Can global war now be outlawed from the world? If so, it would mark the greatest advance in civilization since the Sermon on the Mount. It would lift at one stroke the darkest shadow which has engulfed mankind from the beginning. . . .
>
> You will say at once that the abolition of war has been the dream of man for centuries, every proposition to that end has been promptly discarded as impossible and fantastic. But that was before the science of the past decade made mass destruction a reality. The argument then was along spiritual and moral lines, and lost. But now the tremendous evolution of nuclear and other potentials of destruction has suddenly taken the problem away from its primary consideration as a moral and spiritual question and brought it abreast of scientific realism. It is no longer an ethical question to be pondered solely by learned philosophers and ecclesiastics, but a hardcore one for the decision of the masses whose survival is the issue. . . .
>
> We are in a new era. . . . We must have sufficient imagination and courage to translate the universal wish for peace—which is rapidly becoming a universal necessity—into actuality.

These speeches by the two most highly respected American leaders of World War II should convince any military officer that "peace" and "disarmament" are not dirty words, and that it is his duty to think towards the attainment of the long-term object of his government's foreign policy—a stable and lasting peace.

A preview of the obstacles which an extensive programme of disarmament will meet has been afforded as a result of the cuts which Secretary McNamara has made in areas of defence spending which he has found to be unproductive in the sense of not giving real defence value for the money. Cuts in programmes for the development or continued production of certain weapons systems which the cost-effectiveness evaluation teams found to be redundant met strenuous opposition. It seems, however, that Mr. McNamara and his aides will in general have public support in their economy endeavours, partly because no one wants to pay more taxes than necessary, and partly because the concept of the uselessness of great expenditures to reinforce "overkill" is beginning to sink into the public consciousness.

"Overkill," in the simplest form of the idea, is the present capacity of the United States, measured in megatonnage of nuclear weapons and the means of delivering them, to destroy the main cities and industrial targets in the Soviet Union not only once, but several times. Therefore it is not sensible to keep on adding to the weaponry at great expense. This idea was translated into terms directly applicable to the defence spending of the United States by Secretary McNamara in his speech to the Economic Club of New York on 18 November 1963 (already quoted from on page 178) in which he made the following key statements:

> The most wishful of Soviet planners would have to calculate as a certainty that the most effective surprise attack they could launch would still leave us with the capability to destroy the attacker's society. . . .
> But given the kind of force that the Soviets are building, including submarine-launched missiles beyond the reach of our offensive forces, the damage which the Soviets could inflict on us and our allies, no matter what we do to limit it, remains extremely high. . . .
> Larger budgets for us strategic forces would not change that fact. They could have only a decreasing incremental effect limiting somewhat the damage the us and its allies could suffer in a general nuclear war. In short, we cannot buy the capability to make a strategic bombing campaign once again a unilateral prospect.
> That must, I suggest, be accepted as one of the determinants affecting policy. Another is that the same situation confronts the Soviet leaders, in a way that is even more intensely confining. . . .
> The fact that further increases in strategic forces' size will at last encounter rapidly diminishing returns . . . should be reflected in future budgets. . . . We can anticipate that the annual expenditure on strategic forces will drop substantially, and level off well below the present rate of spending.

James Reston, in an article in the *New York Times* of 15 March 1963, made a number of pertinent remarks on the implications of cuts in defence spending:

Bob McNamara is presiding over a department of government that spends more every year than the net income of every corporation in the United States. He has the power of decision over defense contracts for a large and growing segment of American industry that must work for the government or die.

Not only vast cities but in some cases whole states and regions of the nation prosper if they get the big defense contracts or decline if they don't—and powerful politicians rise or fall with them. . . .

. . . McNamara is doing what he was brought here to do; he is managing the Pentagon; he is establishing civilian control over the officers; and he is not hesitating to scrap expensive weapons systems when they go wrong, no matter who complains.

The article goes on to list some of the programmes Mr. McNamara had cancelled: the nuclear-powered aeroplane, the Skybolt missile (referred to on page 152), the Dynasoar programme and others. He had battled against the appropriation of many billions of dollars for the development and production of the RS70 aircraft, a supersonic (2000 m.p.h.) aircraft intended to replace the B 52's and B 58's when they finally were relinquished by the usaf. In this he encountered the tough opposition of General Curtis LeMay, then Chief of the Air Staff, not only in intra-departmental discussions, but also before the committees of Congress.

In these discussions, and those about the cancellation of Skybolt (see page 152), usaf generals were very loath to admit that the long-range bomber is obsolescent as a vehicle for the nuclear weapon, and will, sooner or later, be entirely replaced by the intercontinental and shorter-range ballistic missiles. For purposes of strategic missions, that is, attacks on the cities that are the centres of production and transportation of the enemy, the great missiles are clearly more efficient, mainly on account of the increasing vulnerability of the bomber. Missiles would seem also to have an advantage in the "counterforce" or retaliatory-deterrent role. They would be more effective instruments for carrying out the carefully controlled responsive strikes contemplated in the announced strategy, because of their relative invulnerability to an enemy pre-emptive strike and the speed with which they could reach their selected targets.

The transformation of the air force function brought about by the development of the ballistic missile is hard for the majority of airmen to accept. They have been brought up to believe in the bomber as the most powerful and prestigious engine of war. The senior air force officers who resist the phasing out of the long-distance bomber are probably committing the same error as the admirals who fought for so long to retain the battleship in navies, until World War II showed once and for all that super-Dreadnoughts were as obsolete as triremes. It is noteworthy that the King-Bomber of the RAF, Sir Arthur Harris, in a passage near the end of his book *Bomber Offensive,* forecast the development of ballistic missiles, and its effect on the function of air forces. He urged airmen not to struggle against it, but to work for a unification of the air, land and sea services.

Military murmurings against the McNamara regime of budget-cutting and junking of service idols were set forth in an article by Mr. Hanson W. Baldwin, military correspondent of the *New York Times,* in an article dated 18 June 1962. It was subheaded "McNamara's Innovations Arouse Plea for Understanding 'Human' Leadership." Most of the article is a quotation from *Army* magazine. After enumerating Secretary McNamara's exceptional abilities, it goes on to say that if the Secretary and his immediate assistants do not understand armies, they don't understand war, and then added: "Perhaps 'understand' is not the right word. There is a certain visceral comprehension which goes beyond what the completely rational man can 'understand.'" Presumably, therefore, the Secretary of Defense and his advisers should begin thinking with their viscera instead of with their heads.

In view of the facts cited, it is trite to say that the US Government is and has been very conscious of the serious effects on the economy of the country which a programme of disarmament might cause. The act which established the Arms Control and Disarmament Agency directed it to conduct research on the economic consequences of arms control and disarmament, including the problems of readjustments in industry and the reallocation of national resources. Mr. John J. McCloy, while he was Adviser on Disarmament to the President of the USA, set up a panel of experts under the chairmanship of Professor Emile Benoit of Columbia University to study this question, and the panel submitted its report in January 1962. It has been published as an official document of the us Arms Control and Disarmament Agency.

The panel concluded that disarmament, in accordance with the provisions of the us Program for General and Complete Disarmament in a Peaceful World, and carried out over the time period indicated in that program, should create little danger of immediate depression in the us economy, assuming sensible adjustment policies and vigorous government leadership to dispel adverse effects.

Further conclusions were:

> That structural problems in particular industries or areas are unavoidable and could be serious for individuals, companies and communities prominently affected. . . .
>
> That the alleviations of these structural difficulties may require a variety of adjustment programs, some providing assistance for the retraining, temporary support, and relocation of individuals and reconversion and diversification of enterprises. . . .
>
> That within wide limits the Nation can afford to have as high or as low a level of defense expenditure as is deemed politically desirable, and should feel no constraint on the economic side in adjusting defense expenditures to whatever level seems best to accord with our political objectives.

The Fifteenth United Nations General Assembly (1960) passed a resolution calling on the Secretary-General to conduct a study of the economic and social consequences of disarmament in countries with different economic systems and at different stages of economic development. The late Mr. Hammarskjöld set up an advisory group, consisting of experts from the following countries: USSR, Sudan, UK, India, Pakistan, Poland, USA, Venezuela, France and Czechoslovakia. The United States was represented by W. W. Leontief, Professor of Economics at Harvard. The group made its report about a year later, and rather surprisingly, reached unanimous agreement. It concluded that "all the problems and difficulties of transition connected with disarmament could be met by appropriate national and international measures" and that "there should thus be no doubt that the diversion to peaceful purposes of the resources now in military use could be accomplished to the benefit of all countries and lead to the improvement of world economic and social conditions."

However, until late in 1963 not much seems to have been done by either the US Government or the firms engaged in armaments production to prepare for a considerable reduction in defence spending, much less for a programme of disarmament. Philip Shabecoff and Joseph Lelyveld, financial and business reporters for the *New York Times*, reported on 24 August 1963 after an extensive survey that the defence industry was doing very little to cope with the impact of possible arms control or disarmament. Many defence contractors simply were refusing to consider that there could be a cutback in arms production of any considerable size in the foreseeable future. Others had thought about the problem and said that a sharp reduction in defence expenditure would hit them hard, but that they had no idea of how to plan to meet such a contingency. A few companies were confident that they could convert to civilian business without much trouble. However, since the article in the *New York Times* was published, most of the largest armaments contractors have begun seriously to study reconversion problems.

A good many of the industries questioned thought that the Government should tackle the problem, since it seems to be beyond the capacity of individual firms. In fact, as the *New York Times* reports, the Defense Department has established an office to assist the communities and corporations that have lost big contracts. The work this office does every day is a smaller-scale version of what would have to be done if an effective programme of disarmament should be agreed upon and put into effect. The final paragraph of the report quotes Mr. Yarmolinsky, then special assistant to the Secretary of Defense, as saying that the notion that the American economy depends on armaments is a "simplistic economic analysis." But, the reporters say, virtually no one predicts that the sophisticated defence industries of today will be able to make the transition to civilian production as easily as was done after World War II. The reason given on all sides is lack of planning.

On 22 December 1963 President Johnson announced that he had appointed a committee of very senior government officials to co-ordinate the work of federal agencies in appraising the economic impacts of disarmament and changes in defence spending. The President said in his statement: "I am confident that our economy can adjust to changes in defense spending or arms reduction that may occur. . . . But the nation as a whole and the communities with heavy concentrations of defense industry deserve assurance that any changes will be made with as little dislocation as possible."

Although a useful start has been made, much more thought and hard work will be needed if the armament-dependent economy of so many areas in the USA, in which are employed so much of its manufacturing labour force, and more important still, so many scientists, engineers and technicians, is to be converted to the uses of peace with a minimum of disruption of the personal and family lives of the people affected, and a minimum check to the economic well-being of the areas and communities where defence spending is now concentrated. Failing a fairly clear picture of where their salary is going to come from if disarmament puts them out of their present jobs, the workers in defence industries, from the manager and engineer down to the sweepers and oilers, are going to be against disarmament, and will go around shaking their heads and growling "you can't trust the Russians," even if they don't join the John Birch Society.

A thorough study of the problems which would face the United Kingdom if general disarmament were agreed upon and implemented is contained in *The Economic Effects of Disarmament*. This work was produced by *The Economist* Intelligence Unit. It analyzes in considerable detail the dislocations in employment and industry which could occur, and, as one would expect, displays an impressive mastery of economic method. While no general conclusions are set out, it appears that the authors believe that with suitable and adequately planned government policies to assist reemployment, retraining or retirement of personnel, and to divert productive capacity and financial resources now devoted to making armaments into other activities, there would not be very great difficulties for

Great Britain in making the transition from the armed to the disarmed world.

The Canadian Peace Research Institute published in 1963 the results of a survey of Canadian opinion on defence and disarmament entitled *In Your Opinion*. Among the questions asked were, "Are you in favour of general disarmament with proper safeguards?" To this, 92 per cent answered yes. Asked if they would favour general disarmament even if it meant a loss of income or that they had to look for another job, 70 per cent still said yes; 13 per cent said no; the balance either didn't know or were against disarmament. The next question was rather more cunning: "Do you think that many people are against disarmament because they are afraid it would cause a depression or recession?" To this, 37 per cent said yes, 38 per cent said no, and the remainder didn't know, or were against disarmament. This indicates that Canadians who depend on military spending for their livelihood are not so altruistic in contemplating the possibility of disarmament as the answers to the previous questions would show.

The chapter on the economic consequences of disarmament in the above survey states that the Canadian Government spends about a quarter of its budget on defence programmes. In addition, a sizable portion of our exports to the United States consists of raw materials and finished products for defence industries. Consequently, disarmament could have a considerable effect on the Canadian economy. The following question was asked: "If all nations in fact started disarming, do you think this would lead to prosperity or depression in this country?" Of the replies received, 31 per cent expected that disarmament would lead to prosperity, 18 per cent, no change, 21 per cent, a minor recession, and 24 per cent, a depression. This was the opinion of the total sample. The views of business leaders were 21 per cent for prosperity, 19 per cent for no change, 48 per cent for a minor recession, and only 10 per cent for a depression. The opinion of labour leaders and politicians questioned was roughly similar to the general sample. Those of the selected groups who thought there might be an economic decline agreed that it could be avoided by suitable advance planning.

The writer has been unable to find records of comparable questions put to the United States public by the American In-stitute of Public Opinion (Gallup poll) or other such organizations. The *Public Opinion Quarterly* for Summer 1963 brings together the results from 1945 on of polls on various aspects of atomic weapons and nuclear energy, but without relevance to disarmament except for questions in the years 1945-48 when the Baruch Plan for control of atomic energy was under discussion. These do not, however, help us in ascertaining whether people at present feel that disarmament would be a good or a bad thing.

One or two of the results are of general interest. For example, when asked how worried they were about the chance of a war breaking out in which nuclear bombs would be used, 22 per cent of those interrogated were very worried, 37 per cent fairly worried and 38 per cent not worried at all (July 1961). In March 1963, 60 per cent thought hydrogen bombs would be used against the United States if there were another world war, 23 per cent thought it unlikely, and 17 per cent had no opinion. In May 1958 the average of opinions was that in a nuclear war between Russia and the West only 3 persons out of 10 would survive. Perhaps some day a candidate for a Ph.D. will trace the relationship between the peaks and lows of the Cold War, the development of armaments, the people's fears and their opinions on what should be done to save them from the dangers which are so obvious to the majority.

# 14

## NATO AND THE CONTROL OF NUCLEAR
## WEAPONS; THE CUBA CRISIS

We have come to the end of our excursion into past history, during which we have seen how the military theories which have led us into the age of nuclear terror were conceived and grew, and how they were put into practice in World War II on a scale which immolated the civil population by scores of thousands. It is impressed on us by frequent reminders in the press that victims in a World War III would be counted not by scores of thousands, but by hundreds of millions. We shall now try to establish a few points of reference for thinking about the situation in the world today of the great powers and the opposing alliances—NATO and the Warsaw Pact.

Sir Alec Douglas-Home, then Prime Minister of the UK, in his reply to Chairman Khrushchev's message of 31 December 1963 proposing the peaceful settlement of territorial disputes, ended by saying that the principal task of statesmen today is to ensure that nuclear war will not break out. How are the statesmen going about that task; what ideas guide them in it? Can the statesmen on the two sides of the Iron Curtain settle their socio-economic-political dialectic peacefully? How firm is governmental control over military hierarchies?

In previous chapters we have examined various strategies proposed for the use of nuclear weapons of mass destruction in war, and considered different kinds of deterrence as catalogued by Mr. Herman Kahn. Mr. Kahn's Deterrence II was the ability of the USA with its nuclear striking power to deter the USSR and its allies from attacking NATO Europe. We have seen that Europeans are disturbed by doubts that in all circumstances an American President would, to protect European interests, give the order for nuclear engagement which could result in a Soviet Union reprisal that would probably kill scores of millions of Americans.

Mr. Kahn points out that most Americans seem to think, rather self-righteously, that although the United States possesses in the SAC and *Polaris* submarines such a terrifying power of destruction, "We would never start a nuclear war." Nevertheless, he goes on relentlessly, the United States would be obliged to do exactly that, to start a nuclear exchange, if the Soviet Union should invade Western Europe with conventional forces and if the existing NATO conventional forces were unable to resist them.

From almost every point of view the US Government would like to avoid being faced with the alternatives, either of initiating a nuclear exchange which could become unlimited, or of failing to meet its commitment to regard an attack on a NATO ally's territory as an attack on its own. One way of lessening the likelihood of this dilemma's becoming actual would be for the European allies to strengthen their conventional forces to the point where they would be able to repulse the *presently deployed* conventional forces of the Soviet Union and its allies. If these were augmented to a point approaching general mobilization, this would betoken a war without limits, in which nuclear weapons would inevitably be engaged.

If the European governments had the will, they could strengthen their armed forces to the required degree. But there are two strong reasons why they do not do it. The first is the political unpopularity that they would incur if they greatly increased defence expenditure and imposed lengthier terms of military service on young people. These two measures, they think, would depress their economy and possibly put them, the governments, out of power at the next election. The second reason is that the military advisers of the European NATO governments, and not only in France, dislike the idea of being second-class troops armed on a lower scale, that is, without the tactical nuclear armament which the American troops have. Moreover, when allied NATO forces do get nuclear armament, they tend to think that tactical nuclear weapons are the answer to inferiority in numbers and conventional armament—a mistaken idea, as has been argued in Chapter 10. They may think that if the Russians know that all the NATO forces have tactical nuclear weapons and will use them as soon as they are attacked and that these actions will probably escalate into all-out nuclear war, then the Russians will not be tempted to venture a surprise invasion. This would make the nuclear-weapon-armed forward troops of NATO a sort of trigger, or trip-wire attached to the detonator of the world explosion (see page 128). Once the nuclear weapons started going off, the United States would be brought into the war without pause, reflection or option. Of course, for the present, the United States' control over the nuclear warheads intended for discharge or delivery by nuclear weapon vehicles in the possession of the allies would seem to be a safeguard against such a thing happening. It is very hard to judge whether the measures of control might some day prove ineffective and whether the nuclear weapons might be fired off whether the United States' consent had been given or not. But in any case, European military men who think in terms of using the tactical nuclear weapon as a device to make any kind of Soviet Union military action into a world-wide nuclear war, are indulging in most dangerous fantasies. The danger is, of course, fully recognized by the Americans, who continue to show themselves determined to resist any dispersion of the control of nuclear forces through which they might be plunged into nuclear war by the action of a reckless ally.

A new strategic concept for the employment of SAC and other nuclear-armed United States forces was announced publicly by Mr. McNamara in his speech at Ann Arbor on 16 June 1962. Previews had been given privately in NATO councils and elsewhere. It was a specific statement of the ideas of "counterforce" strategy, which simply meant that the missiles and bombers of the SAC should be aimed at USSR military units and establishments such as bomber airfields and missile launching pads, and not at cities or industrial targets. "Counterforce" purported to revert to classical strategic doctrine, long departed from by the partisans of mass destruction air warfare, that the most effective line of action in war is to destroy, or otherwise render powerless, the enemy's armed forces. When one side no longer had the means to resist, his territory and wealth would lie at the mercy of the victor in the conflict between the military forces. The vanquished would have to surrender, or agree to the victor's terms of peace.

But given the conditions of war in the nuclear-rocket age, is it really possible to conceive direct combat between national military forces, leaving the civil population relatively unharmed? Of course, a "no-cities" strategy would seem to be free of the moral obloquy attached to the policy of massive retaliation. No American can really be comfortable with the idea of supporting a military establishment which is to function, in case of war, by slaughtering hundreds of millions of Russian people. Still less can they like the idea of being exterminated in scores of millions by Russian reprisals.

The following is the most important passage in Mr. McNamara's Ann Arbor speech:

> The United States has come to the conclusion that to the extent feasible, basic military strategy in a possible general nuclear war should be approached in much the same way that more conventional military operations have been regarded in the past. That is to say, principal military objectives, in the event of a nuclear war stemming from a major attack on the Alliance, should be the destruction of the enemy's military forces, not of his civilian population.
>
> The very strength and nature of the Alliance forces make it possible for us to retain, even in the face of a massive surprise attack, sufficient reserve striking force to destroy an enemy society if driven to it. In other words, we are giving a possible opponent the strongest possible incentive to refrain from striking our own cities.

If the United States is to adopt such a strategy, clearly the United States forces must have (a) a very considerable superiority over the Soviet Union in total number of "invulnerable" missiles and aircraft, and (b) information sufficiently accurate for aiming purposes on the location of a very high proportion of the Russian ICBM's and intercontinental bombers.

It is hardly surprising that when the Russian strategists looked at the new counterforce policy, they found it an obvious disguise for the preventive war, or pre-emptive strike plans which they had previously attributed to the USA. In one of the carefully documented notes in the "RAND" edition of *Soviet Military Strategy* the following occurs:

> Soviet commentators flatly rejected any Soviet commitment to restrict the use of nuclear weapons, and denied the feasibility of avoiding the destruction of cities, especially if the Soviet Union were to use its 50- and 100-megaton weapons according to Mc-Namara's rules. The United States Government, according to Soviet comments, was trying to establish "rules" of nuclear war in order to make it more acceptable to the American people. It was asserted that "McNamara's statement shows concrete and practical evidence of preparation for a preventive war." Khrushchev expressed similar views in his speech of July 10, 1962, and asserted in addition that the new strategy represented an attempt to divert the main weight of Soviet nuclear retaliation to American overseas bases and forces.

Mr. Arthur I. Waskow, of the Peace Research Institute of Washington, has given a very cogent and extensive criticism of the counterforce strategy, together with other strategic concepts of the employment of nuclear power, in a paper originally presented to the Columbia University Research Conference on Disarmament in December 1961, and reprinted in *Survival*, May-June 1962. He remarks that the counterforce theory was worked out by Air Force strategists, in co-operation with the RAND wizards, and their industrial allies. This happened when it was realized that the Soviet ability to retaliate against the US homeland from 1958 had made "massive retaliation" and other previous theories obsolete. So some refinement of these theories which would not involve an intolerable number of megadeaths and destruction in the USA had to be found. What would be the best way to use the armaments, which are now in service in large numbers, such as the B 52 and B 58 bombers and the

*Atlas, Titan* and *Minuteman* missiles? Almost as important as the technical attributes of these vehicles is the means of obtaining accurate information on the location of USSR intercontinental striking forces, that is, their airfields and missile launching sites. Up to 1960, the U 2 high-altitude aeroplane was providing the information; after that, it was expected that the reconnaissance satellite, Samos, would be able to furnish equivalent data.

We shall not discuss the variants of the "models" which the Air Force strategists elaborated, except the one which depicts how the USA might reply, within the counterforce strategy, to an attack by the USSR on the territory of one of the European NATO allies. A less serious "provocation" might be the communist takeover of Berlin, or a Soviet-supported revolution in a Latin American country. The Air Force strategists worked it out that thermonuclear attack, or the threat of it, could be scaled to the seriousness of the provocation. If launched, it would be carefully controlled, and directed, in the first instance, against the enemy's nuclear forces.

It can be agreed that for the purpose of deterring the USSR from attacking NATO Europe, a counterforce programme for applying nuclear weapon power is greatly to be preferred to a threat to commence wholesale destruction. While the USA might, under this policy, still be the first to use nuclear weapons, the responsibility for escalating the conflict would fall on the Soviet Union.

Unless the USSR has more numerous and powerful nuclear weapons than is presently believed, they would know (even if they did not publicly acknowledge) that they would get the worst of it if they responded to the nuclear challenge by any level of exchange up to an all-out discharge of ICBM's and other means of delivering nuclear weapons. The USSR would incur what Mr. McNamara has called, in his statement of 18 February 1965 to the House of Representatives Armed Services Committee, "assured destruction." Mr. McNamara explained this term as the destruction of "the aggressor as a viable society, if he should strike first with nuclear power." He told the Committee that the US armed services had the ability to do this. Translated into more specific terms, "assured destruction" would mean the killing of one quarter to one third of the enemy population (that is, in terms of the Russian population projected to 1970 as 245 million, sixty to seventy-five million people) and the destruction of two thirds of its industrial capacity.

But Mr. McNamara also made it clear that even though the USA has the power to mete out "assured destruction" to the USSR if the nuclear conflict were pushed to the limit, the USSR would nevertheless have the power to inflict enormous losses on the USA, whatever might be done to strengthen the "damage limitation" function of the US armed forces. "Damage limitation" includes all means of defence against nuclear attack, including the active defence of counter-fire on enemy nuclear weapon vehicles installations in the USSR, anti-aircraft and anti-missiles defences in the USA, and civil defence measures, including a vast programme of shelters. Mr. McNamara presented a tabulation of the number of Americans who would probably be killed if such a catastrophic war should occur in the year 1970. (The programme for the armed forces which he presented was projected to this year in general terms, although the armed forces estimates for the year 1966 were what he was specifically explaining and defending. In this era of long "lead times" for the most powerful armaments, it is necessary to assess the current year's programme in the light of longer term plans and purposes.)

Two factors would influence the level of American fatalities in the event of all-out nuclear war in 1970. One would be whether (Case A) the attack on US cities would come at the very outset of hostilities, with practically no warning; or whether (Case B) there would be a certain delay before cities were attacked, which would enable additional defence measures to be taken, reducing fatalities. The second factor would be how much the US Government invested in all the measures of defence or "damage limitation" listed above. If there were no additional investment, 149,000,000 Americans would be killed in Case A; 122,000,000 in Case B. If twenty-five billion dollars were invested in "damage limitation" measures, 78,000,-000 would be killed in Case A; 41,000,000 in Case B. Mr. McNamara solemnly warned that nothing that could be done would be likely to reduce the fatalities below the eighty million mark in the event of a sudden attack directed at US cities.

So we have the two super-powers deterring each other from any armed aggression against themselves or their allies by the ultimate threat of mutual slaughter of eighty to a hundred million of their citizens. This could perhaps be described as deterrence under the threat of Mutual Megamurder.

One is happy to record that the United States Government recognizes the basic insanity of this state of affairs. Mr. McNamara said, in the course of the same statement:

> We see a world in which long-frozen positions and attitudes are beginning to thaw . . . and in which the struggle against Communism continues unabated. But we also see a world in which new opportunities to advance the cause of peace may arise and we intend to take full advantage of them. We have long recognized that as the arms race continues and the weapons multiply and become more swift and deadly, the possibility of a global catastrophe, whether by miscalculation or design, becomes ever more real. We also recognize that more armaments, whether they be offensive or defensive, cannot solve the dilemma. The United States and the Soviet Union as the two great nuclear powers, are the nations most directly endangered by these weapons, and we, therefore, share a common interest in seeing that they are never used. Accordingly, we intend to pursue every step, no matter how small, which might lead to a peaceful understanding with the Soviet Union that would lessen the danger to us all. And we intend to stand fast against the presently implacable animosity of Communist China until that nation, too, realizes that its security and prosperity can be better served by a more peaceful policy.

Mr. Waskow has also criticized counterforce strategy as being based on the belief that nineteenth-century rules of warfare can be applied in the nuclear-missile age, that wars can still be *won*, that the fighting elements of the nation can be kept separate from the non-combatant elements and that the latter can somehow be protected from the worst results of a thermonuclear war, namely, megamurder. It supposes that the cataclysmic power in the possession of each side could be directed and used, in a situation where tensions would be immeasurably greater than in any previous state of war or threat of war, with the cool detachment and iron control of a successful gambler at cards or in the stock market. Does all or any of this appear likely?

In discussing later the balanced deterrent strategy, which he said tended to be favoured by the Navy and Army brass in the Pentagon, Mr. Waskow said that when a balanced deterrent position was established, it would "constitute a plateau in the arms race." When both sides had reached the level of the invulnerable deterrent, they could agree to arrest the arms build-up, while trying to settle outstanding difficulties by negotiation. Perhaps the present United States Administration considers that this point has actually been reached.

President Johnson, in his message of 21 January 1964 to the Eighteen-Nation Disarmament Committee, made the following proposal:

> While we continue our efforts to achieve general and complete disarmament under effective international control, we must first endeavour to halt further increases in strategic armaments now. The United States, the Soviet Union and their respective allies should agree to explore a verified freeze of the number and characteristics of strategic nuclear offensive and defensive vehicles. For our part, we are convinced that the security of all nations can be safeguarded within the scope of such an agreement, and that this initial measure preventing the further expansion of the deadly and costly arms race will open the path to reductions of all types of forces from present levels.

At this point, let us review briefly the consequences of the Cuba episode of October 1962. Many people have thought that this may have been the culminating crisis of the Cold War and of the arms race of which it is the prime cause. It is conjectured that the agreements during 1963 on the partial nuclear test ban, the "hot line" and on abjuring nuclear weapons in space were essentially the result of the "moment of truth" which both President Kennedy and Chairman Khrushchev experienced when the decisions they had to take could have unleashed unlimited nuclear war.

A great deal has been written about the reasons which Mr. Khrushchev and his advisers may have had for attempting to establish Soviet Union intermediate-range ballistic missiles in Cuba, and about why they miscalculated. If they had succeeded, the military advantages would have been great: the complex of air missile bases in the Southern States and the

Middle West could have been brought under the fire of these IRBM's, thus raising the counterforce ability of the Soviet Union relative to that of the United States. The Soviet Union had many hundreds of IRBM's, but relatively few ICBM's, according to *The Military Balance*, 1963-64, published by the Institute of Strategic Studies. The political advantages would have been correspondingly great; the Soviet Union would have demonstrated its power to defend a Latin-American nation which joined the socialist camp, and this could have become a decisive factor for other Latin-American nations on the verge of going the same way as Cuba. A point scored against the USA by establishing bases in Cuba would have greatly increased Soviet prestige, especially within the communist bloc of nations in which the struggle for predominance between the Soviet Union and Red China was becoming acute. Mr. Khrushchev might also have used the position established in Cuba as a bargaining counter in a negotiation over Berlin and a German peace treaty —objectives far more important for him than anything in the Caribbean. All of these possible prizes must have seemed worth the risk. It was probably calculated that the bases could be established and operative before the United States had acquired sufficiently precise intelligence about them for deciding on the necessary counter-action.

But Mr. Khrushchev and his advisers miscalculated, first on the speed with which the American forces got the vital information, and secondly on President Kennedy's resolution, which they may have discounted following the Bay of Pigs fiasco and the lack of direct response to the building of the Berlin Wall the year before. They may have also reckoned that the NATO allies and the Latin-American members of the OAS, fearing an outbreak of world-wide nuclear war, would press the United States to refrain from military measures.

What happened is extensively documented history. The United States air and naval forces were completely predominant in the Caribbean, and without using nuclear weapons could have arrested the Soviet ships bringing their remaining rockets and other material for the bases; they could have destroyed the work in progress at the sites, and probably could have inflicted heavy casualties on the Russian armed forces there. What could Mr. Khrushchev have done to prevent this happening? It was feared at the time that he would put pressure on Berlin; blockade it as the USA was going to blockade Cuba. But he evidently calculated that this would be only one step removed from the direct threat of attacking the USA by ICBM's. If, in the Berlin area, where the NATO and Warsaw Pact forces were in close contact, and where many tactical nuclear weapons were deployed on both sides, conventional force were applied in a tense situation, someone might easily set off a nuclear weapon and the conflict might escalate into all-out nuclear war. American forces in Europe were far from being isolated as were the Russian forces in Cuba. Above all, given the preponderance of American power to deliver nuclear weapons intercontinentally, the destruction the Soviet Union would experience if nuclear war should break out would be such that the risk of going on would far outweigh any possible gain.

So the order to the Russian ships to alter course was given, and in due time the missiles and auxiliary equipment and the Russian military units in Cuba were withdrawn. Soviet Union propaganda tried to salvage what it could from the general defeat by stressing President Kennedy's promise not to invade Cuba if the Soviet Union withdrew its rockets and the military build-up, and rather pathetically praising Mr. Khruschev's statesmanship in saving the world from the nuclear war his Cuban gamble could have initiated.

General Thomas D. White, retired Chief of the Air Staff, writing in *Newsweek* of 14 January 1963, headed his article "Great National Orgy for Self-Congratulation." General White thought that in fact the Government and the military had not so much to congratulate themselves on; they had nearly been caught napping, and, keeping in mind Mr. Khrushchev's implacable determination to "bury" the United States, there would be another time. And Cuba still was a potential source of danger.

Also dangerous to the world's safety is the exuberance with which some Americans hailed the bloodless victory over the Soviet Union. This could be put into a proposition along these lines: "They backed down when we showed ourselves firm and resolute; they will always back down if we only take the tough line and keep ourselves strong." If such an attitude ever became accepted United States Government policy and was applied in situations where the special circumstances of the Cuban crisis were not present, it would add greatly to the danger of outbreak of nuclear war. But we can be thankful that it has become apparent that President Johnson and his advisers will never fall into this cardinal error.

The Cuban crisis and its outcome may have produced a delayed effect on the coherence of the NATO alliance. Most commentators on the events of October 1962 stress the loyalty with which the NATO allies rallied to the American decision to challenge the Soviet Union in the Caribbean. The final decision to impose the blockade was taken by President Kennedy on Sunday, 21 October. Mr. Dean Acheson, sent as a special envoy, told what had been decided to President de Gaulle during the afternoon of Monday, 22 October, approximately ten hours before President Kennedy's announcement to the nation on television. President de Gaulle is reported to have received the news with splendid loyalty, assenting without qualification to the decision of the United States, and his attitude during that time of crisis has been frequently referred to since, when other attitudes of his have not been equally acceptable to the United States and other NATO nations. One may perhaps wonder whether some of his subsequent actions taken without consultation with and contrary to the views of the USA and other NATO allies may not have been due to, or at least reinforced by, his reflection that on 21 October 1962 a decision of the utmost importance, and one that could have involved France in a nuclear war, had been taken without consulting him. It has been reported that some time later an American admiral who was conferring with the French President remarked that if the USA had had to use armed force to prevent Soviet ships reaching Cuba, they anticipated having great trouble from Soviet submarines operating in the Caribbean and western Atlantic. In that case, the US Navy woud have had to attack the bases of the Russian submarines with nuclear weapons. This specific information on how conventional armed action in the Caribbean could have escalated into nuclear war in Europe probably was not needed by President de Gaulle, who must have long since worked out for himself the possible consequences of the Cuban affair and similar clashes in the future.

On the same day, October 22, the other NATO allies were informed of the United States Government's decision by cabled letter, and the NATO council was briefed by Mr. Dean Acheson. All the allies, sooner or later, expressed the same loyal acceptance of the decision as President de Gaulle had. But the whole episode seems to demonstrate that the balance of nuclear power and the absolute urgency of decision being what they are, it is probable that if there should be a future crisis, it will be the United States which will decide what is to be done, and decide alone.

Let us now return to the problem of what policy NATO should adopt for the use of nuclear weapons. Not only has the problem not been solved to the satisfaction of the members of the alliance, but its existence is producing a divisive effect and shaking the solidity of the NATO structure. There are, broadly speaking, three policies which NATO could adopt to use the nuclear weapon as a deterrent to aggression.

Policy No. 1 would be for the USA to have full responsibility for a "strategic" response to a Soviet Union threat of or initiation of nuclear or conventional war, and for the USA also to have control over the initiation of the use of the tactical nuclear weapons with which NATO forces in Europe are armed. This, essentially, is the existing policy. It has been accepted until now, but it will probably not be valid for many years longer for reasons which nearly all European NATO members acknowledge privately, and which President de Gaulle has voiced publicly. We have seen (page 149) his view that France, and presumably any other nation which wants to retain real independence in its foreign policy, cannot rely indefinitely on protection by the US nuclear deterrent power against threats which may develop to its territory and interests. We have also seen that de Gaulle recognizes that neither France nor Britain, nor presumably Germany, could expect to build up a nuclear striking force which would approach in power and dimensions those of the USA and USSR. Yet he believes that France and other European countries could, with national resources, create forces under their national control which could give pause to any aggressor.

So Policy No. 2 would be for each of the larger NATO nations to have its own nuclear deterrent, which it could use at its own discretion to protect it against threats to its national existence or vital interests. This is the theory elaborated by General Gallois in his *Stratégie de l'Age Nucléare*.

General Gallois asks his readers whether, if it is unlikely that the United States would be willing in all cases to risk enormous devastation in order to protect the interests of European countries, it would be reasonable to rely for protection on a nuclear deterrent force possessed in common by the European members of NATO. If it were possessed in common, the decisions to employ it would have to be taken in common. Would not some nations either hesitate or refuse to use the reprisal force, fearing the total destruction which the USSR could visit on them? General Gallois makes the prime point that the effectiveness of a deterrent is the product of the power of the weapons composing it, plus the means to deliver them on the chief cities of the potential aggressor, multiplied by the known resolution of the authority having the power to order the deterrent force into action in case of invasion or nuclear attack. He doubts whether any combination of nations could act with the speed and resolution required to make credible a deterrent of limited size, such as one which the nations of Europe could create.

Any structure of nuclear defence built up on the mosaic of the European states, apart from the initial disadvantage of separating the interests of Europe from those of North America, would collapse at the first test. The credibility of a deterrent depends upon what the opponent thinks. If fifteen states had to agree before a nuclear deterrent were put into action, a calculating aggressor would not be likely to believe that it would actually be used. The deterrent power of the United States, exhibited in the Quemoy-Matsu affair and more recently in the Cuba episode, resides in the power of the President to order retaliation instantly.

Having analyzed the problem, and considered various alternatives, General Gallois came to the conclusion that for Europe, national deterrents are the only solution. They wouldn't be easy to create, and wouldn't solve all problems. But it is reasonable to believe that a nation which possessed nuclear armament would use it if there were a threat to its national existence. Under national control, a deterrent would be credible, or at least would raise a doubt in the mind of a potential aggressor. It would have the advantage that it would only be usable as a defence against nuclear blackmail or a threat of subjugation. To be effective, it would only have to represent a potential for destruction which would cancel the advantages which an aggressor could gain by taking over the country threatened. That is, national deterrents could be of limited power.

Another argument in favour of national deterrents is that as technology develops (especially in limiting the vulnerability of long-range nuclear weapon vehicles), no nation will be able to adopt a counterforce strategy against the Soviet Union, and all would be obliged to resort, for credible deterrence, to an anticities policy. National deterrent forces, of limited size, would fit in with this.

General Gallois's theories have been attacked, especially by American strategists, who argue that national deterrents will inevitably be too weak to be effective against a great nuclear power such as the USSR. Furthermore, institution of national deterrents would be disruptive of the NATO alliance. General Gallois admits the last objection, but says it would not be so serious, since the NATO alliance, like many alliances in the past, would have fulfilled its purpose for the necessary time.

More recently, criticisms of American theories on the use of nuclear weapons have been offered by Général d'Armée Beaufre. He contends that American theory goes wrong because the Americans think of how nuclear weapons *can be used* in war. But these weapons should be thought of only as a means of *dissuading* any nation from initiating war.

The latest American formula for a nuclear strategy is graduated response, announced by Mr. McNamara. This involves somehow communicating to the enemy the intended limits of this response, so that he will decide not to escalate the conflict, and so incur the "assured destruction" which the USA could launch. But, argues General Beaufre, the nuclear weapon only retains its power to deter (dissuade) if there is uncertainty in the enemy's mind as to how it will be employed: "It is peace through danger, a formula at first sight paradoxical, but which constitutes the essential arcanum of our century, so astonishing in many ways."

Well-intentioned but naïve disarmament proposals or stabilization formulae which don't recognize this law (of the necessity of uncertainty), the General argues, can only reduce the dissuasive value of nuclear weapons, to the point at which a third great war of the same kind as those which devastated Europe twice in the present century might break out.

General Beaufre contends that the continental NATO countries, having lived for years with the danger of destruction which now menaces the USA, have realized during this period that it is the danger reciprocally shared with the enemy which guaranteed the status quo. To rely once more on defence by conventional arms would be great folly. It is to be feared that too many elaborate and subtle declarations about the use of nuclear weapons will indicate a lack of resolution and annul the deterrent value. The Germans demand an atomic detonator placed close to their frontiers; France has affirmed her determination to unleash an immediate strategic retaliation to any attack, using what means she has.

This subtle argument on the need for some uncertainty to ensure deterrence appears to rest on the generalization from military experience, namely, that if any system of defence is known with a fair degree of certainty, an offensive can be designed to defeat it. But if there is uncertainty in regard to who will let off the nuclear weapons, responding to unspecified aggression, threat of provocation, is this a happy situation for the general population? When severe international tension occurs, whole populations of the biggest cities will never know from minute to minute whether or when they will be blasted into nothing. It is to be remembered that in the theory of nuclear warfare propounded by Generals Gallois and Beaufre, the nuclear weapon will be directed against the great centres of population, without ambiguity. It is difficult to imagine that the general population—of France or any other country—(if they ever thought about the matter seriously for more than two minutes) would be content to live in a "security" dependent on uncer-

tainty; a contradiction in terms which may perhaps be swal-
lowed by professionals, sufficiently imbued with a triply-dis-
tilled *mystique.*

Turning from the examination of the French theories which
justify national deterrents, we come to the point that the main
argument against them is that general dissemination of nuclear
weapons in the NATO community would be followed by their
dissemination among other countries.

For many years it has been a policy of nuclear powers to
prevent the dissemination of nuclear weapons. The subject has
been perennially debated at the United Nations. Provisions
against the dissemination of nuclear weapons are included in
the plans for general and complete disarmament of both the
USA and the USSR. They are also proposing arrangements to prevent further nuclear weapons dissemination before concrete
measures of disarmament are agreed upon. But although both
sides profess to want this sort of arrangement, progress was
blocked because of the United States' commitment to the plan
for a multilateral nuclear force for NATO, which the Soviet
Union denounced as a barely camouflaged proposal for giving
nuclear weapons to the Federal Republic of Germany.

The objection to dissemination is well known: the more nations that have nuclear weapons, the more likely it is that these
will be used in war. The difference between nuclear and conventional weapons maintained rather precariously until now
would disappear. First use by a minor nuclear-armed power
could touch off a general nuclear war in which the great
powers would loose their vast arsenal of destruction. If ownership of nuclear weapons was widespread, their use in war
would be looked on as inevitable. Without progress towards
disarmament, and a stable, peaceful world, it would become
much more difficult to prevent war than under the present balance of power and distribution of the nuclear weapons.

It is therefore quite understandable why the present nuclear
powers desire to keep the possession of nuclear weapons to
themselves, and are, in principle, opposed to a larger number
of nations getting them. The US Congress passed the McMahon
Act to forbid the Administration to give any other nation nuclear weapons or information. But in the zeal to prevent further

dissemination, diffusion or proliferation of nuclear weapons, which is enshrined in the United Nations "Irish Resolution" of 1961, no one seems to have thought much about what would happen if the nuclear powers do not within a few years begin to divest themselves of their power to destroy half the world. The Irish Resolution, and the whole idea that the spread of nuclear weapons should be arrested, is based on the assumption that the nuclear powers themselves are going to disarm in the foreseeable future. If the nuclear weapons and the danger of nuclear war are eventually to disappear, it is logical to stop the spreading of the power to start a nuclear war. But what if the nuclear "haves" don't disarm? In that case will the world remain for ever divided into nuclear powers and non-nuclear powers as at present—five nuclear powers and a hundred and twenty or so of other states which are "nuclearly under-developed," to use a favourite United Nations adjective?

It has been generally acknowledged for some years now that there are a dozen or so nations which would have the technical competence and the industrial base to become nuclear powers. The reasons they have not done so are first, the general distaste of their publics for setting up the apparatus to use this weapon of mass destruction in war, and secondly, the very great cost under present conditions of becoming a nuclear power, a nuclear power being defined as a nation which produces nuclear warheads and the means of delivering them by its own resources. Representatives of the present nuclear powers seem to consider the abstinence of the uncontaminated nations as rather like the virtue of those individuals who haven't the money to enable them to sin agreeably.

But the nations of the world cannot always be divided into nuclear sheep and non-nuclear goats. Either the existing nuclear powers must renounce and eventually abolish these weapons, to which action they are committed by UN resolution, or there will be an increasing number of nations which will possess the power to begin a nuclear exchange on their own initiative. Non-nuclear nations do not consider that the virtue and wisdom of the present nuclear powers are so extraordinary that they should be forever entrusted with the fate of the world. In this connection a glance at the history of disarma-

ment negotiations between the two world wars should be illuminating. Unequal treaties in this respect, as in most others, do
not carry a lasting obligation. That is to say, that if certain
nations insist on maintaining heavy armaments, they cannot expect other nations to refrain from arming themselves to the extent that their wealth allows and in the manner which the dangers confronting them seem to make necessary.

So much for the policy of national nuclear deterrents. The
third policy open to NATO would be to organize a nuclear deterrent force under the control of all the allies or a directorate
appointed by them. Two variations of this policy have recently
been considered. The first is that the British V-Bomber force
and the French *force de frappe,* together with a United States
component, probably of *Polaris* submarines, should constitute
the NATO nuclear deterrent force under NATO control, possibly
exercised by a directorate of the three contributing powers.
The British and French bombers would eventually be replaced
by the nuclear submarines that they are planning to construct,
with the *Polaris* missiles still being supplied by the United
States. This proposal, sometimes described as a "multinational
force," was put by President Kennedy and Prime Minister
Macmillan to President de Gaulle after the Nassau conference,
but he rejected it.

The second variation was to create a NATO multilateral nuclear force. This proposal had been under active discussion
since early 1963, and had been incubated in Washington for
some time before that. The multilateral force was to consist of
about twenty-five surface warships from which *Polaris* missiles
could be fired. As many of the European NATO countries as
possible were to participate. The ships' crews would be mixed
in nationality. This provision was to guard against a captain
and crew of a ship, all of the same nation and all inspired with
the same patriotic fervour, firing off their missiles without NATO
(or USA) authorization.

The first idea had been that the force should be made up of
nuclear submarines; their great cost and the time that it would
take to build them ruled that out. The proposal generally was
recognized as intended to solve a political problem: how to
decide and control nuclear strategy in NATO. European naval

and other military men tended to regard it generally with a good deal of scepticism. However, in default of any better idea, several of the NATO nations agreed to participate in the trial of an experimental mixed-manned ship, a destroyer lent by the US Navy. France rejected participation outright; Norway, Denmark and Canada abstained; while Great Britain, Italy and Holland agreed to go along with the study and experiment, Greece and Turkey accepted with less reserve. The plan was accepted with more satisfaction by the Federal German Republic, and this aroused the deepest suspicion in the Soviet Union. They thought that if the West Germans got to handling and familiarizing themselves with IRBM's in the multilateral force, this would be a first step towards their gaining complete possession and control of them, and the *Polaris* is an intermediate-range ballistic missile which from German territory or waters could reach the most vital targets in the western Soviet Union.

How Western Germany's possession of an independent nuclear deterrent could threaten Soviet Union interests in central Europe needs little elaboration. Soviet Union spokesmen profess to fear that once in possession of strategic nuclear weapons, the "militarists and *revanchistes*" of the Federal Republic, unreconstructed Nazis in the opinion of the Soviets, would set about recovering their lost territories now occupied by the Soviet Union and Poland. To this end, the *revanchistes* might engage conventional forces, perhaps calculating that the Kremlin authorities could no longer, without second thought, warn the West German Chancellor—as Mr. Khrushchev did—that Germany would "burn like a candle" if there were war. The Soviet Union could doubtless destroy Germany, and every sane German knows it, but it might be at the cost of having many torches lit in the Soviet Union. One has to admit that the danger against which the Soviet Union leaders inveigh must appear real to them.

Other NATO nations recognized that there would be a danger in the long term. The essential purpose of the multilateral force was to provide an alternative to national possession of nuclear armaments, to the de Gaulle-Gallois policy which we have just examined. It seemed clear that the Federal German Republic, which provided the bulk of the land force of NATO Europe, could not forever be refused entitlement to nuclear weapons if France and the United Kingdom continued to have them. Unless a NATO deterrent force could be constituted in such a way that Germany as well as other European partners in the alliance could have their proper say as to how and when the nuclear weapons would be used in Europe's defence, there was a danger that President de Gaulle's solution might be adopted. So ran the thought of the proponents of the plan for a NATO multilateral nuclear force.

However, the multilateral force does not appear to all members of the alliance as a satisfactory solution. It has a built-in contradiction. This relates to whether the United States, as one of the partners in the force, shall have a veto over its use or not. From the viewpoint of United States interests, if there were no US veto, the European allies might begin a nuclear war which the United States alone has the power to finish, and which could involve her in tremendous destruction and loss of life. The counterforce strategy, and the methods of response by nuclear weapons to a Soviet Union aggression against NATO Europe (discussed on page 210), would require centralized control of the tightest kind over all nuclear weapons owned or shared by all members of the alliance. It is thus easy to understand and sympathize with the strong objection of American strategists to nationally-owned nuclear deterrents or any system of a combined NATO nuclear force which would not allow a United States veto on firing, and a preponderant American voice in strategic planning.

This American view was expressed clearly by Secretary McNamara in his statement of 18 February 1965. He said:

> Furthermore, any such agreement we enter into must reinforce our basic policy of non-dissemination of nuclear weapons, i.e. the consent of the United States must be obtained prior to the firing of nuclear weapons. If, however, the major nations of Europe some day achieve political unity with a central political authority capable of making the decision to use nuclear weapons, the United States recognizes that this will create a new situation in which it might be appropriate to reconsider any agreement which might be made in the present circumstances. In any event, the

revision of such an agreement would be possible only with the unanimous approval of the members.

The Soviet Union doubtless felt that its apprehensions of the result of creating a multilateral force were justified by the suggestion that eventually the USA might hand over nuclear weapons to be controlled by a European political authority, in which the strongest voice might be that of Western Germany.

If the USA retained a veto on the use of the weapons of a multilateral force, there would be essentially no difference from the present state of affairs. In European eyes, the danger of the USA's compromising with the USSR in cases where vital European interests were involved would remain, and any system of deciding by some kind of majority voting whether the weapons or the force were to be used would be open to the objections cited by General Gallois (page 218).

Except for the Federal German Republic, the European countries which had originally accepted the multilateral force idea and had engaged in the studies and experiments gradually became disillusioned. It was an open secret that the Pentagon had never liked the MLF. Late in 1965 President Johnson issued instructions to the State Department not to press the plan on the European NATO partners. During 1966 press stories appeared from time to time announcing that the MLF was dead. Whether these stories reflected a firm administrative decision or not was not clear. In the disruption and confusion caused by President de Gaulle's withdrawal of French forces from the integrated NATO defensive organization, the attention of the other fourteen members of the organization was fully occupied in the attempt to reorganize and restore the solidity and effectiveness of the defence, less France. The question of a mulilateral force receded into the background, and no decision to proceed with it or to declare it finally dead was taken during the summer and autumn of 1966.

However, political and military planners were working on another approach towards giving the European partners a say in the use of nuclear weapons for the defence of NATO Europe. The idea was that while there would be no additional "hardware"—long-range rockets on ships or on land, or other "strategic" nuclear armament—the European allies would be given a greater share in the process of determining the policy and planning the strategy for the use of nuclear armaments; a share in fashioning the shape and functioning of the nuclear deterrent. In principle, such responsibilities had always been shared by all the allies, operating through the North Atlantic Council, the political body of the Alliance, and its military adjuncts. But in practice, as the nuclear weapons belonged to the United States (except for the relatively small British and French nuclear forces), the equal sharing of responsibilities tended to be on the "one horse—one rabbit" formula. Enough has been written in previous chapters to show the variety of concepts which existed at various times in the USA and in NATO as to how the nuclear weapon should be used if deterrence should fail. The allies which did not possess nuclear weapons relied on the USA nuclear umbrella, but they never really knew how and when it would be opened, and what degree of protection it would afford, if the rain came.

In justification of what might seem a lack of confidence in their allies, or an ignoring of their right to be informed and consulted, it should be said that USA military men had some reason to mistrust the security of information in NATO; data on less top-secret matters than plans for nuclear war had a way of leaking out. Furthermore, an alliance in which no nation is acknowledged leader, in which all are equal, is a most unsatisfactory organization for waging war, or planning for it.

The problem to be solved is how to share responsibility in nuclear armament matters, while avoiding an unwieldy and inefficient organ for the direction of strategy. It appears the solution is being sought by setting up a sort of inner circle in NATO. If the composition of this inner circle has been settled, it has not been disclosed. It would obviously have to include the nuclear powers, and also the Federal Republic of Germany, and possibly one or two other allies. Germany's claim to membership is based on the size of her contribution to the conventional forces of the Alliance, and also on the fact that her territory constitutes the forward zone of defence for the Alliance. It is to be hoped that the problem of the sharing of nuclear responsibilities within NATO can be solved along these lines, which should not be a bar to the hoped-for treaty on non-proliferation.

Nuclear armaments cannot in the long run provide security for the European nations under any of the policies discussed above. The reunification of Germany and the related political problems of central Europe cannot be solved by force, as this would inevitably entail the engagement of nuclear armaments carrying with them devastation on such a scale that no political object could be worth the monstrous price to be paid. The existence of this tremendous nuclear force deployed on either side of the Iron Curtain at present deters aggression, or any military adventure, and may continue to do so for some years. But it does threaten the European nations of NATO and the Warsaw Pact with obliteration, and will continue to do so as long as overkill armament exists. It is and will continue to be a tremendous economic burden. And for what purpose? Must we acknowledge that the civilized nations of the world can only be restrained from attacking one another by the threat of an immediate hell on earth?

As nuclear armaments are seen to be useless as instruments of policy and at the same time enormously dangerous, it would seem logical to get rid of as many of them as possible as soon as possible, while, in the process, *not upsetting the present equilibrium which constitutes mutual deterrence*. All nations in both alliances profess to believe this, and have subscribed to plans of disarmament which propose finally to abolish nuclear armaments. There are political leaders and thousands, perhaps millions, of ordinary citizens who believe in disarmament and are making some effort to achieve it. But, sad to say, there are also those who hold to the old belief that security is only to be guaranteed by national armies, navies and air forces. The conflict between those who sustain the traditional concept, and those who are convinced that the nuclear age has made this old concept obsolete, has up until now created an almost total impasse, a paralysis of will to move forward towards disarmament and a peaceful world. The impasse exists in the communist-ruled countries as well as in the Western democracies, as is evidenced by the speeches and writings of military and political leaders and of influential journalists. On both sides of the

Iron Curtain the question—armament or disarmament—is being weighed in the scales of debate. On both sides the scales
must dip towards disarmament before there can be real progress towards a safer world.

The main purpose of this book is to persuade military men,
especially those in high office, to think again and again of their
responsibility in this nuclear-missile age. It is argued that if
they continue to think and act in the patterns on which air war
has developed into nuclear war, they will have fallen away
from their true function as protectors of the civil population,
and will have delivered them over to mass slaughter. It is hard
to believe that the military officers who have directed the step-
by-step development of methods of warfare in the twentieth
century have ever, with full deliberation and without flinching,
faced the horror that will be the ultimate result of the course so
far followed. Doubtless they have been acting in accordance
with what they conceive to be their highest duty: to defend
their country against all enemies. But have not some of the
greatest crimes of history been perpetrated with the highest
motives? So there should be an examination of conscience by
every military man, every scientist, every government servant
engaged in the business of defence, and especially by those
who have the responsibility of advising the statesmen who
must take the decisions for peace or war. Is the continued
building up of nuclear armaments, or even their retention at
present levels, the best way to ensure the safety of the nations
they serve? In the world today the safety of any single nation
cannot really be separated from the safety of the whole community of nations.

I suppose that everyone likes to think that in pursuing the
trade or calling by which he gains his sustenance he is fulfill-
ing some necessary social function, or at least gratifying some
need or desire of his fellows. If nuclear war is entirely immoral
and illegitimate, the military officers, scientists, administrators
and armaments manufacturers engaged in preparing for that
war are all in anti-social employment. If it is legitimate and
moral, then they are carrying out a necessary task of fearful responsibility.

In seeking guidance on the moral problem of whether prepa-

ration for a nuclear war is justifiable, and whether participation
in such preparation can be approved on moral principles, we
naturally turn to the professors of ethics, the religious leaders,
and moral philosophers. A great deal has been written and
preached about the question of whether nuclear war can be
reconciled with the moral teachings of Christianity or Judaism.
It will be useful for our purpose to cite a few comments from
*God and the H-Bomb*, a symposium of opinion published in
1961 and distributed by Random House.

In a foreword, Mr. Steve Allen, the television and motion
picture celebrity, puts the moral question before the American
people (and the people of their allies) very bluntly. He writes:

> The Nazis are regarded as animals in human form because they
> gassed, shot or burned perhaps as many as six million Jews. To-
> day the people of the United States are quite prepared, if pro-
> voked, to actually burn alive *hundreds* of millions of innocent men
> and women, young and old.

The pieces which follow Mr. Allen's foreword are addressed
to various aspects of the problem, and are by eminent laymen
as well as by priests, Protestant ministers and rabbis. Perhaps
the most apposite to the theme of this book, which is the
historic development of the concepts of nuclear war, are the
articles which trace or refer to the development of Christian
thinking on war, especially the articles that discuss whether
there is any longer a case for categorizing some wars as "just,"
as was done by St. Thomas Aquinas, a judgement that was followed by Catholic theologians and moral philosophers for
many centuries.

But an answer to the question of whether wars can any
longer be regarded as just is not the end of it. If a thermonuclear war will result in the nearly total destruction of just and
unjust alike, the question of which side has the just cause and
which the unjust becomes irrelevant; the problem is not to distinguish between causes for which a thermonuclear war is to be
fought, but to prevent it happening. Obviously, no one who
believes in a just God can believe that it is his intention that
the human race shall be immolated in a thermonuclear war.

The theologian Franziskus Stratmann, O.P., writes:

. . . the deliberate killing of innocent persons is "murder" (according to international law, noncombatants, i.e. the entire civil population, are considered to be "innocent persons"). Thus an atomic war would lead to mass murder more surely than the type of mass bombings hitherto employed.

Stratmann later observes:

> The extreme limit to which one may tolerate atomic armament is its being set up as a deterrent . . . [If] the opponent should nevertheless start a war, in my opinion, uncontrollable atomic weapons may even then not be used in defense, because this means is bad in itself. And the end does not justify the means. The principle laid down by Catholic moralists . . . that the good to be expected from the defensive war must outweigh its enormous damage, cannot be realized by a defense carried out with atomic weapons.

The final quotation which I shall give from *God and the H-Bomb,* which on almost every page contains arguments on the moral problem of nuclear warfare calculated to make all but the wilfully blind see, is, appropriately, from Jerusalem. It is by Israel Goldstein of the Jewish Agency. He wrote:

> Thousands of years of civilization have taught us that what is morally wrong is in the long range insane, and what is morally right in the long range is practically wise. Let us resolve, each for his own sake, as well as for the sake of the world, that never again shall nuclear power be used for destruction . . . let us not fail to recognize the small steps on the long and difficult road. For every step is important as long as it is in the right direction—looking to the ultimate goal of total disarmament.

Another book in which are collected a number of essays on the moral problems relating to the use of nuclear weapons is *Nuclear Weapons and the Conflict of Conscience* edited by John C. Bennett, published 1962. Among the authors are social and political scientists, as well as theologians and professors of ethics. Dr. Paul Ramsey is the only one among the seven authors who can find any moral justification for nuclear war. In his essay "The Case for Making a Just War Possible," he gives a succinct statement of the doctrine of the Church in past centuries, and comments:

It was never supposed that non-combatants were morally immune from indirect injury or death on however colossal a scale, if there is proportionate grave reason for doing this.

He later goes on to say:

Acts of war which directly intend and directly effect the death of non-combatants are to be classed morally with murder, and are never excusable. If the excuse is that victory requires this, then we would be saying that the end justifies an intrinsically wrong means or that men may be murdered in order to do good.

This dictum would seem to condemn a great deal of the massive bombing of German and Japanese cities in World War II, recorded in Chapters 4 and 5.

Printed on the dust-cover of *God and the H-Bomb* is a rather discouraging comment by Congressman Chet Holifield, Chairman of the Joint Committee on Atomic Energy. He says:

Its [the book's] over-all content will no doubt be received with approval by minds made receptive by adherence to Judaic-Christian and some Asiatic religious principles. It will not be convincing, in my opinion, to those minds that have been exclusively indoctrinated with atheistic communism.

To this one might reply that while Communists would not respond to religious exhortations, they use the same kind of moral arguments against the use of nuclear weapons in war as are contained in *God and the H-Bomb,* and have been doing so since they began their "Ban-the-Bomb" campaign in 1946. Of course, the purpose of this campaign was mainly to serve Soviet Union interests in world politics and defence. The mere declaration that the nuclear weapon will be abolished, without any apparatus for verifying that nuclear weapons and their vehicles have really been destroyed, would be no protection for the world against the menace of devastating nuclear war. But the slogan of "Ban the Bomb," crude and deceptive as it is, seems to have aroused sympathetic response in the majority of non-aligned peoples. An examination of the voting lists on any of the United Nations resolutions relating to the use of nuclear weapons in war and to nuclear testing will show that this is a fact. Why? The North American and European peoples have become acclimatized to the changing ideas of air warfare. Others, who have not had this experience, accept less readily the prospect of being incinerated in scores of millions. They do not forget that when the atomic bomb was used it was used against an Asiatic nation, and they probably feel uneasily that the "imperialists" would have fewer scruples against using it against a nation of coloured people than against Caucasians. The Soviet Union, by propagandizing throughout the years for the unconditional removal of the means of waging nuclear war, has reinforced its self-proclaimed status as a peace-loving nation, and has done its best to create for the United States the image of a bomb-loving nation.

# 15

## THE PROSPECTS FOR DISARMAMENT

In 1963 hopeful people thought that they might be witnessing the beginning of a halt to the arms race, that the course of history might be turning, and that the world could gradually be freed from the terror of a nuclear holocaust. But as 1964, 1965 and 1966 have passed with no further move in the direction of disarmament, some have begun to fear that the production of the engines of megamurder will go on, and at a more frenetic tempo, until in the end men's nerves will imperiously call for action, an end to the waiting and fearing. But this could be the end of everything for hundreds of millions.

There is still hope that the great nations can begin to move again to ease international tensions, and to limit the armaments build-up. But the decisions that can lead to a safer world should be taken soon, or it may be too late, and the trend towards more armaments and nuclear war will become irreversible.

The break in the pattern of increasing stresses came some seven months after the Cuba crisis. It dates from President Kennedy's speech on 10 June 1963 to The American University, in Washington. It was after this speech, received with relief and applause by the USSR, that the moves started which produced the signature of the Moscow Treaty banning nuclear testing, and the agreements on the hot line and the preclusion of nuclear weapons from outer space. These moves could well be the prelude to other, more important moves towards real peace and disarmament. The thoughts expressed in this speech were so vital that it is essential to quote it in part here.

> Some say that it is useless to speak of peace or world law or world disarmament—and that it will be useless until the leaders of the Soviet Union adopt a more enlightened attitude . . .
>
> But I also believe that we must re-examine our own attitude—as individuals and as a nation—for our attitude is as essential as theirs. . . . First examine our attitude towards peace itself. Too many think it is unreal. But that is a dangerous, defeatist belief. It leads to the conclusion that war is inevitable—that mankind is doomed—that we are gripped by forces we cannot control.
>
> And second; let us re-examine our attitude towards the Soviet Union. It is discouraging to think that their leaders may actually believe what their propagandists write.

President Kennedy then went on to summarize certain passages in the recently-published book *Soviet Military Strategy*, edited by Marshal Sokolovsky. These were to the effect that the American imperialists were preparing to unleash a preventive war, and that the aims of the United States were to enslave European and other countries economically and politically. President Kennedy said that it was sad to read these statements and to realize the gulf between the two nations. (Or the mirror reflection of attitudes between the militarists of the two sides? These militarists include the politicians and functionaries who follow the "hard-nosed" line in all dealings with and thoughts about the adversary super-power.) The President continued:

> It is also a warning—a warning to the American people not to fall into the same trap as the Soviets, not to see only a distorted and desperate view of the other side, not to see conflict as inevitable, accommodation as impossible and communication as nothing more than as exchange of threats . . .
>
> . . . [Both] the United States and its allies, and the Soviet Union and its allies, have a mutually deep interest in a just and lasting peace and in halting the arms race. Agreements to this

end are in the interests of the Soviet Union as well as ours—and even the most hostile nations can be relied upon to accept and keep those treaty obligations, which are in their own interest.

The stark alternatives before humanity, and more especially before the United States and its allies on one side and the Soviet Union and its allies on the other, are either a continuation of the arms race and the cold war which is the excuse for it, or else reaching understandings for maintaining and strengthening peace, first between the two great alliances, and eventually between all nations. Such understandings must halt the arms race, and as quickly as possible must dismantle the horrific apparatus of megamurder that has been built up on both sides of the Iron Curtain.

What are the prospects for achieving these understandings? We can begin to answer this question by examining the position reached in the disarmament negotiations which for the last seven years have been carried on in Geneva, supplemented by discussions in the United Nations in New York. On page 176 the agreements reached in 1963 are cited. These are the treaties signed at Moscow, prohibiting tests of nuclear weapons in the atmosphere, in outer space, and under water; the so-called "hot line" agreement for a direct communication link between Washington and Moscow, to allow rapid consultation in a crisis, and so to ensure that war would not break out through a misunderstanding of intentions; and the agreement not to put weapons of mass destruction into outer space.

The Eighteen-Nation Disarmament Committee met at Geneva from January until September 1964, with a month's recess. Then the disarmament discussions shifted to the United Nations, in the expectation that there would be the annual review of the subject, complete with hortatory resolutions. However, as mentioned on page 182, disputes over the payment of the costs of UN peace-keeping operations disrupted the normal proceedings, and the usual debate on disarmament in the First (Political) Committee did not take place. However, there were references to the problems of disarmament in speeches in the general debate with which the assembly opened. Mr. Gromyko, Foreign Minister of the USSR, in his statement showed a change of emphasis which was widely noticed. Ever since Mr. Khrushchev had introduced the Soviet Union formula for general and complete disarmament during the UNGA of 1959, USSR spokesmen had been declaiming that complete disarmament in four years was the only way in which the world could be made safe from the perils of nuclear warfare. They had been demanding, whether sincerely or not, that the negotiations should concentrate on the rapid working out of a programme to put general and complete disarmament into effect. But while Mr. Gromyko, in his statement of 6 December 1964, cursorily reiterated this standard USSR position, he had more to say about partial and preliminary measures of disarmament—collateral measures in the terminology of the ENDC. He followed up his speech by circulating a memorandum on "Measures for the further reduction of international tension and limitation of the arms race"—the USSR preferred list of collateral measures. It would be encouraging if we could be sure that the Soviet Government has concluded that the "great leap forward" of general and complete disarmament is not the most feasible way to move towards a peaceful and disarmed world, but that, on the contrary, it will be more profitable to move forward by smaller steps, opening the way, as confidence is increased, to more substantive measures of disarmament.

Since the United States and the Soviet Union were hardly on speaking terms because of the peace-keeping costs dispute, for some time it could not be settled how to continue disarmament negotiations. Eventually it was agreed to hold sessions of the United Nations Disarmament Commission. This is a committee of the whole of the UN Membership, and the scope of discussions in it is about the same as in the more usual forum, the First (Political) Committee. The last time it had met was in 1960, to determine what should be done to resume negotiations after the Ten-Nation Disarmament Committee had broken off talks in June 1960, through the walk-out of the USSR and its allies, as recounted on page 172.

The meetings of the UNDC lasted about two months, and, after an interval during which it was uncertain whether the USSR would return to the disarmament negotiating table, it was agreed to reconvene the ENDC, which met from about mid-July 1965 to early September. There followed a recess, as had become standard practice, to allow for the discussions of disarmament in the 20th UN General Assembly. The General Assembly passed several resolutions on the subject, intended to serve as guidance to the ENDC, which was requested to reassemble and continue with its work. It did so on 27 January 1966, continuing, with a recess from 10 May until 14 June, to allow for consultations between delegations and their governments, until shortly before the convening of the 21st UN General Assembly.

During these meetings of the several bodies the main stress has been laid on the urgent need to get an international agreement to stop the proliferation of nuclear weapons, and another to put an end to underground testing of nuclear weapons. The latter would complete the Moscow Treaty, which had not prohibited testing in this environment. Both of these measures fall into the category of "Arms Control" (as defined on page 163) rather than disarmament. The emphasis on the need to agree on them as a first step, is a sign that those who have been closely concerned with disarmament negotiations have tacitly agreed that while general and complete disarmament remains the eventual goal, it is necessarily a distant one, and that what is important now is to agree on some measure or measures which will help to bring the arms race to a halt. These should be followed by other measures which, even if limited in degree, would in fact reduce the stocks of nuclear and other armaments in national arsenals, and thus begin the process of disarmament. I shall therefore give a brief account of the position reached in the negotiations on non-proliferation, and the prohibition of underground nuclear tests as of November 1966. I shall also mention some other proposals which have been under discussion in the ENDC and the United Nations, which can be described as "collateral," preliminary, or "Arms Control."

On pages 221 to 223, in the context of a critique of the various possibilities for policies for nuclear armaments in NATO, I have set out the main reasons why it has been agreed by the present nuclear powers (with the exception of the People's Re-

public of China) that the dissemination of nuclear weapons*
would be a most undesirable development, which ought to be
prevented. If further proliferation or dissemination of nuclear
weapons takes place, it could result in upsetting the present
balance of deterrence on which we rely to prevent nuclear war,
or indeed any large-scale war. The following are other important points relating to this problem.

When, as has been the case in the European theatre since
1948, the antagonists are clearly identified, in a two-polar confrontation of two super-powers leading coalitions, it is relatively simple to foresee possible threats to security, and determine what is necessary to deter them. But if, in the course of
the next two, three or x decades several other nations should
develop into major or minor nuclear powers, it will become
very much more difficult to predict whether and how nuclear
weapons could be used in response to clashes of interest or
threats to security. The simple balance of deterrence as it now
exists will exist no longer. The sort of complex situation which
could become increasingly prevalent with the multiplication of
nuclear powers, ambitious and with an inflated notion of their
military strength, can be illustrated by projecting the position
of Communist China. In the recent past, she has had the assurance of Soviet Union support if she were attacked. But it is not
certain today—and probably will be less so tomorrow—that if
she should become embroiled in hostilities with the USA, and
the latter should escalate the conflict by using nuclear weapons,
the USSR would risk the chances of nuclear war. Looking at the
hypothetical situation in another way, the United States might
decide that they could safely use tactical nuclear weapons
against superior Chinese manpower, calculating that the Soviet
Union would not intervene. And the USA could be mistaken.

Consider the tensions and hostilities existing between nations
in various geographical regions, and note that some or many of
them can become independent nuclear powers. The NATO and

* "Non-proliferation" has become accepted as a more comprehensive term
than "non-dissemination," since the former would cover the event of a
non-nuclear nation developing a nuclear weapon without specific outside
aid, while "dissemination" would have the more restricted meaning that
some nuclear power had either given a non-nuclear nation the weapons or
assistance in making them.

Warsaw Pact alliances may disintegrate, and the technically-advanced non-nuclear nations included in them may decide to furnish themselves with nuclear armament. It is apparent that if these transformations are allowed to occur, the dangers and insecurities illustrated in the relatively simple Chinese case could be multiplied manifold.

If this proliferation of nuclear power should occur, it would follow that the nuclear arm would more and more be regarded as one of the kinds of armament that would be employed in warfare. Or, as it is sometimes expressed, tactical nuclear weapons would become "conventional." And, as has been argued in previous pages, and is contended by more writers on the subject, once nuclear weapons are used in a "tactical" situation, there is no cut-off point in size. There is nothing to stop the successive use of more and more powerful weapons until the largest and most powerful are brought into play, and there is all-out nuclear war.

Non-dissemination, or non-proliferation, has been on the agenda of the ENDC, as a collateral measure, since 1962. However, the explosion of a nuclear device by the People's Republic of China in October 1964, which has been followed by their testing of other nuclear weapons, has focussed the attention of the members of the United Nations on the problem. The Chinese authorities announced, after their break-through, that they would never be the first to use the nuclear weapon. This did not greatly reassure China's neighbours, especially India, which could compare this promise with the Chinese endorsement of the peaceful principles of Bandoeng—and what had happened in 1962. So there is an incentive for India, and perhaps Japan, to become nuclear powers. They both have the capacity to make the bomb, and to acquire the means of delivering it. After them could come Pakistan; in the Middle East Israel and the United Arab Republic—perennial enemies; and in Europe perhaps Sweden and Switzerland. Several authoritative books have been published on the subject of how nuclear weapons could spread throughout the nations, and the chances of preventing this. The latest is *Must the Bomb Spread?* by Leonard Beaton; others are listed in the bibliography.

The United Nations Disarmament Commission in June 1965

passed a resolution calling on the ENDC to give priority in its discussions to developing an agreement on the non-proliferation of nuclear weapons. Most of the time of the ENDC in its ensuing two-month session was devoted to this subject.

The British and Canadian disarmament organizations had been working since early 1965 on drafts of a treaty to achieve this purpose, and began comparing their texts while the UNDC was still in progress. The USA also produced one, and a consolidation of the three was submitted to the disarmament conference in Geneva on 17 August 1965. The Soviet Union lost little time in pointing out that it would not provide a satisfactory basis for a treaty, since it did not categorically prohibit creation of a collective nuclear force such as the Multilateral Nuclear Force which had been discussed by NATO. According to the USSR, the creation of such a force would open the way for "militarists and *revanchistes*" to make the Federal German Republic into an independent nuclear power. While it was true that the USA text was so drawn as to permit the creation of a multilateral nuclear force within NATO, the US delegate explained that this could only come about if a present nuclear power were to turn over its entire stock of nuclear weapons to a collective entity and voluntarily renounce its rights of veto over the collective force. But this would only occur if a European political entity were set up with sufficient authority to speak for all the participating nations in such a vital decision as the use of nuclear weapons. The USA delegation maintained that in all circumstances the American veto would be maintained over the use of US nuclear weapons in a multilateral force and that the Germans would not have "access" to the secrets of construction of nuclear warheads. All these explanations convinced the Russians not a whit. For the rest of the ENDC sessions little substantive progress was registered.

When the discussion of non-proliferation began in the 20th UN General Assembly, the USSR produced a draft treaty which they felt would completely block the way to the acquisition of nuclear weapons by the Federal German Republic. The Soviet Union treaty was very tightly drawn and included a provision that the states possessing nuclear weapons should not accord to states not possessing such weapons the right to participate in their control or use. Representatives of NATO objected that this provision of the USSR draft purported to prohibit certain existing arrangements between the USA and its allies involving the defensive use of nuclear weapons. The USSR representative did not publicly dispute such an interpretation. Discussion of the subject went on for several weeks, and in the end a resolution was adopted, almost unanimously, which called for all states "to take all steps necessary for the early conclusion of a treaty preventing the proliferation of nuclear weapons," and for the ENDC to reconvene and get on with negotiating it. The principles upon which the treaty should be based included the following: that it should be "void of any loopholes" (meaning that it should prohibit an MLF or other exception to non-proliferation) and that it should "embody an acceptable balance of mutual responsibilities and obligations of the nuclear and non-nuclear powers." Debate had made it clear that the non-aligned, non-nuclear nations thought that if they were to promise not to acquire nuclear weapons, the nuclear powers should give some sort of guarantee not to use the nuclear weapons against them and should agree upon and put into effect some real measures of nuclear disarmament which would halt or at least check the course of the arms race. But the measure to which the non-aligned nations attached the greatest importance, and which they urged should accompany or closely follow a non-proliferation agreement, was the stopping of all further testing of nuclear weapons; making the Moscow Nuclear Test Cessation treaty comprehensive by prohibiting underground testing.

During the seven months of its 1966 sessions the Eighteen-Nation Disarmament Committee devoted most of its effort to the questions of non-proliferation and underground nuclear testing. Progress was painfully slow, but, as the members of the Committee reported to the 21st UN General Assembly in October, there was a clarification of positions on both questions. The USSR pointed out that the language of the US draft treaty left "loopholes" (their favourite metaphor) for proliferation; particularly for the Federal Republic of Germany to acquire "access" to nuclear weapons, through possible arrangements for a NATO multilateral nuclear force. Through such "access" (a term never precisely defined) "revanchistes" and "militarists" would eventually acquire possession of nuclear weapons, and West Germany would become another independent nuclear power. This would indeed be proliferation, and the USSR was determined it should never be allowed to happen.

The United States representatives, and those of the UK, Italy and Canada, pointed to the impossibly restrictive language of the USSR draft, which would have prevented members of the alliance which did not possess nuclear weapons having any voice in the alliance's nuclear policy and strategy. It also would have prohibited the existing arrangements under which, if war came, USA nuclear weapons, in peace held tightly under USA control, could be put to use in vehicles owned by the non-nuclear allies.

One notable feature of the discussions was that, while representatives of the USSR and its allies would periodically deliver denunciations of the United States "aggression" in Vietnam, couched in familiar agitprop terms, the leaders of the USSR delegation made it clear that their strong opposition to the USA on the Vietnam question would not prevent their continuing negotiation on a non-proliferation treaty, and if possible reaching agreement on its terms.

Early in October 1966, shortly after the opening of the 21st General Assembly, Mr. Gromyko had a long interview with Secretary Rusk. The two foreign ministers continued their talks in Washington. Subsequent cautious comment by both sides allowed it to be deduced that the long and repetitious discussions in Geneva had borne some fruit, and that each side felt that the other was prepared to bridge the remaining gap between the opposing positions. After his subsequent interview with President Johnson, Mr. Gromyko said to reporters: "We discussed questions relating to disarmament problems, among them the question of proliferation of nuclear weapons. It looks like both countries, the United States and the Soviet Union, are striving to reach agreement to facilitate an international agreement on this question . . . exchange of views on this question will be continued." And President Johnson, in his press conference on 13 October, said, in a generally hopeful passage about improvement in USA-Soviet Union relations: "We have hopes that we can find some language that will protect the national interests of both countries and permit us to enter into the thing that I think we need most to do—that's the non-proliferation agreement."

When discussion of the subject began in the First Committee of the UNGA, Ambassador Federenko for the USSR and Ambassador Goldberg for the USA led off, each expressing cautious hopes for progress in continued bilateral negotiations to find agreed language. This was followed up by the almost unanimous passage of a resolution, co-sponsored by the USSR and the USA, calling on all states to do nothing to hamper the conclusion of a non-proliferation treaty.

The omens looked brighter for an agreement than they had for years. If a non-proliferation treaty should indeed be concluded between the USA and the USSR and their respective allies in NATO and the Warsaw Pact, what could follow? It is expected that, as happened when the Moscow Nuclear Test Cessation Treaty was agreed, a great majority of the members of the United Nations would hasten to add their signatures to those of the originators of the treaty. Some of the non-aligned nations not possessing nuclear weapons have expressed reservations, and call for balancing obligations on the part of the nuclear powers. As previously mentioned, their principal demand is that the nuclear powers should follow a non-proliferation agreement by real disarmament, adopting and putting into effect some of the proposals which will be briefly described in the following pages. But first we might look at another problem —which can be simply expressed: What will be the use of a non-proliferation agreement, or any other relating to disarmament, if the People's Republic of China is not party to it?

The world has been concerned by the absence of China from the Geneva negotiations, ever since they began. It has always been perfectly well realized by the negotiators that general and complete disarmament, their final goal, cannot be reached unless China eventually becomes a party to the negotiations, and to any agreements for really extensive disarmament. But it has unfortunately been clear that up to the present, and probably for several years to come, there have been and will be great obstacles to bringing China to the disarmament table. The main obstacle is the hostility between the United States and the

People's Republic of China (PRC), which has resulted in keeping it out of the United Nations. The United States, of course, is not alone in greatly disliking the communist régime on mainland China, nor is the PRC's absence from the United Nations and disarmament negotiations the sole unfortunate result.

It has been described how the emergence of China as a nuclear power has complicated the balance of deterrence (see page 240). The Chinese took a further step along the road to acquiring an effective nuclear force, carrying out their fourth nuclear test explosion on 27 October 1966. The fission-type nuclear weapon was carried about 400 miles to a target area by a guided missile. This experiment showed China to be slightly in advance of the progress in the development of nuclear weapons and their vehicles which had been forecast by USA military authorities. Secretary McNamara had told the NATO Council of Ministers in December 1965 that

> [The Chinese] appear to be making an intensive effort to develop a medium-range missile which possibly could become operational as early as 1967. It is estimated they could probably deploy several launchers by 1968 or 1969, and several dozen by 1976. It is probable that they have already begun an intercontinental ballistic missile programme. This programme could result in an initial deployment as early as 1975. (*New York Times*, 29 Oct. 1966)

For some time USA strategists have been taking future Chinese nuclear capabilities into account in their calculations and hypotheses. For instance, some of them deduce that the Chinese nuclear threat will be of relatively minor dimensions for the next decade and that therefore it might be worth while to build up an anti-ballistic missile (ABM) defence which could neutralize the comparatively few missiles China could throw at the USA. It is generally thought that the much greater USSR missile potential would make effective ABM defence against them practically impossible.

These developments have of course reinforced the previously held view that the People's Republic of China should be taking part in the disarmament negotiations. There have been rumours that the subject was broached by the American ambassador during one of the periodical conversations which he holds with his PRC homologue. The latter is understood to have rejected the suggestion contumeliously. But a more ambitious effort to secure Chinese participation was made early in 1966. This followed the passage of a resolution in the 20th UN General Assembly, which requested a group of non-aligned nations to carry out preliminary studies for the convening of a world disarmament conference. This was not to be under the auspices of the United Nations. It was thought by this device that it would be possible to remove one of the obstacles to Chinese attendance. But when the proposal was conveyed to the PRC, with the utmost diplomatic discretion, it was rejected out of hand. The attitude of the Chinese régime to the current disarmament proceedings has been set out more than once in statements published in the press. The most recent pronouncement occurred in the communiqué published 28 October 1966, which was mainly devoted to announcing the successful test of the nuclear-tipped missile. The statement about disarmament ran:

> The imperialists headed by the United States and the revisionists with the leadership of the Communist Party Soviet Union as their centre working hand in glove are now stepping up their collaboration and contriving to strike a bargain on the question of so-called prevention of nuclear proliferation so as to maintain their nuclear monopoly and sabotage the revolutionary struggle of the people of various countries. China's purpose in developing nuclear weapons is precisely to oppose the nuclear monopoly and nuclear blackmail by the United States and the Soviet Union, acting in collusion . . .
>
> The conducting of necessary and limited nuclear tests and the development of nuclear weapons by China are entirely for the purpose of defence, with the ultimate aim of destroying the nuclear weapons. We solemnly declare once again that at no time and in no circumstances will China be the first to use nuclear weapons.
>
> As in the past, the Chinese people and Government will continue to carry on an unswerving struggle, together with all the other peace-loving peoples and countries of the world, for the noble aim of completely prohibiting and destroying the nuclear weapons. (*New York Times*, 28 Oct. 1966)

As indicated in the last sentence, the PRC's standard reaction to suggestions that they should participate in disarmament negotiations is the counter-proposal that a world conference of all heads of states should be held, for the purpose of reaching an agreement to destroy all nuclear weapons and their means of delivery. In brief, Communist China takes the same position that Communist Russia used to take in the late 1940's, with their own variations of invective. Nevertheless, hopeful viewers of the international scene, including disarmers, still think it probable that one day, possibly when their nuclear weapons programme has reached a fairly advanced stage, China will come to the disarmament negotiating table. This possibility would seem to be tied in with the solution of the question of the People's Republic's admittance to the United Nations; a complicated problem which it is not appropriate to discuss here.

Let us now revert to the discussion of what further steps towards disarmament might be taken, if a non-proliferation treaty is achieved. We have noted briefly the views of the non-aligned, non-nuclear nations about this. In particular, they think that a minimum *quid pro quo* for their promise to abstain from acquiring nuclear weapons would be for the nuclear powers to conclude an agreement to stop all further nuclear testing, including underground testing.

Ever since the treaty prohibiting nuclear tests in the air, the sea and space was signed in August 1963, non-nuclear states have been urging that the treaty should be completed by banning underground tests also. The argument is that nuclear testing is for the purpose of developing new and potentially more destructive forms of nuclear weapons; hence it is one of the more blatant manifestations of the arms race. While underground testing goes on, it signifies that whatever the superpowers may say about their devotion to the ideal of disarmament, what they are actually doing is continuing to pile up nuclear armaments. Furthermore, underground testing is expensive, and technically rather difficult. So, to allow testing underground while prohibiting it in the air constitutes a discrimination in favour of the nuclear sophisticates. How this operates is demonstrated by the positions taken by France and China, latest members of the "nuclear club." President de

Gaulle's policy is that France shall simply ignore the existing three-environment test-prohibition treaty. However, in deference to strong protests by African countries about air testing in the Sahara, later French tests were carried out underground. We have already noted the view of the People's Republic of China, as expressed in their communiqué of 28 October 1966, announcing their fourth nuclear weapons test.

The Eighteen-Nation Disarmament Committee has, regrettably, made no real progress towards an agreement to stop underground testing, either in its meetings in 1964, 1965 or in 1966. What causes the deadlock is the opposed positions of the United States and the Soviet Union as to what is necessary in order to verify that no underground tests have taken place. The Soviet Union declares that it is possible to detect and identify all significant underground explosions from outside the territory of the nation testing—just as nuclear explosions in the other environments could be detected from outside the territory of any delinquent state which might breach the treaty. The United States, supported by the United Kingdom, and other Western nations which have made a serious scientific study of the problem, maintain that while the means of detecting underground tests at great distances by seismological and other scientific means have been greatly improved in the last ten years, information obtained from these devices alone cannot be relied upon to give positive assurance that no underground testing in violation of an agreement could take place without being detected.

In the 1965 and 1966 sessions of the ENDC, United States and British representatives described the improved methods of detecting underground nuclear explosions at a distance. The greatest improvement was achieved by deploying large arrays of seismometers in certain critical geographic areas. But in spite of the improvement in the instruments, and better interpretation of the records they produce, the British and American scientists working in this field state that whatever further advances in distant detection may be brought about by following this line, there will still be a residue of events which it will be impossible to identify as either earthquakes or explosions. Therefore some on-site inspections should be provided for in the eventual treaty to prohibit underground nuclear tests, to provide full assurance that it could not be clandestinely violated by any party.

Soviet Union representatives, however, stick firmly to the position they have held since 1962: viz., that national means of detection would give entirely adequate verification of compliance, and that the USA only wants to make on-site inspections for purposes of espionage. The argument of the USSR is weakened by their refusal of frequently repeated requests of the other members of the ENDC to demonstrate, in a sub-committee of scientists, what means they use to detect distant underground tests, for which they claim results so superior to those which Western scientists have found possible to achieve.

The non-aligned participants in the ENDC have made various suggestions, in the course of the negotiations, with the hope of breaking the deadlock. Among these suggestions are that there might be an agreement to stop underground tests above a certain magnitude, which it could be agreed would be likely to be detected and identified. Swedish representatives have begun to organize a "nuclear detection club" to consist of nations not possessing nuclear weapons, who would exchange seismological information from a great many quarters of the globe, which could improve the possibilities of detecting and identifying underground nuclear explosions. But no suggestion so far made seems likely to break the deadlock.

Non-aligned nations, both in the ENDC and in the United Nations disarmament debates, have shown discouragement and exasperation in the face of the rigidity of the opposed positions of the super-powers. Several of them go so far as to suggest, privately, that neither the USA nor the USSR really wants to stop underground testing, and that the dispute over methods of verification is really an elaborate comedy played out between them, to camouflage their real reasons for not wishing to complete a treaty.

Besides the non-proliferation and underground test ban problems, the Eighteen-Nation Disarmament Committee has for some years had before it a series of other proposals by the United States and a different series proposed by the Soviet Union for measures preliminary to disarmament. These, as mentioned, are termed "collateral measures" in the vocabulary of the conference. According to their sponsors, they are all intended to reduce tensions, slow down the arms race, and pave the way for further advance towards the goal of general and complete disarmament. Unfortunately, there is no agreement as yet by both sides on which, if any, of these measures it would be profitable to negotiate.

President Johnson put the following five proposals, some of which were new and some old, before the ENDC when it began its 1964 sessions and renewed them, with slight variations, in January of 1966. They included stopping the production and development of strategic nuclear weapons vehicles (called in disarmament jargon "The Freeze"); stopping the production of fissionable material for nuclear weapons, and turning over a quantity of this fortified uranium for peaceful uses (called respectively "The Cut-off" and "Reconversion"); setting up a system of observation posts in mid-Europe which would prevent surprise concentration or mobilization of forces; and of course, non-proliferation of nuclear weapons and underground test cessation. Later there was added a proposal for the simultaneous destruction of equal numbers of United States and Soviet Union bombers of a type, which though becoming obsolescent, could carry the nuclear bomb over medium ranges. This was nicknamed by the British "The Bomber Bonfire."

The Freeze, Cut-off and Reconversion and the Bomber Bonfire have received some favourable notice by the non-aligned participants in the ENDC, particularly since they are seen as measures which the nuclear powers might take to balance the obligations not to make or acquire nuclear weapons which the other parties to a non-proliferation treaty would assume. But the Soviet Union representatives have found reasons to reject all of these ideas and to refuse to negotiate seriously on them. The Freeze, they say, would not be disarmament, and nuclear powers would retain weapons with which they could unleash a nuclear war, yet the controls for verification of the measure would inevitably disclose the most important USSR defence secrets, leaving their nation vulnerable to destruction or "nuclear blackmail." In rejecting these measures, by attacking the verification provisions, the Soviet Union negotiators' favourite formula is that there would not be control over disarmament, but espionage.

The same objections are raised to Cut-off and Reconversion. As for the Bomber Bonfire, the USSR countered the USA idea by proposing that *all* bombers of every category should be destroyed in some agreed period of time. This, they knew, would not be accepted. The United States representatives tried to keep the idea open for negotiation by letting it be known that the bonfire idea could be extended to take in missiles as well as bombers and other categories of armaments. This met no response from the Soviet Union. The idea of setting up observation posts in the territories on each side of the Iron Curtain and exchanging military missions, all with the object of reducing the possibility of surprise attack and reducing existing tensions, seemed like a possible starter for a while in 1964. Then the USSR made their acceptance of this plan conditional on the reduction and elimination of military forces in Western Europe, which is unacceptable to the NATO partners, and the idea has been dormant ever since.

Mr. Gromyko's December 1964 exposé of the Soviet Union's collection of measures leading to the reduction of international tension and limitation of the arms race, as they describe them, includes the following:

(1) *Withdrawal or cut-back of "foreign troops"* (i.e. troops of one nation stationed on the territory of another);
(2) *Dismantling of foreign military bases;*
(3) *Prohibition of the use of nuclear weapons.*

During the meeting of the United Nations Disarmament Commission in 1965, the Soviet Union delegation introduced one resolution inviting the Commission to recommend action in accordance with the first two of these propositions, and a second calling for a world conference to be organized to produce a treaty prohibiting the use of nuclear weapons. The representatives of the United States and its allies pointed out that if "foreign troops" were withdrawn and "foreign bases" were dismantled, this would destroy the defensive power of NATO. The effect of the provisions of the second draft would be to destroy the credibility of the nuclear deterrent and to confer strategic superiority on communist nations which had larger conventional forces in being, and had no need of "foreign" bases if they should feel the need to extend the benefits of communism to unwilling neighbours.

As the debate continued through the lengthy session of the UNDC, the USSR delegation apparently concluded that they had miscalculated the support their resolutions would attract. Several representatives of non-aligned nations pointed out that any nation had a sovereign right to invite the forces of another nation to be stationed on its own territory in the interests of its own defence. The "Ban-the-Bomb" resolution would probably have got a majority if it had been put to the vote, as a similar resolution sponsored by Ethiopia and other Afro-Asian countries had in the 1961 session. But it would not have been an impressive majority, partly because a resolution had already been passed, calling for the UN to organize a world conference on disarmament generally. This cut away the ground from under the proposal to have a world "Ban-the-Bomb" conference. So in the end, both of the USSR draft resolutions were withdrawn without having been put to the vote. The Western delegations generally thought that the fate of these two resolutions showed that the non-aligned nations represented in the UNDC had grasped the point that if there was to be progress in disarmament, it had to be through measures on which both sides —NATO and Warsaw Pact—would be willing to negotiate.

The other favourite Soviet Union measures are the reduction of military budgets and the reduction of military forces. These ideas were advocated before the Vietnam war involvement had driven both the military spending of the United States and the numbers of its serving military personnel upwards. In early 1964, however, the USSR could point to recent reductions in military spending announced by themselves and the United States, and so proposed a larger cut of 10 to 15 per cent in military budgets of all the more important military powers. This proposal, of only academic interest at present, was opposed by the NATO negotiators because of the difficulty of verifying the real military expenditure of the USSR. In Western democracies, where military spending has to be approved by parliamentary bodies, very detailed accounts of where the money goes are public property. Certainly this is not so in Communist-ruled countries.

As for the proposal to reduce manpower in the armed services of the great powers, the USSR cited unilateral reductions that had been made in its forces at various periods, and proposed that other states should follow its lead, either under formal agreements or through a "policy of mutual example." A multilateral agreement for reduction of forces would be most difficult to negotiate, nations having fixed their force levels in accordance with what they believe to be the requirements for their national defence. Several nations besides the USSR and the USA (prior to the Vietnam build-up) have reduced their forces, desiring to save money and manpower. On the other hand India, formerly such an ardent proponent of pacifist policies, was obliged to increase its army and air force because of aggression and threats from the People's Republic of China.

Another method to halt the spread of nuclear weapons and the consequent danger of nuclear war is to establish geographical zones in which, by agreement between the countries within these zones, no nuclear weapons would be allowed. The Latin American countries have made better progress than elsewhere in developing this approach. A number of meetings of a conference to produce a treaty have been held, and after the latest, in May 1966, optimistic statements were made to the effect that there was agreement on 90 per cent of the draft treaty provisions, and that the difficulties in regard to the remainder would be soon overcome. The attitude of Cuba and the United States' concern over Cuba create obstacles which might perhaps necessitate a restriction of the territory which the remainder of the Latin American states would like to include in their agreement.

The Organization of African Unity in its Cairo conference in July 1964 asserted that Africa should be considered a nuclear-free zone under an international convention. This demand had already been expressed in a resolution of the 1961 General Assembly. However, little appears to have been done since by the African states to advance this idea.

The Soviet Union, besides supporting initiatives respecting nuclear-free zones in Latin America and Africa, proposes that they also should be created in areas where military forces with nuclear weapons presently confront one another—such as mid-Europe and the Balkan area. Poland has had on the table since 1958 the well-advertised Rapacki Plan, which has been through successive amendments. Essentially, it proposes that there should be a nuclear-free zone, comprising the two Germanies, Poland, and Czechoslovakia. A variant of this idea has been the so-called Gomulka plan, which proposes that there should be a freeze on the nuclear armament (and its means of delivery) in this area, prior to effective disarmament. All such plans for nu-clear-free zones in areas where nuclear weapons systems are deployed have been rejected by the West, because Western military forces rely on nuclear weapons to offset Communist superiority in conventional forces. Furthermore, it would weaken the effect of the nuclear deterrent, and upset the equilibrium of forces in the areas concerned.

This concludes the list of measures preliminary to larger steps in general disarmament which have been proposed by the United States and its allies on the one side, and the USSR and its partners on the other. The number and variety of the proposals should show that there has been no lack of zeal and ingenuity on the part of the officials dealing with disarmament (and behind them many academics) who have been trying to find ways to get the process started. How to begin? That is the vital question. Effort has been concentrated for the past three years on the negotiation of a non-proliferation agreement, and an agreement to prohibit underground testing, thus completing the Moscow Treaty on the Cessation of Nuclear Tests. As has been suggested in the discussion of these particular measures on the preceding pages, there are no insurmountable obstacles to agreement, once the political will for agreement emerges in Moscow and Washington—as it did in 1963.

But the war in Vietnam casts its shadow over the disarmament negotiations as it does over other possible ways of reducing tensions and improving relations between the power blocs in several parts of the world. There are two features of this unhappy war which relate to the themes of this book. The first is that it substantiates the widely-held belief that it is not possible to foresee a generally peaceful and disarmed world while the Soviet Union and those nations which follow its lead proclaim that "wars of liberation" are virtuous, and accordingly encourage and support insurrectionists and guerillas.

The second feature is that the fighting in Vietnam again demonstrates the tendency of air warfare to escalate. In the earlier chapters of this book it has been described how the independent or "strategic" role of air forces in World War II was extended, intensified and increased in ruthlessness, and in the end brought about the slaughter of great numbers of the civil population.

In reporting on the air operations against North Vietnam, the USA military authorities have stressed the care they have taken to spare lives of civilians to the greatest extent possible. It is clear, from what appears in the press, that the USA Administration has always in view the danger that Communist China may come into the war if the scope of bombing in North Vietnam is extended beyond a certain point. And the Administration seems even more wary of air actions carrying a danger of bringing in the USSR. Nevertheless, the chain of events since the attacks on targets in North Vietnam began in July 1965 shows again that, if bombing of the enemy's homeland is adopted as an important element in war strategy, there is an inherent tendency for it to expand in scale, range and intensity. It may begin with attacks on specifically military targets. Such limited use of the air arm usually fails to produce the decisive effect which the proponents of independent or semi-independent air action anticipate. When this happens, they advocate extending the scope of the air offensive. Press reports make it clear that a faction among the USA Administration's military advisers—and a few politicians—have been in favour of hitting North Vietnam harder from the air. But up to the time of writing, November, 1966, the Administration has heeded the warnings of its other advisers, who see the dangers of further extension of the war.

Let us turn again to the point that the Vietnam war exemplifies the danger inherent in the Communist doctrine regarding "wars of liberation." The following statement by Mr. Kosygin, Chairman of the Council of Ministers of the USSR—or Prime Minister as we might say—reported by James Reston, sets out the point clearly. He said: "We believe that wars of national

liberation are just wars, and they will continue as long as there
is national oppression by imperialist powers. . . . In South
Vietnam there is a national liberation war. These peoples do
not want to be governed by United States puppets. If you continue to fight there, the people will go on rising up. The people
will always fight against oppression for their freedom and independence. . . . This war in Vietnam and the war in the Dominican Republic and others—you believe that this reflects
your doctrine of peace? . . . Your policy of support for colo-
nialism will cause the peoples to rise against the United States.
There is a growing feeling of hatred for United States policies
because of your support for the colonialists and oppressors."

That is the communist position. How much truth is there in
it? Probably good communists believe it to be true. But does
the advance of communist rule mean the advance of freedom?
The Western democracies believe its meaning is exactly the
contrary. And the weight of evidence is that the mass of non-
aligned, less-developed countries which have passed recently
from the status of colonies to that of independent nations do
not want to be further "liberated" by a Communist-led revolution.

The communist position on the war in Vietnam having been
set out briefly but authoritatively by Mr. Kosygin, it should be
balanced by the American position, which is based on principles accepted by most of her allies.

Secretary of State Rusk, in his testimony before the Senate
Foreign Relations Committee on 18 February 1966, made the
following statements:

> Why are we in Vietnam? Certainly we are not there merely be-
> cause we have power and like to use it. We do not regard our-
> selves as the policemen of the universe. . . . We are in Vietnam
> because the issues posed there are deeply intertwined with our
> own security and because the outcome of the struggle can pro-
> foundly affect the nature of the world in which we and our chil-
> dren will live. . . . What we are seeking to achieve in South
> Vietnam is part of a process that has continued for a long time—
> a process of preventing the expansion and extension of communist
> domination by the use of force against the weaker nations on the
> perimeter of communist power.

There, in short, is set out the United States purpose in Vietnam. While Mr. Kosygin's words "hatred for United States policies" are communist rhetorical exaggeration, it is difficult to deny that during the progress of the Vietnam war not only non-aligned nations but also some allies have become doubtful as to the rightness of United States policy. The Vietnam war has to some degree shaken the confidence built up by all the many initiatives the United States has taken since the end of World War II for the purpose of maintaining peace and stability and resisting communist expansion in many quarters of the world. Why has this happened? It would seem to be that, while all allies approve the ends, they do not believe that the means used to attain them in Vietnam are justified.

As for the non-aligned "emerging" nations (whose insulation from communism is one of the long-term United States purposes), they tend to see the picture as of the world's most powerful nation waging war against a small and weak nation, using tons upon tons of high-explosive bombs, combined with napalm and "riot-control" gases. It looks the worse because it has become more and more a white nation fighting an Asiatic nation—not merely white military forces helping one side in an Asian civil war. The cause of the fighting, that there is danger of communists taking over control of the southern half of this nation as they have of the north, does not weigh too heavily in the scales of public opinion in the neutral countries, many of which lean towards socialism in their economies.

Having summarily surveyed the particular case of Vietnam, let us consider the more general danger to peace, or obstacle in the way of achieving a peaceful world, which is created by the communist dogma that "wars of liberation" are just and should be supported. Is there no escape from the prospect of innumerable conflicts, in which the communist-ruled nations and the Western democracies would find themselves on opposite sides? If they support native pro- and anti-communists, in any of these, as in Vietnam, it may lead them into active military participation: in short, they may be drawn into war with each other, with no limit to its scale.

In this generally stormy prospect, there are some patches of bright sky. One of them is the attitude of the non-aligned "less-developed" countries to the competitive programmes of the Western democracies and the communists for their future social and economic organization. Put in brief, what they want most is for both sides to give them economic aid but to leave them alone to work out their own political problems. This basic position of the under-developed countries in the so-called world revolution was illustrated in the debate on "non-intervention" in the 20th General Assembly of the United Nations, in December 1965.

The USSR had inscribed an item on the agenda entitled "The inadmissibility of intervention in the affairs of states." The purpose of this was apparently to set the stage for attacks on USA "imperialist interventions" in Vietnam and the Dominican Republic. However, once discussion of this agenda item began in the First (Political) Committee of the UNGA, a number of nations took up the theme that (to quote one of the preambular paragraphs in the final resolution) "subversion as well as all forms of indirect intervention are contrary to these principles, and consequently a violation of the charter of the United Nations." "These principles" were "the basic principles on which peaceful international co-operation between states should be built."

The debate was long and vigorous, and several groups of representatives produced amendments to the original USSR draft. What came out in the end was a massive and rather discursive document, containing ten preambular clauses setting out, for the most part, the preoccupations of the newer ex-colonial states, plus Latin American states, over threats to their independence and political integrity. There were also eight operative clauses. Of these the following are the most important:

> No state has the right to intervene, directly or indirectly, for any reason whatever, in the internal or external affairs of any other state. Consequently armed intervention as well as all other forms of interference or attempted threats against the personality of a state or against its political, economic and cultural elements, are condemned;
>     . . . Also, no state shall organize, assist, foment, finance, incite

or tolerate subversive, terrorist or armed activities directed to the violent overthrow of the regime of another state, or interfere in civil strife in another state. (UNGA Resolution 2131 xx)

This last clause, directed against "subversion, terrorist or armed activities," was due mainly to the efforts of Latin American countries. Of course, the organizers of the amendments desired that direct armed intervention on the Dominican Republic pattern should be ruled out, but they also had experienced the dangers of foreign-based subversive and terrorist activities intended to overthrow existing regimes. Such dangers came, or were thought to come, from Cuba and its powerful though distant communist-ruled patrons.

The reader will perceive, on examining the clauses of the resolution quoted above, that if all nations and particularly the larger powers would behave in accordance with its principles, the world would be very different from what it is now. Looking at the Vietnam situation in the light of the desiderata set out in the resolution, *prima facie,* the presence of USA forces constitutes an intervention, contrary to the principles. But that intervention had been preceded and caused by actions of the Democratic Republic of Vietnam, which had infringed the principles by organizing and assisting subversive, terrorist and armed activities directed to the violent overthrow of another state.

It will be noted that the prohibition extends to interference "in civil strife in another state." In other words, outside parties must refrain from taking sides in a civil war, and aiding the chosen side with political support, arms, money, and in other ways. It is not within the scope of this book to argue whether North and South Vietnam are separate states, or whether the conflict which has gone on since 1956 is a civil war in the single state of Vietnam. There are plenty of other publications dealing with this question with more expertise than I can summon. In any case, this is a legal and somewhat unreal distinction. What is real about the struggle is that there is an attempt to extend the area of communist rule by subversion, terror and force, which is being resisted by force of arms by an indigenous non-communist government and population, with massive support from the USA and some of its allies in the Pacific zone. And this contest is one which may be typical of others which will be brought about in other parts of the world.

Will the leaders of the Soviet Union adopt the "more enlightened attitude" which Mr. Kennedy said was a prerequisite to progress towards peace and disarmament? Will they show themselves willing to place this object ahead of the extension of communist rule to other countries by subversion and intrigue? This is the essential problem as most Westerners see it. But we should not forget that Soviet attitudes tend to reflect the attitudes of the Western democracies towards them. This has been revealed by the chronicle of reciprocal moves in armament since 1945 and in political postures since the revolution of 1917. So we should think of President Kennedy's plea again.

In closing, I should like to summarize the argument of this book.

The way in which methods of waging war have developed since the introduction of aircraft, through to the nuclear and missile age, leads to the conclusion that if war between great powers should occur, it would be unlimited in scope and cause immense, catastrophic damage to the most highly civilized countries. The greatest danger against which all nations have to be protected is the outbreak of nuclear war.

The present state of balance—deterrence from warlike acts or policies through fear of the destruction of nuclear war—although it can be expected to preserve peace between great powers for some time to come, will not be of indefinite duration. While the arms race goes on, the balance and thus the stability and effectiveness of the nuclear deterrent is threatened. If additional nations become independent nuclear powers, the balance will become less stable and war more likely.

At present, what has been described as a "plateau" in the arms race between the USA and the USSR and their allies on both sides may have been reached. That is to say, it does not appear likely that in the immediate future, additions to the quantity of nuclear armament or development of new arms systems will produce additional security for either side, only additional unproductive expenditure. Mr. McNamara has made this point on several occasions, recently in a speech to the American Society of Newspaper Editors in Montreal, on 19 May 1966. Therefore, the present offers an opportunity to halt the arms race and begin serious negotiations for the reduction of nuclear and other powerful armaments.

Seven years of negotiations since Mr. Khrushchev introduced his programme of general and complete disarmament have shown no progress in the attempt to agree on a treaty to effect such a tremendous change in the organization for the security of nations in the short period proposed by the USSR.

Agreement in 1963 was achieved on several measures of arms control, and a number of others offer the possibility of successful negotiation if the political intention to achieve agreement is present on both sides. This is the best way to move towards disarmament and a peaceful world.

Finally, there is the duty of the military men and scientists who advise governments on questions of defence. In this connection a significant statement was made by Air Force Secretary Eugene Zuckert in an address to the Harvard Business School Club on 8 January 1964. He outlined the principles upon which Air Force planning for future years was to be based, with a view to determining the airmen's tasks in the defence of the nation and the means, including armaments, that they would need for this. What is arresting and encouraging is that the first place in the list was given to arms control. Secretary Zuckert said:

> Arms control is now a military requirement in itself. Military men are concerned with it, not because it might make them technologically unemployed, but because it is a necessary part of the defense package. It is both an end—in terms of possible relief from the burden of arms investment—and a means—in terms of the job that the military has to perform.

It is to be hoped that all military men, not only the airmen but the soldiers and sailors, not only in the United States but in allied countries and also in the armed forces of the Warsaw Pact countries, will come to perceive that there can never be peace and safety, and that the freedoms and rights of men cannot be secure in a world under the threat of nuclear war. Is it not their true duty to their countrymen to find ways to remove that threat? A way must be found to protect liberty and the values of civilization which does not depend on the ultimate possibility of Megamurder.

# NOTES AND BIBLIOGRAPHY

# NOTES

## Chapter 1

1. References to the Hague Convention IV of 1907 were taken from *International Law: Cases and Materials* by William W. Bishop (Little, Brown & Company, 1962).
2. For Kahn's anticipated casualties in a nuclear war, see *On Thermonuclear War*, table, p. 113.
3. For conscientious scruples of scientists, see Gilpin's *American Scientists and Nuclear Weapons Policy* and many issues of the *Bulletin of Atomic Scientists*.

## Chapter 2

1. For the account of the development of bombing from aircraft in World War I and the creation of an independent air force, Saundby's *Air Bombardment* is the main authority. A biography of Marshal of the Air Force, Lord Trenchard, by A. P. Boyle has also been drawn upon.

## Chapter 3

1. The Douhet theories of air war are extracted for his book *The Command of the Air*, especially pp. 20-22, 59, 61, 181, 188.

2. For Kahn's theories of credible deterrence, see *On Thermonuclear War*, pp. 29, 32.

3. For Douhet on the use of poison gas, see *op. cit.*, pp. 181 *ff.*, and for his quote of Fokker, *op. cit.*, p. 255.

4. Regarding Brigadier-General Mitchell's theories, see his book *Skyways*, p. 253 for his definition of the object of war, and p. 255 for his view of the change brought about by air power.

5. For the use of the RAF to control Iraq and other colonial or mandated areas, see *Air Bombardment*, p. 38, and *Bomber Offensive* by Harris.

6. Lord Trenchard's view of air warfare is taken from *Trenchard*, pp. 576 *ff.*

7. The Hague Rules of Air Warfare, 1923, are given in Appendix VI of Greenspan's *The Modern Law of Land Warfare*.

8. For disarmament efforts, especially regarding air forces, between World Wars I and II, see *Air Bombardment*, pp. 53-56, and Spaight's *Bombing Vindicated*, p. 15.

## Chapter 4

1. The principal authorities for this and the following chapter are *Air Bombardment*, *Bomber Offensive*, and the British official histories, *The Strategic Air Offensive Against Germany* by Webster and Frankland, Vols. I and II, and Collier's *The Defence of the United Kingdom*.

2. For the forcing of Czechoslovakia to capitulate, see Wheeler-Bennett's *Munich: Prologue to Tragedy*.

3. For the bombing attack on Rotterdam, see David Irving's *The Destruction of Dresden*.

4. On the dispute between British scientists over the effects of bombing, see Blackett's *Studies of War: Nuclear and Conventional*.

5. For Harris's proposal to win the war against Germany by concentrating all resources on the bombing offensive, see *The Strategic Air Offensive Against Germany*, Vol. 1, p. 340.

## Chapter 5

1. An additional authority to those listed for Chapter 4, in so far as American bombing operations are concerned, is *Army Air Forces in World War II*, Vols. II and V, ed. Craven and Cate.

2. For the attacks on Hamburg, Dresden and other German cities heavily bombed, see *The Destruction of Dresden* and Rumpf's *The Bombing of Germany*.

3. Mr. Irving in his book gave the number of killed in the Dresden

raids as 135,000. Casualty records which subsequently came to light caused him to accept the lower figure of 35,600 for deaths. See article by Peter Lust in *Parallel* magazine (Montreal), September-October 1966.

## Chapter 6

1. For reactions of American scientists to the use of the atomic bomb in war, see *American Scientists and Nuclear Weapons Policy* and Teller's *The Legacy of Hiroshima*.

2. For the decision to use atomic bombs against Japan, see *Year of Decision*, Vol. 1 of the memoirs of President H. S. Truman.

3. *Chronology of Negotiations on Nuclear and Conventional Disarmament*, a study prepared for the Sub-committee on Disarmament of the Committee on Foreign Relations of the US Senate, was used as a general reference in these matters.

4. For negotiations on the Baruch Plan, see also Noel-Baker's *The Arms Race*, Part 3, p. 16.

5. Extracts quoted from General Arnold's report of 12 November 1945 were taken from Emme's *The Impact of Air Power*.

## Chapter 7

1. For the extension of communist rule over Eastern European countries, see Mackintosh's *Strategy and Tactics of Soviet Foreign Policy. Staff Study No. 5 on Disarmament and Security in Europe*, made for the Sub-committee of the Committee on Foreign Relations of the US Senate, was also used as a reference in writing this chapter.

2. Extracts from "Survival in the Air Age" and Lieutenant-General Doolittle's speech were taken from *The Impact of Air Power*.

## Chapter 8

1. References the same as for Chapter 7, plus Ismay's *NATO, The First Five Years*.

2. For the development of the hydrogen bomb, see *American Scientists and Nuclear Weapons Policy* and *The Legacy of Hiroshima*.

3. Extracts from Mr. Finletter's article on Korean experience are taken from *The Impact of Air Power*.

## Chapter 9

1. The theories of massive retaliation, preventive war, and preemptive attack are dealt with in Brodie's *Strategy in the Missile Age*, Chapter 7.

2. Mr. Dulles' article modifying his previous position on massive retaliation was in "Foreign Affairs," October 1957 issue.

3. The latter part of the chapter, dealing with tactical nuclear weapons and NATO, includes comments on views expressed in Kissinger's *Nuclear Weapons and Foreign Policy* as noted in the text.

*Chapter* 10

1. As indicated in the text, much of the discussion in this chapter is related to the argument concerning tactical nuclear weapons and the defence of NATO Europe contained in *Nuclear Weapons and Foreign Policy* and *The Necessity for Choice* by the same author.

2. Since the text of *Megamurder* was written, Dr. Kissinger has published another book, *The Troubled Partnership: A Reappraisal of the Atlantic Alliance*. In it he further reconsiders his earlier views on the use of nuclear weapons for the defence of Europe. It seems fair to give some excerpts which show his present thought on these matters—nearer to the mark than that of any other military writer, it seems to me.

On page 156 of *The Troubled Partnership*, after reviewing the history of the multilateral force project and giving the pros and cons, Dr. Kissinger writes:

The MLF, as orginally conceived, is not likely to be realized. So much opposition exists that even the most passionate advocates will have to modify the scheme. It may be useful, however, to inquire what lessons can be drawn from the experience. . . .

The most important one is not to try to solve political problems with technical expedients . . . ends and means become confused. At its best the MLF was irrelevant to the fundamental problems of NATO. It would have repeated within its framework many of the disputes which it was supposed to overcome.

Concerning the use of so-called tactical nuclear weapons in a limited war, on pages 102-3 Dr. Kissinger cites opinions by Messrs. McNamara, Gilpatrick, and Enthoven to the effect that it is hardly possible to conceive that a war situation could remain limited if nuclear weapons of any dimension were used. Dr. Kissinger draws the following conclusion:

If any use of nuclear weapons is likely to lead to an uncontrolled general nuclear exchange, it follows that many of the Administration's strictures against independent nuclear forces apply also to the tactical nuclear weapons on the Continent. Administration statements have made clear that the tactical nuclear weapons in

Europe were too vulnerable to serve as reliable second-strike weapons, and thus were not needed to deter or fight a general nuclear war.

Dr. Kissinger sums up his thinking about the use of tactical nuclear weapons in Europe at the end of Chapter 6. After reviewing the problems, difficulties and uncertainties that exist in determining how they are to be used, he writes: "All this suggests that it is imperative to reconsider the mission and deployment of the tactical nuclear arsenal on the Continent." He goes on to suggest that, mainly because the potential enemy possesses tactical nuclear weapons as well as superior conventional military forces, it is necessary for NATO to have tactical nuclear weapons. Their main purpose should be to bring aggression by major military forces to a halt, and to inflict sufficient punishment on them to oblige the aggressor to enter negotiations. He goes on: "To achieve these objectives, the tactical nuclear establishment must be adapted along the following lines: (1) its mission must be redefined; (2) its vulnerability must be reduced; and (3) its deployment must be changed."

Dr. Kissinger concludes this chapter by saying, "However, no arrangement of military forces will, of itself, solve the problems of the Alliance. The ultimate challenge lies in the political field."

3. Halperin's *Limited War in the Nuclear Age* also deals with the subject.

4. Jerome Wiesner, formerly President Kennedy's Special Assistant for Science and Technology, writes in his recently published book, *Where Science and Politics Meet* (p. 16):

Most people appreciate that strategic nuclear weapons cannot be used without total destruction for everyone as the result. Some people still search for ways of using small tactical weapons to advantage in limited wars. If nuclear weapons were introduced in a conflict whose outcome is vital to both sides, each would use the weapons required to assure victory. They might begin with ten-ton weapons, but would almost certainly move up to weapons large enough to destroy airfields and munition dumps and, in the end, probably cities. I have examined dozens of war games carried out to learn how to use tactical nuclear weapons, and they all ended inconclusively. The only certain conclusion was the escalation and the thorough destruction of the territory over which the fighting took place. It is important to remember that there are no experts on nuclear war, that anything that anyone says is based on analysis, experiences gained in World War II, conjecture or ignorance.

*Chapter* 11

1. The quotation from the letter from Bulganin to Eden is taken from the *New York Times*, 10 November 1956 (AP and Reuters). It is also referred to in *Strategy and Tactics of Soviet Foreign Policy*, p. 188.

2. The reference for Kahn's discussion of the credibility of American response to an attack on Europe is mainly from *On Thermonuclear War*, Chapter 1; for "Scenario," see *ibid.*, p. 28.

3. In his latest book, *On Escalation: Metaphors and Scenarios*, Mr. Kahn elaborates his classification of deterrence. The book is intended to stimulate thought on how a nuclear war could start and on whether it could be fought and terminated without entailing wholesale death and destruction. In pursuit of this purpose, various metaphors are employed, as the title indicates. The chief of these, the "escalation ladder," refers to a series of steps, each of which represents an intensification of the conflict between the two antagonists (USA and USSR). These steps, or rungs, in the escalation ladder number forty-four. The lowest is an "ostensible crisis," and there are twenty rungs before nuclear weapons are used, for "exemplary" purposes, in a "local nuclear war." Mr. Kahn remarks ". . . as this would be the first unmistakably deliberate use of these weapons since World War II, it would be a profoundly consequential act, even if very limited and specialized." Too true. After this rung is passed, escalation could go on up to the forty-fourth rung, "Spasm or Insensate War," in which the nuclear powers would fire off every nuclear weapon they had, with the aim of inflicting as much damage on the enemy as possible.

Mr. Kahn discusses the possibility of halting the escalation on the various rungs, before and after the fateful first use of nuclear weapons. Of course, if communications can be established between the antagonists, it is theoretically possible to do this. But it is equally possible that the escalation will go on upward, rung by rung, or more probably by jumps of several rungs at a time. Communication between resolute antagonists for the purpose of stopping an escalation and negotiating an armistice is not at all easy, as current experience in the relatively slow-paced Vietnam conflict has shown us.

The skein of thought in Mr. Kahn's latest book is very intricate, and it is often difficult to understand because of the many new terms introduced, denoting tactical, strategical, or political concepts. Some of these terms have been invented by the author; others are taken from the proliferating jargon of the faculty of "strategic analysts." In an end chapter, Mr. Kahn endeavours to clarify matters by classifying and defining these terms, but this does not greatly ease the burden on the reader.

The present writer does not find that Mr. Kahn's examination of the possibility of preventing the use of nuclear weapons in a war between great nations, or of conducting such a war without its ending in "Spasm," makes one feel any safer than one did after reading his previous books.

*Chapter* 12

This chapter has been written mainly from personal recollection. I have been closely connected with all disarmament negotiations since January 1960, when I became Adviser on Disarmament to the Canadian government. I have, of course, checked my memory against the Conference records of the Ten-Nation and Eighteen-Nation Disarmament Committees and those of the UN General Assemblies of 1960-63. But since this is not a book for the specialist in disarmament negotiations, it seemed unnecessary to give references for every statement.

1. The speculation about the influence of communist internal politics on the decision to withdraw from the Ten-Nation Disarmament Conference is based on material from the chapter on the Bucharest Conference in Crankshaw's *The New Cold War, Moscow v. Peking.*

2. Sir Michael Wright, in his recently published *Disarm and Verify,* gives an excellent summary of, and commentary on, recent disarmament negotiations.

3. The extracts from the speech of Mr. McNamara to the Economic Club of New York are taken from the text published in *Survival,* January-February 1964.

4. William C. Foster, an engineer and business executive who had served successive administrations with distinction in many important posts, as well as directing ACDA, has since 1963 been the chief USA representative in the Eighteen-Nation Disarmament Committee.

5. The committee of thirty-three continued to meet at intervals between the 20th (1965) and 21st (1966) General Assemblies, but with no better result. During the 20th General Assembly, Ireland attempted to promote a resolution which would establish principles for the financing of UN peace-keeping operations. Owing to the indifference of the majority of members, it was not brought to a vote.

*Chapter* 13

1. The quotation is from Noel-Baker's *The Way to World Disarmament—Now!*

2. The references to President Johnson's Budget message are taken from the text published in the *New York Times,* 22 January 1964.

3. The reference by Sir Arthur Harris to obsolescence of the bomber is from *Bomber Offensive,* p. 272.

4. Extended discussion of the matters covered in this chapter is to be found in Cook's *The Warfare State* and Swomley's *The Military Establishment.*

5. A report issued on 5 September 1965, by a special committee headed by Mr. Gardner Ackley, chairman of the President's Council of Economic Advisers, confirmed the conclusions reached in the previous investigations of the problem of the effect disarmament would have on the world economy, and on the economy of the United States. The Ackley report said, in short, that a shift in defence spending, or even general and complete disarmament, would present no insuperable problems for America's economy. It could even open new opportunities for American citizens and step up economic growth.

*Chapter* 14

1. The relevant passages from Secretary McNamara's speech at Ann Arbor, on 16 June 1962, are taken from the text published in *Survival,* September-October 1962.

2. The quotation from *Soviet Military Strategy* is to be found on pp. 166-7 of the "RAND" edition. "RAND" is the research and development corporation sponsored by the US Air Force. It has on its staff a large number of scientists of different disciplines who try to provide answers to problems set them by the Air Force. Translation of and comment on *Soviet Military Strategy* was just one of their jobs.

3. A chronology of the Cuban crisis was published in the *New York Times,* 6 November 1962.

4. Général de l'Armée Beaufre's arguments on nuclear deterrents are from an article "Dissuasion et Stratégie" in *Revue de Défense Nationale,* December 1964.

5. Falk's *Law, Morality and War in the Contemporary World* has been published more recently than the books referred to in the text. It contains very extensive references to other writings on the subject and its conclusions seem to me to support the general argument in this chapter.

275 |

*Chapter* 15

1. The quotations from President Kennedy's speech to the American University are from the text given in the *New York Times*, 11 June 1963.

2. During the presidential electoral campaign of 1964, certain questions of defence policy became issues. On these issues Mr. Goldwater, the Republican candidate, adopted a hard line which was interpreted by the press, for the most part, as likely to lead towards war, and indeed nuclear war. Probably a more warmongering image was created for Mr. Goldwater than he really deserved. Nevertheless statements which he made before and during the electoral campaign furnished ample ammunition to his critics. For example, in a speech to the Veterans of Foreign Wars, in Cleveland, on 25 August 1964, he suggested that NATO should be given a stock of "small, tactical nuclear battlefield weapons." He casually said these were no more powerful than the firepower already faced on the battlefield. He implied that the authority to order these weapons to be fired should be devolved on Saceur, perhaps lower down the echelons of command. It should be recorded, however, that Mr. Goldwater had on other occasions denounced the proposed NATO multilateral force; and also opposed giving any other nation or group control of the long-range, more powerful nuclear weapon systems, which he said should be kept under US control.

President Johnson firmly rejected Senator Goldwater's argument in his first campaign speech, in Detroit, on 7 September 1964. He said: "Make no mistake about it, there is no such thing as a conventional nuclear weapon. . . . To [make use of atomic weapons] now is a political decision of the highest order. It would lead us down an uncertain path of blows and counterblows whose outcome none may know. No President of the United States can divest himself of the responsibility for such a decision."

On 27 August 1964, speaking to the same convention of veterans which Senator Goldwater had addressed the previous day, Deputy Secretary of Defense Cyrus E. Vance pointed out that the typical "tactical" nuclear weapon had several times the yield of the atomic bomb that had destroyed Hiroshima. "Small" and "conventional" were dangerously misleading and totally inappropriate adjectives to apply to any nuclear weapons. (See *New York Times*, 26, 28 August and 8 September 1964)

3. For Mr. Kosygin's statement to James Reston, see *New York Times* 8 December 1965.

4. The quotation from Secretary Zuckert's speech of 8 January 1964 is taken from an excerpt of the *Congressional Record* giving remarks of the Hon. Melvin Price in the House of Representatives.

# BIBLIOGRAPHY

AIR WAR—HISTORICAL

Blackett, P. M. S., *Studies of War: Nuclear and Conventional.* Edinburgh, Oliver & Boyd Ltd., 1962.

Boyle, A. P., *Trenchard.* London, William Collins Sons & Co., 1962.

Collier, Basil, *The Defence of the United Kingdom,* London, Her Majesty's Stationery Office, 1957.

Craven, Wesley F. and Cate, James L., ed., *Army Air Forces in World War II.* Chicago, University of Chicago Press, 1949. vol. II.

———— *Army Air Forces in World War II.* Chicago, University of Chicago Press, 1953. vol. V.

Douhet, Giulio, *The Command of the Air.* New York, Coward-McCann, Inc., 1942.

Emme, Eugene M., *The Impact of Air Power.* New York, D. Van Nostrand Company, Inc., 1959.

Greenspan, Morris, *Modern Law of Land Warfare.* Berkeley, University of California Press, 1959.

Harris, Air Chief-Marshal Sir Arthur, *Bomber Offensive.* London, William Collins Sons & Co., 1947.

Irving, David, *The Destruction of Dresden.* London, William Kimber & Co. Ltd., 1963.

Mitchell, General William, *Skyways*. Philadelphia, J. B. Lippincott Company, 1930.

Rumpf, Hans, *The Bombing of Germany*. London, Frederick Muller Ltd., 1963.

Saundby, Air Marshal Sir Robert, *Air Bombardment*. New York, Harper and Row Publishers, 1961.

Spaight, J. M., *Bombing Vindicated*. London, Geoffrey Bles Ltd., 1944.

Webster, Sir Charles Kingsley, *The Strategic Air Offensive Against Germany*. London, Her Majesty's Stationery Office, 1961.

Wheeler-Bennett, Sir John, *Munich: Prologue to Tragedy*. London, Macmillan & Co. Ltd., 1943.

## POLITICAL

American Friends Service Committee, *Peace in Vietnam*. New York, Hill & Wang, Inc., 1966.

Crankshaw, Edward, *The New Cold War, Moscow v. Peking*. Harmondsworth, Middlesex, Penguin Books Ltd., 1963.

Fall, Bernard, B., *Viet-Nam Witness*. New York, Frederick A. Praeger, Inc., 1966.

Fulbright, J. W. (introduction), *The Vietnam Hearings*. New York, Vintage Books, 1966.

Gettleman, Marvin E. (ed.), *Vietnam, History, Documents and Opinions*. New York, Fawcett World Library, 1965.

Gordon, Bernard K., *Dimensions of Conflict in Southeast Asia*, Englewood Cliffs, N.J., Prentice-Hall, Inc., 1966.

Graebner, Norman A., *Cold War Diplomacy: American Foreign Policy, 1945-1960*. New York, D. Van Nostrand Company, Inc., 1962.

Harriman, Averell, *Peace with Russia?* New York, Simon and Schuster, Inc., 1959.

Ismay, Lord, *NATO, The First Five Years, 1949-1954*. Utrecht, Bosch & Keunig N. V., 1955.

Kennan, George F., *Russia, the Atom and the West*. London, Oxford University Press, 1958.

Mackintosh, J. M., *Strategy and Tactics of Soviet Foreign Policy*. London, Oxford University Press, 1962.

Mills, C. Wright, *The Causes of World War Three*. New York, Ballantine Books, Inc., 1960.

—— *The Power Elite*. New York, Oxford University Press, 1956.

Roberts, Henry L., *Russia and America*. New York, Mentor Books, 1956.

Thompson, Sir Robert, *Defeating Communist Insurgency*. London, Chatto and Windus, 1966.

Whitney, Thomas P., ed., *The Communist Blueprint for the Future*. New York, E. P. Dutton & Co., Inc., 1962.


NUCLEAR WAR—POLICY, STRATEGY AND MORALITY


Abel, Elie, *The Missile Crisis*, Philadelphia, J. B. Lippincott Company, 1966.

Bennett, John C., ed., *Nuclear Weapons and the Conflict of Conscience*. New York, Charles Scribner's Sons, 1962.

Brodie, Bernard, *Strategy in the Missile Age*. Princeton, Princeton University Press, 1959.

Buchan, Alistair, *NATO in the 1960's: The Implications of Independence*. London, Weidenfeld & Nicolson Ltd., 1960.

———— and Windsor, Philip, *Arms and Stability in Europe*. London, Chatto & Windus Ltd., 1963.

Burdick, Eugene, and Wheeler, Harvey, *Fail-Safe*. New York, McGraw-Hill Book Co., Inc., 1962.

Cook, Fred J., *The Warfare State*. New York, The Macmillan Company, 1962.

De Seversky, Alexander P., *Air Power: Key to Survival*. New York, Simon and Schuster, Inc., 1950.

————, *America, Too Young to Die*. New York, McFadden Bartell Corp., 1962.

Falk, Richard, *Law, Morality, and War in the Contemporary World*. London, Pall Mall Press Ltd., 1963.

Gallois, General Pierre, *Stratégie de l'Age Nucléaire*. Paris, Calmann-Lévy, 1960.

Garthoff, Raymond L., *Soviet Strategy in the Nuclear Age*. New York, Frederick A. Praeger, Inc., 1958.

Gilpin, Robert, *American Scientists and Nuclear Weapons Policy*. Princeton, Princeton University Press, 1962.

Halperin, Morton H., *Limited War in the Nuclear Age*. New York, John Wiley & Sons, Inc., 1963.

Hart, B. H. Liddell, *Deterrent or Defence*. London, Stevens & Sons Ltd., 1960.

Herzog, Arthur, *The War-Peace Establishment*. New York, Harper & Row, Publishers, 1965.

Kahn, Herman, *On Escalation: Metaphors and Scenarios*. New York, Frederick A. Praeger, Inc., 1965.

———— *On Thermonuclear War*. Princeton, Princeton University Press, 1961.

———— *Thinking About the Unthinkable*. New York, Horizon Press, 1962.

Keys, Donald, ed., *God and the H-Bomb*. New York, Bernard Geis Associates, 1961.

Kissinger, Henry A., *The Necessity for Choice*. New York, Harper & Row, Publishers, 1961.

———— *Nuclear Weapons and Foreign Policy*. New York, Harper & Row, Publishers, 1961.

———— *The Troubled Partnership*. New York, McGraw-Hill Book Co., Inc., 1965.

Knebel, Fletcher and Bailey, Charles W., *Seven Days in May*. New York, Harper & Row, Publishers, 1962.

Legault, Albert, *Deterrence and the Atlantic Alliance*. Toronto, Canadian Institute of International Affairs, 1966.

Lilienthal, David E., *Change, Hope, and the Bomb*. Princeton, Princeton University Press, 1963.

Moch, Jules, *Non à la Force de Frappe*. Paris, Editions Robert Laffont, 1963.

Osgood, Charles E., *An Alternative to War or Surrender*. Urbana, University of Illinois Press, 1962.

Power, General Thomas S., *Design for Survival*. New York, Coward-McCann, Inc., 1965.

Rosecrance, R. N., ed., *The Dispersion of Nuclear Weapons*. New York, Columbia University Press, 1964.

Russell, Bertrand, *Common Sense and Nuclear Warfare*. New York, Simon and Schuster, Inc., 1959.

Schelling, Thomas C. and Halperin, Morton H., *Strategy and Arms Control*. New York, Twentieth Century Fund, Inc., 1961.

Sokolovsky, Marshal V. D., ed., *Soviet Military Strategy*. Englewood Cliffs, N.J., Prentice-Hall, Inc., 1963.

Swomley, John M. Jr., *The Military Establishment*. Boston, Beacon Press, 1964.

Taylor, General Maxwell D., *The Uncertain Trumpet*. New York, Harper & Row, Publishers, 1960.

Teller, Edward and Brown, Allen, *The Legacy of Hiroshima*. New York, Doubleday & Company, Inc., 1962.

Truman, Harry S, *Memoirs, vol. I: Year of Decision*. New York, Doubleday & Company, Inc., 1958.

Wiesner, Jerome B., *Where Science and Politics Meet*. New York,

McGraw-Hill Book Co., Inc., 1965.

Young, Wayland, *Strategy for Survival.* Harmondsworth, Middlesex, Penguin Books Ltd., 1959.


## DISARMAMENT AND ARMS CONTROL

Barnet, Richard J., *Who Wants Disarmament?* Boston, Beacon Press, 1964.

Beaton, Leonard, *Must the Bomb Spread?* Harmondsworth, Middlesex, Penguin Books, Ltd., 1966.

Bloomfield, Clemens & Griffiths, *Khrushchev and the Arms Race.* Cambridge, Mass., M.I.T. Press, 1966.

Bull, Hedley, *The Control of the Arms Race.* London, Weidenfeld & Nicolson Ltd., 1961.

Cousins, Norman, *In Place of Folly.* New York, Harper & Brothers, 1961.

*Daedelus* (Special issue on arms control). Boston, American Academy of Arts and Sciences, 1960.

Dean, Arthur H., *Test Ban and Disarmament.* New York, Harper & Row, Publishers, 1966.

Frisch, David H., ed., *Arms Reduction—Program and Issues.* New York, Twentieth Century Fund, Inc., 1961.

Hadley, Arthur T., *The Nation's Safety and Arms Control.* New York, Viking Press, Inc., 1961.

Howard, Michael, *Disengagement in Europe.* Harmondsworth, Middlesex, Penguin Books Ltd., 1958.

Melman, Seymour, *The Peace Race.* New York, Ballantine Books, Inc., 1961.

———— ed., *Disarmament: Its Politics and Economics.* Boston, American Academy of Arts and Sciences, 1962.

———— ed., *Inspection for Disarmament.* New York, Columbia University Press, 1958.

———— ed., *No Place to Hide.* New York, Grove Press, Inc., 1962.

Noel-Baker, Philip, *The Arms Race: A Programme for World Disarmament.* London, Atlantic Book Publishing Co. Ltd., 1958.

————, *The Way to World Disarmament—Now!* London, Union of Democratic Control, 1964.

Nutting, Anthony, *Disarmament, An Outline of the Negotiations.* London, Oxford University Press, 1959.

Stone, Jeremy J., *Containing the Arms Race.* Cambridge, Mass., M.I.T. Press, 1966.

Szilard, Leo, *The Voice of the Dolphins, and Other Stories*. New York, Simon and Schuster, Inc., 1961.

Wright, Sir Michael, *Disarm and Verify*. London, Chatto & Windus, Inc., 1964.

# INDEX

Holifield, Chet; Chairman of Joint
Committee on Atomic Energy;
comment on *God and the H-
Bomb*, 232

"Hot Line" Washington–Moscow
telephone link, 124, 175

Hungary, establishment of communist government, 88

Intercontinental Ballistic Missiles
(ICBM's); limit possibility of
successful preventive war, 121

International Atomic Development
Authority; proposed in Acheson-Lilienthal report, 75

INTERNATIONAL LAW; re air
war; Trenchard's views, 34

Geneva Protocols, 1925, against
gas warfare, 28

Hague Convention, 1907, 3

jurists' rules of air warfare,
Hague, 1922–23, 35

Irish Resolution; against dissemination of nuclear weapons, 1961,
222

Johnson, Lyndon B., President of
the USA; announces cutback of
U 235 production, 1964, 181

"disarmament is everybody's
business," 185

measures preliminary to general
disarmament proposed, January 1964, 213

policies advocated during 1964
presidential election, 273

proposes balanced destruction
of bombers, January 1964,
251

proposes freeze on development
and construction of nuclear

weapon vehicles, January
1964, 179, 213

sets up committee to appraise
economic effects of disarmament, 202

Kahn, Herman; American commitments and acceptable casualties, 27, 147

categories of deterrence, 154,
206

defensive measures needed to
make deterrent credible, 26

*On Escalation* etc., 270

*On Thermonuclear War*, 4, 6

Kellogg-Briand Pact, 36

Kennedy, Pres. John F.; attitudes
towards peace and USSR,
speech June 1963, 235

Cuba crisis; action, 214

Nassau Conference, 152

Khrushchev, Nikita S., Chairman
of USSR Council of Ministers;
announces reactors to produce
fissile material will not be
built 1964, 181

presents plan for GCD to UNGA,
September 1959, 79

proposes peaceful settlement of
territorial disputes, 205

threats against Berlin, 92

West Germany will "burn like
a candle" in war, 224

warns USSR would intervene if
People's Republic of China
were attacked, September
1958, 116

re withdrawal of USRR from
TNDC, 173

Kissinger, Henry A., 6

on use of tactical nuclear weapons, 125

*The Necessity for Choice*, views